Creative Ideas for Children's Worship

Creative Ideas for Children's Worship

*Based on the Sunday Gospels,
Year A*

Sarah Lenton

Theological consultant:
Andrew Davison

Morehouse Education Resources
A division of Church Publishing Incorporated

First published in the UK under the title:
Fresh Expressions in the Sacramental Tradition
by the Canterbury Press Norwich
Editorial office, 13–17 Long Lane,
London, EC1A 9pn, UK

Canterbury Press is an imprint of Hymns Ancient and Modern Ltd
(a registered charity)
13A Hellesdon Park Road, Norwich,
Norfolk, NR6 5DR, UK

www.scm-canterburypress.co.uk

First published in the United States in 2012 by
Morehouse Education Resources
a division of Church Publishing Incorporated
Editorial Offices: 600 Grant Street, Suite 630
Denver, Colorado 80203

Typeset by Regent Typesetting, London

Library of Congress Cataloging-in-Publication Data
(to come)

Printed in the United States of America

10 9 8 7 6 5 4 3 2 1

ISBN-13: 978-1-60674-094-1

This book is dedicated to the memory of
Fr. Joe McGeady SSCC

See Script 16

Contents

Acknowledgements   xi

Introduction   xiii

Setting up a Children's Church Team   xvi

How to Use this Book   xxv

Frequently Used Prayers   xxxvi

THE SESSIONS

Script 1 –   "Watch Out" (Advent 1)   1

Script 2 –   "Repent!" (Advent 2)   7

Script 3 –   "Rejoice!" (Advent 3)   12

Script 4 –   St. Joseph (Advent 4)   18

Script 5 –   The Word (Christmas 1)   22

Script 6 –   The Flight into Egypt (Christmas 2)   28

Script 7 –   The Baptism of Jesus (Epiphany 1)   33

Script 8 –   Behold the Lamb of God (Epiphany 2)   38

Script 9 –   Fishers of Men (Epiphany 3)   43

Script 10 –   Wedding at Cana   48

Script 11 –   The Beatitudes (Epiphany 4)   52

Script 12 –   Lights and Bushels (Epiphany 5)   60

Script 13 –   Staying Good (Epiphany 6)   64

Script 14 –   Turning the Other Cheek (Epiphany 7)   69

Script 15 –   Trusting in God (Epiphany 8)   74

Script 16 –   The Transfiguration (Last Epiphany)   80

Script 17 –   Jesus in the Desert (Lent 1)   85

Script 18 –   Nicodemus (and Noah) (Lent 2)   92

Script 19 –   The Samaritan Woman (Lent 3)   99

Script 20 –   Jesus heals a Blind Man (Lent 4)   104

Script 21 –   Lazarus (Lent 5)   109

Script 22 –   Palm Sunday   114

Script 23 –   Easter Sunday   120

Script 24 –   Doubting Thomas (Easter 2)   125

Script 25 –   The Walk to Emmaus (Easter 3)   130

Script 26 –   "I am the Gate" (Easter 4)   135

Script 27 –   Mansions (Easter 5)   139

Script 28 –   Jesus Packs Up (Easter 6)   144

Script 29 –   Staying Together (Easter 7)   149

Script 30 –   Detecting the Ascension (Ascension Day)   153

Script 31 –   Pentecost (Pentecost)   158

Script 32 –   Trinity Sunday   163

Script 33 –   The Two Builders (Proper 4)   169
              The Sunday closest to June 1

Script 34 –   The Call of Matthew (Proper 5)   174
              The Sunday closest to June 8

Script 35 –   Jesus' Twelve Friends (Proper 6)   178
              The Sunday closest to June 15

Script 36 –   Shouting from the Housetops (Proper 7)   183
              The Sunday closest to June 22

Script 37 –   A Cup of Cold Water (Proper 8)   187
              The Sunday closest to June 29

Script 38 –   My Yoke is Easy (Proper 9)   193
              The Sunday closest to July 6

Script 39 –   The Sower (Proper 10)   198
              The Sunday closest to July 13

Script 40 – Wheat and Tares (Proper 11) 203
The Sunday closest to July 20

Script 41 – Mustard Seeds (Proper 12) 208
The Sunday closest to July 27

Script 42 – The Feeding of the 5,000 (Proper 13) 215
The Sunday closest to August 3

Script 43 – Walking on Water (Proper 14) 220
The Sunday closest to August 10

Script 44 – Foreigners (Proper 15) 224
The Sunday closest to August 17

Script 45 – St. Peter's Keys (Proper 16) 229
The Sunday closest to August 24

Script 46 – Take up Your Cross (Proper 17) 233
The Sunday closest to August 31

Script 47 – Time Out (Proper 18) 237
The Sunday closest to September 7

Script 48 – The Ungrateful Servant (Proper 19) 241
The Sunday closest to September 14

Script 49 – The Laborers in the Vineyard (Proper 20) 246
The Sunday closest to September 21

Script 50 – The Two Sons (Proper 21) 251
The Sunday closest to September 28

Script 51 – The Farmer and his Tenants (Proper 22) 255
The Sunday closest to October 5

Script 52 – The King's Party (Proper 23) 260
The Sunday closest to October 12

Script 53 – Render unto Caesar (Proper 24) 265
The Sunday closest to October 19

Script 54 – The Great Commandment (Proper 25) 270
The Sunday closest to October 26

Script 55 – Happy Endings (David and Goliath) (Proper 26) 275
The Sunday closest to November 2

Script 56 – Happy Endings (The End of the World) (Extra Lesson) 281

Script 57 – The Wise and Foolish Virgins (Proper 27) 286

The Sunday closest to November 9

Script 58 – The Parable of the Talents (Proper 28)   291
The Sunday closest to November 16

Script 59 – Christ the King (Proper 29)   296
The Sunday closest to November 23

Script 60 – Saint Spotting (Any Saint's Day)   302

Stories for Children in Distress   309

Index of Biblical References   310

Acknowledgements

This book is the result of seventeen years of ecumenical (and exhilarating) work in the London churches of Our Lady of Lourdes, Acton (Catholic), and St. Michael and All Angels, Bedford Park (Anglican). Both churches were unstintingly generous in their provision of space, time and resources, and to everyone involved, priests, congregations and children, I offer heartfelt thanks.

The children's church in Acton owes its existence to the enlightened leadership of Bishop Pat Lynch (then the parish priest) and his lay administrator Ellie McKeown. Ellie, working on the "vocation by compulsion" principle, roped in a large and varied group to look after the children, and in the fullness of time her net caught me. The immediate cause of my recruitment was Nicholas Rodger, one of the founder members of the group, who brought his fine scholarship—and scarcely less remarkable dramatic skills—to an already talented team. Among them I am particularly grateful to Sr. Miriam McNulty, Janusz Jankowski, Peter Robertson, Margaret Fry, Joan Hughes and Susan Cunningham. To Deacon Tito Pereira, whose devotion to the gospel was the dynamo that powered our team meetings, and whose ideas I have shamelessly plundered, I owe more than a mere acknowledgement can express.

In Bedford Park, Fr. Kevin Morris has been equally generous in his encouragement and support. The press gang is as active at St. Michael's as it is at Our Lady's, and among our "volunteers" I am extremely grateful to Wendy Callister, Bernadette Halford, Nicola Chater and Pamela Bickley, all of whom have led the team with a commitment that went way beyond the call of duty.

To my family, who have endured seventeen years of disrupted Sunday mornings, my brothers Christopher and Andrew, whose features I default to whenever I draw the Apostles, and my sister Jane for giving my dialogue some sort of street credibility, I offer as always my love and thanks.

Fr. Andrew Davison's meticulous reading of the text, as theological consultant, has ensured the scripts are faithful to the teaching of the Church (any errors that have crept in since his scrutiny are my own). I am deeply grateful to him and to Christine Smith of the Canterbury Press, a paragon of encouragement and patience, David Beresford for doing the photo shoots, Anne Tennant, a friend in need when the unedited scripts threatened to overwhelm me and, last of all, Margaret Stonborough, who insisted that I responded to Nicholas's call in the first place, and has found it involved her in more prop making and keyboard bashing than she can ever have anticipated.

Introduction

Children

Children are part of the Church. Everyone knows that, and most churches do their best to make them feel at home. Even so, there are times, particularly at the beginning of the Eucharist, when it seems appropriate to offer the kids an alternative to a full set of Bible readings and the sermon.

Enter Children's Church! Or Sunday School, Children's Liturgy, Children's Club, it doesn't matter what you call it.

The idea is that the children are shepherded out of church to a hall—or somewhere suitably out of earshot—where they hear the Gospel and worship Almighty God in their own way, and at their own pace. They reappear at Communion time to rejoin their families at the altar, ready with a presentation to share their discoveries with the rest of the congregation.

Such a group presupposes adult leaders, and if you're one of them—and don't have time to think up children's activities week after week—this book is for you.

Scripts for Children's Church

Our purpose is to provide material that will help children acquire a familiarity with the life of Christ and the events of the church year, in a way that is vivid and memorable. Better still, they'll enjoy it. The material does not require a great deal of preparation, nor a degree in theology, in fact you and the children will probably learn the faith together.

This book provides a session for every Sunday of the liturgical year A,* in the form

---

* The readings for the Eucharist are arranged in three cycles, A, B and C, and run from the beginning of the liturgical year (Advent Sunday) to its end (Christ the King). Sets of scripts will be published in time for year B (2011) and year C (2012), followed by a book for the festivals that come up every year, such as harvest festival and all the major saints' days.

of an easy-to-use script. Each one is headed up by the theme of the day, a list of the toys, props and pictures you'll need, the prayers that open and close each session, the Gospel reading and (most importantly) your "lines:" the sort of things you'll say to the kids, their (probable) response, and the games and activities that will reinforce the Gospel message. Given a modicum of preparation (see below), all you'll have to do on Sunday is set up the hall, spend fifteen minutes with a photocopier, and the children's session should practically run itself.

Pictures

The book is full of pictures and each session comes with its own set of images: these can be found on the CD-ROM attached to the back cover.

Children's Church and the Eucharist

The main act of worship on a Sunday is the Eucharist. The service is composed of two sections: the Liturgy of the Word, and the Liturgy of Holy Communion. The Liturgy of the Word is, naturally, centered on the Bible: it reaches its climax with the Gospel reading and is concluded by the sermon that follows. The Liturgy of Holy Communion is centered round the altar as bread and wine are consecrated and we receive the Body and Blood of Christ.

These sessions provide a child friendly Liturgy of the Word that parallels the adult version going on in church, and allows the children to return to church in plenty of time for the Liturgy of Holy Communion. As a result they follow the structure of the Eucharist closely.

The normal pattern in churches where I have worked is: the children are sent out by the priest, with their own Gospel Book, at the beginning of the service. They reassemble in the church hall and join in a simplified version of the prayers of penitence and the Opening Prayer. Then they turn their attention to the Gospel—which is where the fun begins.

The Gospel passages are so rich that we've found the most effective way to teach them is to concentrate on one leading idea. The Prodigal Son, for example (Luke 15:11-32), could be about the crucial moment when the young man, sitting among the pigs, "comes to himself" and repents, or it could be about the way his father runs to greet him before he's even got to the front door, or it could be about the furious sulk of his older brother. There's no time to do all this, so the script focuses on one of these themes and underlines it with prayers, pictures and games.

The children might not realize immediately that the Prodigal's Pig Hunt (see *Creative Ideas for Children's Worship, Year C*) they've just enjoyed is an illustration of what the younger son really found in that sty (that is, himself), but they'll have got the idea by the end of the session; particularly as it ends with a pithy summary of the Prodigal's adventures, geared for a presentation back in church.

Growing in the Christian Faith

A major advantage of these scripts is that the children hear exactly the same Gospel as the rest of the church, so their contribution at the end of the service will tie in with something the adults have already encountered. Added to which, living with these scripts, Sunday by Sunday, means that children and leaders experience a whole Christian year together and discover that church is more interesting (and a great deal more energetic) than they'd realized.

Setting up a Children's Church Team

Recruitment

Recruitment to a Children's Church team is usually done via a general invitation. All the same, an assurance that the load will be spread evenly over the year usually calms people down—that, and a guarantee that all a leader has to do is follow a script: everything else will be provided.

Leaders

The liturgies in this book assume that a "leader" is someone who feels OK about getting up in front of children and presenting a script, but there's plenty of scope for more nervous types who may prefer to help from the side. It's good to have a variety of "voices" presenting the session, so two leaders are the basic minimum to make it effective, four leaders mean you can give people Sundays off, and twelve leaders are practically ideal.

Team Meetings

You will find it helpful to meet at least once a quarter. There will be rotas and practical matters to discuss of course, but the core of these meetings should be a read through of the sessions coming up. Each script comes with its Gospel reading, notes on understanding the passage, and suggestions for activities and devotions. Talking this through will help you get on top of the material and indicate what toys and props you'll need to gather. This is also the moment to modify the scripts to suit local circumstances.

Child Protection/Safeguarding

Churches have clear rules about child protection; find out what they are and follow them. If you have any uncertainties about your church's requirements, consult the website of your diocese and consult the resolution of The Episcopal Church titled Protect Children and Youth from Abuse, found here: *http://www.episcopalarchives. org/cgi-bin/acts/acts_resolution.pl?resolution=2003-B008.* You may also want to consult the U.S Department of Education's excellent document titled Safeguarding Our Children: An Action Guide, found at *www2.ed.gov/admins/lead/safety/act-guide/action_guide.pdf.* Additionally, the Church Pension Group offers materials for Safeguarding God's Children; you'll find these resources online at: *https://www. cpg.org/administrators/insurance/preventing-sexual-misconduct/overview/.* It is now mandatory for all volunteers to have a background check; it is also important to note that at least two adults must always be present with the children in your care. Larger churches may have a children's advocate who will help advise you and sort out the paperwork. It's good practice to take attendance at all sessions—it helps you identify which kids are where at what time.

The School Year

Children's Church usually only operates during the academic year, as there can be a sharp decline in numbers over the summer. However, we've provided a session for every Sunday in the year—just in case the church is heaving with children after all.

Young Children

As a rule of thumb liturgy works best with children who have started school: they're used to basic school rules, like sitting quietly on the floor, putting up their hands before they speak and playing games in an organized way. It may be difficult for a toddler. If parents want to bring small children along, ask them to remain to look after them. Sending little ones in under the care of a sibling doesn't usually work.

Teenagers

You'll find that some of the older children don't want to move on, partly because they like you and partly because they feel children's liturgy is more fun than adult church. Obviously you'll know your own kids and how to deal with this. Teenagers can be very helpful as auxiliary helpers, as long as they are *never* allowed to stand along the back wall! See below . . .

Cool Dudes

Cool dudes who hang around at the back are the death of liturgy. From about the age of eleven onwards, kids have a tendency to drift to the back wall, lean up against it, and watch the proceedings with their friends. With all the sympathy in the world for teenage angst, you can't let this happen. If you do, you'll get a hall divided between enthusiastic little kids, cool dudes, and a middle group who want to copy the big ones. Liturgy is about participation; big kids are fine if they want to join in, otherwise—back to the service in church.

Discipline

Children's Church is not school. Nobody has to come but, as kids have to be *somewhere* in the church complex, they're either with you—and behaving—or back in church. The irritating thing about sending children back to church is you have to accompany them there, or call their parents out to collect them. Fortunately the resulting interview between parent and child usually ensures it never happens again.

Some subversive types might think it great fun to shout out silly answers but you can usually block this by applying a "hands up" only rule. Gameboys and iPods are a total bore. We killed an outbreak of texting once by saying, "Hands up who's got a mobile?" Up shot the hands. "OK, bring them down the front and leave them on the table." (Of course this only works once.)

Parents

Some parents process out with their children to settle them, or look after the little ones. "Spare" parents should be encouraged to return to the main service.

Helpers

They can be parents, big kids, Confirmation candidates, or nervous adults thinking about committing to Children's Church at a future date: they are unbelievably useful. Be realistic about what they can actually do.

Runners

You need to know when to bring the children back into church and it's useful to have some well disposed people in church ready to come around and tell you when the Offertory (or whatever your agreed cue is) is about to start. Teenagers can be very helpful here—especially if they're able to tell you the news via a mobile.

Clergy

As the children's and adults' liturgies should form an organic whole, make sure your priest knows what's going on, particularly when it comes to the presentation. Some priests prefer to be the one who asks the children what they've been doing, others are happy to let the team lead. Either way, check there's time for a presentation at the end—if there isn't, don't rehearse it.

There's nothing worse than a pew full of disappointed kids.

Also make sure what Gospel is actually going to be read that Sunday. The Gospels in this book are the "normal" ones, but a feast may be transferred to its nearest Sunday. As long as the priest knows you're following the normal Gospel all should be well. (Alternatively, we have provided a "filler" script which can be adapted to practically any saint: "Script 60—Saint Spotting.)

Setting Up

The most basic requirement is a separate room. Obviously you have to take what is given, but it is surprising how quickly you can adapt any space to your needs.

Rooms/Halls

If you are given a room, clear away as much furniture as you can and make an empty space at one end. If you're given the church hall, mark off one bit as the holy area—the place from which you'll be leading prayers and reading the Gospel. Limits are important in church halls as the mere sight of acres of open space makes children want to rush around.

Furniture

Try to appropriate some shelves or filing cabinet to store your props. You'll need a lectern or a little table on which to place the Gospel Book (see p. xxxi under *Gospel*). Another table at the front is also very useful: you can drape it in the liturgical color of the day, and use it to focus attention on the icon, candle, toy, or whatever you are going to use in the liturgy.

Chairs, oddly enough, are not a great idea. They inhibit the children from acting together, and the kids usually can't resist the temptation to swing their legs and kick the chair in front. Cut the chairs down to a couple for the leaders and visiting grown-ups.

The Floor

Nothing really beats getting the kids to sit on the floor. On mats, if your church has them, but the floor if need be. Children are used to sitting on the floor for assembly at school. In small spaces it means you can accommodate more children and bring them nearer the front to see what's going on. If you're up to it, sitting on the floor yourself among the children works very well—especially if you're telling them a story.

Props

Every liturgy comes with a list of the props you'll need; the most frequent are listed below. It looks formidable, but most churches have a fair amount of equipment and a few visits to the toy store should supply the rest.

Ordinary Equipment

- Either a flip-chart, an easel, or a whiteboard, or a place you can stick up sheets of newsprint or poster board.
- A reusable adhesive putty.
- Large colored markers for the leaders or white board markers.
- Matches—but use tapers to actually light the candles; they look nicer and are easier to handle.
- Candle snuffers.
- The use of a photo copier.

Useful Extras

- Any costumes: all-purpose Shepherd, King or Angel. Burglars are handy as DIY villains, a mask and any stripped top will do.
- Crowns, even paper ones, are invaluable.
- Any helmets: Policeman, Roman Soldier, Knight.
- Wooden dowels, all sizes.
- Large dice—made by covering square (or near square) cardboard boxes in stout white paper and marking gigantic dots on the sides. (Some party stores sell blow-up dice, which are superb for group games.)
- Some large, nice-looking rocks, picked up on the beach, at least one large shiny one.
- Toy animals—particularly sheep.
- Crook or old-fashioned wooden walking stick.

- At least one football.
- Toy props: plastic swords, crowns, doctor's sets, handcuffs and those useful plastic scythes and pitchforks you can get at Halloween.
- Torches.
- Treasure—plastic pearls, any tacky jewelry, preferably in a "Jewel Box."
- Gold covered chocolate money.
- If you find a confectioner selling chocolate fish at Easter, buy a few—they'll come in handy later on.

Art Extras

- Coloring markers and colored pencils in working order.
- Ordinary white paper.
- Child-friendly scissors.
- Scissors.
- Gold and silver paper.
- Index cards.
- Glue.
- Masking tape.

Holy Props

- A Gospel Book: use one of the recognized translations of the complete Bible rather than a "children's Bible." The latter may not have the complete Gospel and much of it will be paraphrased. We recommend the New Revised Standard Version of the Bible (the NRSV).
- The use of a lectionary—that's the list of readings for the church year. Your priest should have one.
- A crucifix or a cross.
- Pieces of cloth to hang over the table in the liturgical colors—green, red, purple, white (and gold if you come across some lamé). Synthetic material doesn't crease as badly as the good stuff.
- Candles in portable candlesticks.
- Small handbells.
- A stout candle that can stand securely on its own.
- And, if your church uses them:

A holy water stoup and sprinkler.

A spare thurible, charcoal and incense (though check the latter won't set the fire alarm off).

Holy Extras

- Icons, posters or postcards of holy pictures, small statues of the saints (plastic is fine!). Try to have at least one image of the patron saint of your church. The National Gallery has an excellent range of posters and postcards on holy subjects by some of the greatest painters in the world. Their website is <u>www.national gallery.org.uk</u>. Alternatively you can use images from the Web Gallery of Art for slide presentation, or simply displayed on your laptop screen, absolutely free. Their website is <u>www.wga.hu/</u>. You'll find references to the pictures they offer in some of the sessions.
- CDs with kids hymns, Taizé chants and quiet mood music are very useful.
- Sweet-smelling oils—you can get cheap flasks of myrrh and frankincense at cathedral gift shops but aromatherapy oils from drug stores are good substitutes.
- Any holy toys, like a Noah's Ark or a crib set.
- Artifacts from the Jewish faith are also very helpful, such as a Torah scroll, Seder plate for the Passover and a Menorah candle stand.

Images in Church

Look round your church. Even the plainest building can yield a surprising number of pictures. They can be anywhere: in the windows, carved on the memorials, embroidered on the vestments and painted on the banners. Everything is worth noticing—flames, lambs, keys, clusters of grapes—as well as the more obvious pictures and statues of saints.

DIY Props

"Our Father" cards are a good standby for those moments when you've got five minutes to fill. You make them by putting the Lord's Prayer, phrase by phrase, on various sheets of newsprint, laminating them—and shuffling.

The idea is that the children go for a land speed record in reassembling the prayer and then, when they've quietened down, pray it. It works for any prayer or creed you wish the children to learn.

High Tech Helps

- All forms of projection: scoop up any offers of unwanted projectors (provided they work). (See if you can borrow the church's overhead projector, slide projector, or—in very lucky churches—a digital projector. The latter only works with a laptop.)
- A CD player.
)• Keyboard.
- Extension cords.
- Gaffer tape or masking tape to stick over cords and ensure the kids don't trip.
- A roving mike, for the presentation back in church, is a great asset.

How to Use this Book

Once you've got your team, a hall and some children—you'll need a liturgy.

Simply find out what Sunday Gospel you should be preparing for, and look it up in the contents list. The Sundays are listed in chronological order, so once you've found your first, all should be SMOOTH sailing.

However, church being what it is, there are a couple of complications. Given the variable date of Easter, we have to allow for some extra Sundays before Easter (in case it's late) or some extra Sundays after Easter (in case it's early).

Photocopying

After you've established what Gospel you're going to do, gather the toys and props during the week, and photocopy the script for any leader without a book. You might also like to photocopy the sections of the Kyries (the "Lord have mercy" prayers) on three separate strips of paper for individual children to read out.

If there are pictures involved, find the set suggested on the CD-ROM and print them as large as possible. All the pictures that make a "scene" are provided separately, so you can copy them on to newsprint.

Getting Ready

- Set up the hall on the day, with all the objects and scripts you'll need.
- Read the script through and agree on who says what with the other leader.
- Alert the children's music group (if you have one) to the hymns planned.
- Some scripts call for help from a couple of children, find your volunteers and run through their parts (it's always very easy).
- That's it, you're ready to go.

Following the Scripts

The scripts follow a simple format. Each section is headed up in bold and, as long as there are no lines for you to speak in the section, the font looks normal.
Like this:

SET UP

- A list of props, extra people, etc.
- A crook (a walking stick will do).
- Toy sheep, etc.

If a section contains remarks by you, your lines stay in normal font, but any instructions now appear in italics, like this:

Put the toy sheep on the floor, and grasp the crook.

Leader   OK, now there are a couple of things you need to know about sheep.

Any question you ask the children comes with the expected answer in bold font, enclosed in round brackets.

Leader   Today we're thinking about sheep—and the people who look after them.
Anyone know what they were called?
(Shepherds)

The only other font change happens when you pray. Prayers said by one person come in normal font, prayers said by everyone are in bold.

Lord have mercy
Lord have mercy

Christ have mercy
Christ have mercy

God's Capital H

You'll notice that God's personal pronoun (He, Him or His) always has a capital H. In the pilot sessions for this book we found this a helpful way of remembering just who we were talking about (especially when doing the liturgy at speed).

A Typical Script, Section by Section

SENDING OUT

The first thing you need to do is organize your exit from the church. Ask if you can place the children's Gospel Book on the altar and gather your group together. At a given moment (usually after the entrance hymn or during the sequence hymn) the celebrant hands the Gospel Book to one of the children (chosen in advance) and sends them out. The whole team processes out, following the Gospel as it is held aloft.

You'll probably find that you pick up stragglers and shy kids as you leave church.

WELCOME

Once you're all in the hall, welcome the children. Keep it brief and go straight into:

THE SIGN OF THE CROSS

If this is not a usual devotion in your church, you may find it helpful to run through the Sign like this:

The Sign of the Cross

+ In the Name of the Father, *(On "Father" you touch your head, that's the Father in Heaven.)*

and of the Son *(Bring your hand down—the Son came down to earth.)*

and of the Holy Spirit. *(Touch your heart, the Spirit lives in our hearts.)*

Amen. *(Finish the Shape of the Cross by touching your right side then your left.)*

A little cross **+** in the text flags up the times it is usual to make the Sign of the Cross.

Making the Sign of the Cross can have an extraordinarily quietening effect on children. However, if they *are* slightly chatty at the beginning, do the old trick of going silent yourself until they get unnerved and stop talking. Reinforce this by saying things like, "Thank you Charlie" to any phenomenally well behaved child.

One leader I knew surprised everybody one Sunday by asking the children to make the Sign of the Cross very quietly (he had a hangover). The kids looked sideways at one another. "How do you do a *noisy* sign of the cross?" you could see they were thinking—even so, a breathless hush ensued.

THE KYRIE

Preface the Kyrie with a brief, "Let's look back at the week—is there anything we wish we hadn't done? Anything we'd like to say sorry for?" Keep it light.

If you've got three children prepared to read the three petitions of the Kyrie, have them at the front, give them a hand if necessary, and join the children in the response:

Lord have mercy
Christ have mercy
Lord have mercy

It's extremely important that all grown ups in the room take part in the prayers and follow the proceedings as seriously as the children. Gossiping adults at the back should be politely banned.

PRAYER FOR FORGIVENESS

This is the "layman's absolution" and can be said by a leader, or repeated by everyone. If the children don't know it, you may ask them to repeat it after you, line by line.

OPENING PRAYER

The moment when the theme of the day starts to appear.

BEFORE THE GOSPEL

A huge change of gear takes place as you prepare for the Gospel reading. The idea is that the children should be able to follow the Gospel when they hear it and to achieve this the scripts try everything: games, mini-dramas, startling demonstrations (like how stupid it is to build a wall out of jelly). Anything to get them going.

It's here that you begin to interact with the children. Ask them questions, the simpler the better. Children love putting their hand up (some toddlers do it automatically but all you get from them is a sweet smile).

As soon as the Gospel Book has been set up, move into:

THE GOSPEL PROCESSION

Obviously the Sunday Gospel is the dynamo of the whole session. Everything—songs, prayers and games, derives from it and, when it's read, it either sets up the message for the day, or clinches it. Either way Jesus calls the shots.

To make this apparent to the children it's helpful to read the Gospel with some ceremony. Depending on how your space is shaped, you can place the Gospel Book on its own special lectern, or table, at the back of the hall and process it to the front, or you can place it down the front and process it into the middle of the children. Or you can just move it from a small table at the front to a lectern beside it. The point is, it should be moved.*

You can't replicate the solemn reading of the Gospel in church (unless you have a deacon or priest present). You can, however, set it apart. Hold the Gospel Book up as it's processed—Jesus is present in His Word, just as He will be present later on in the Bread and Wine of the Eucharist. Flank it with candles—you'll have no lack of volunteers—and invest in some hand bells. Dinging the bells as the Gospel is processed is a marvellous job for very small kids.

---

* The Eastern Orthodox invented the Gospel procession to dramatize Jesus' wanderings through Galilee: they directed that the Gospel, and its reader, should process from the altar, "wander" through the church and land up in the midst of the people.

If you're blessed with a music group you might like to sing some "Alleluias" as the Gospel is processed.

There is no Gospel Procession in Advent or Lent. This is not something we've taken over from church—actually Gospel processions happen all year round—but it's a helpful way of marking these seasons with the children. You'll see the rationale for this change when you do the sessions.

THE GOSPEL

Normally you read the Gospel straight; however, keep an eye on the script because in some cases we give you a paraphrase to read out instead. All our paraphrases contain at least one sentence (usually many more) of a recognized translation of the Bible. The children must hear the genuine Word of God.

If you are reading straight from the Bible, think of ways of making it accessible: make the dialogue sound real, cut verses not dealt with in the session, change *denari* into dollars or *tunics* into shirts. Having said that, it is often appropriate to offer the kids an old-fashioned phrase as part of their cultural heritage. Many of them know already one shouldn't hide one's light "under a bushel," or that the Rich Fool said to himself that he could "eat, drink and be merry." Take a view: stylistic gear changes are part of the modern Christian package.

AFTER THE GOSPEL

You wrap the Gospel up: sometimes in a pithy sentence or two, more often in an extended activity. This might be a game, or a devotion, or some music. The activity always includes a rehearsal for a presentation back in church (if you're doing one).

DIY ART

Coloring pictures is not a major feature of this book. When it happens it appears as a group activity, and is usually timed—so the children produce art work at speed (this seems to motivate the less artsy). However, some of the pictures on the CD-ROM are in black and white, to give the kids who like to color in a chance to show their skill.

 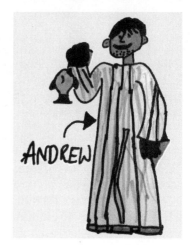

There are many occasions when the children can make their presentation as well as perform it, particularly if the presentation involves pictures. There's no reason, except time, why they should hold up versions of the pictures on the CD-ROM. The congregation is going to be much more interested in stuff the children have produced themselves.

GAMES

All the board games can be played either by a group of children crowded round the board, or a large group, split into teams, who play via a representative. In the latter case, most members of the team get a chance to roll the enormous Children's Church dice.

Energetic games which normally require rushing around have been offered in two versions. One for spaces in which children *can* run around, and another for more restricted venues.

Jesus appears to have been deeply uninterested in people who came first, so make sure you cheer the losers.

MUSIC

Hymns, traditional and modern, are a wonderful way to finish the session, but they depend on somebody having the musical confidence to lead them. If you can't rustle up a piano or guitar player, you can download karaoke style music for many popular hymns via the internet, and there are CDs available with children's songs.

If you are intending to sing, think about the words: writing them up on a flip-chart works better than children fiddling round with hymn books. (On the other hand some kids find it thrilling to look up "number 143.")

REHEARSING THE PRESENTATION

The congregation deserve to hear what the children have been up to. Choose good readers and run the presentation through with the kids. It's almost bound to be fun, try to get it slick and well timed as well.

PRAYER

You won't be able to have an extended session on prayer every Sunday, but get the children used to the idea of a prayer circle. Put a large candle in the middle (the sort that can stand on its own base) as a focus of attention. Or pass round one of the many objects suggested in the scripts.

Give the children alternatives to verbal prayer, sprinkle them with water, bless them with incense. Let them wave their arms about to the movements of an interactive hymn, or reflect on the power of the Holy Spirit by feeling a fan blowing in their faces. Explore the Catholic tradition: most children like bells, icons, holy bookmarks and statues, and they are usually up for making some of these objects themselves. Give the children a chance to pray privately.

Quiet music in the background is a help, but keep the sessions fairly short. There is a moment beyond which even the most pious child can't concentrate.

Every now and then these sessions will provoke a distressing revelation. A child might be anxious about a sick relative, or show an awareness of a family grief they only dimly understand, like a miscarriage. In the immediate situation, give the child time to talk, and see if you can offer them a story that will help. (There are a couple suggested on p. 309.) Afterwards, have a private word with the parents.

THE FINAL PRAYER

Make sure you gather for a formal prayer before you go back to church: a brief "Glory Be . . ." is fine.

COMING BACK TO CHURCH

When you come back depends on your priest and the number of children. Some churches like the children to help with the Offertory procession, others prefer them back at the moment when the people are coming to the altar.

Depending on numbers, you may want the children to rejoin their parents or (if this is too disruptive) reserve a couple of pews for them down the front. Their presentation happens either at the Offertory or, more usually, after Communion.

Do your best to promote a "guaranteed success" atmosphere in the church—and congratulate the kids yourself.

EXTRAS

Mass/Holy Communion/Eucharist

Anglicans use different names for this great sacrament—this book uses all three.

Gender

The sessions acknowledge that Jesus and the Apostles were male, the Virgin Mary and many of Jesus' disciples female, and that Angels, though technically neuter, often appear as "a young man in white." However, though the pronouns are gender specific, there's no reason for the kids to be. You'll find that most girls are happy to play St. Peter or the good Samaritan, boys don't mind being angels, and everyone enjoys being sheep, lepers and so on. Do your best to cast the children even handedly.

Health and Safety

Obviously anybody leading an organized activity for children needs to be aware of health and safety. All these scripts have been test run three times with no problems, but venues differ (as do children). Look at each script beforehand to work out potential flash points (the gallop from "Emmaus" to "Jerusalem," for example) and follow the health and safety protocols of your own church.

Frequently Used Prayers

The Sign of the Cross

✠ In the Name of the Father,
and of the Son
and of the Holy Spirit.
Amen.

The Prayer for Forgiveness

May God our Father
Have mercy upon us
✠ Forgive us our sins
And bring us to eternal life.
Amen.

The Lord's Prayer

Our Father, who art in Heaven,
hallowed be thy Name,
thy Kingdom come,
thy will be done,
on Earth as it is in Heaven.
Give us this day our daily bread.
And forgive us our trespasses,
as we forgive those who trespass
   against us.
And lead us not into temptation,
but deliver us from evil.
For thine is the Kingdom,
the power and the glory,
for ever and ever.
Amen.

Modern Version of the Lord's Prayer

Our Father in Heaven,
hallowed be your name,
your Kingdom come,
your will be done,
on Earth as in Heaven.
Give us today our daily bread.
Forgive us our sins
as we forgive those who sin
   against us.
Lead us not into temptation
but deliver us from evil.
For the Kingdom, the power,
and the glory are yours
now and for ever.
Amen.

Glory Be

Glory be to the Father, and to the Son, and to the Holy Spirit:
as it was in the beginning, is now, and ever shall be.
Amen.

Hail Mary

Hail Mary full of grace,
the Lord is with thee.
Blessed art thou among women
and blessed is the fruit of thy womb Jesus.
Holy Mary, Mother of God,
pray for us sinners now
and at the hour of our death.
Amen.

Script 1 · "Watch Out!"

Advent 1

Matthew 24:42-44

THEME

Advent starts the Church year and Jesus' message is: "Get ready, keep awake!"
The Gospel is full of these wake up calls. Jesus' countrymen, who had waited so
long for the coming of the Messiah, appear not to have noticed He'd arrived. And
Jesus' friends seem to have needed prodding as well.

So what are children to keep awake for? Christmas obviously—not Santa Claus
and presents (important though they are)—but Jesus' arrival as a tiny child on
Christmas morning. It's also worth practicing being alert, you never know when
the Lord might turn up...

SET UP

- The liturgical color is Purple or Sarum Blue: highlight
  by wearing something purple or blue.
- An Advent Wreath.*
- A box full of stuff for Christmas, put a Bible in and
  then add anything you've got—a toy crown, a lamb,
  some candlesticks if you're stuck, even a nativity figure, anything portable.
- Burglar kit: a party mask (preferably black), a striped
  shirt and a floppy bag or sack (like a laundry bag)
  labelled "loot."
- Somebody prepared to dress up as the burglar—a
  grown up or an older child.
- Letter with "Wanted" poster inside (from the CD-
  ROM) and a small Bible with the version of the Gospel used below slid between its
  pages. (This goes in a Leader's pocket.)

---

* Keep the Advent Wreath for all four Advent Sundays; and the loot bag and burglar outfit for next
week. Note: the burglar kit gets used from time to time throughout the year.

WELCOME *the children and start the session with one Leader saying*

Leader   Okay, we have a special message from Jesus today—it is...
All Leaders   **Watch out!**

Lead the children in **The Sign of the Cross + (p. xxxvi).**

INTRODUCING ADVENT

Leader   This week the color has changed in church.

Depending on what you use to indicate liturgical colors in your church, run a dialogue along these lines:

> What color did we have on the Altar today? (**Purple or Blue**)
> What color was the priest wearing? (**Purple or Blue**)
> Check out my socks, what color are they? (**Purple or Blue!**)
> The church has gone purple or blue.
> When the church gets into purple or blue it's a sign we're getting ready for something. Any idea what we're getting ready for?

Give some outrageous hints (I'm ordering a turkey next week, must get a tree, etc.).

> (**Christmas**)
> Brilliant, we're getting ready for Christmas and the four weeks before Christmas are called "Advent."
> Advent means "coming." So in Advent we're looking out for somebody who's coming.
> Anybody know who that is?

Take all answers—one child is bound to say "Santa Claus." Sum up by saying:

> We're getting ready for Jesus, when He comes as a tiny child on Christmas Day.
> One way to get ready is to clear up all the things we've done wrong. Let's do that now.

THE KYRIE   Lord Jesus, you came on earth to tell us how much God loves us,
Lord have mercy.
Lord have mercy.

Lord Jesus, you came on earth to help us say sorry,
Christ have mercy.
Christ have mercy.

Lord Jesus, you came on earth so our sins could be forgiven,
Lord have mercy.
Lord have mercy.

Ask the children to repeat **The Prayer for Forgiveness** *after you* **(p. xxxvi).**

THE ADVENT WREATH

An Advent Wreath helps define the Sundays in Advent. The children like lighting the candles—and love the countdown. Traditionally there are three purple or blue candles (for Sundays 1, 2 and 4), a pink one for the cheerful Sunday (number 3) and a white candle in the middle, for Christmas Day.
Help a child light a purple or blue candle for the first Sunday of Advent.

OPENING   God our Father,
PRAYER   We thank you for sending your Son Jesus into the world at Christmas.
                Help us to be really wide awake this Advent, so that we will be ready
                to greet Him when He comes as a Baby on Christmas Day. *Amen.*

Leader   Okay, we've started Advent.

BEFORE THE GOSPEL

Leader 2   My Advent started very strangely...

Produce letter from pocket.

                     I got a letter this morning, listen to this.

Open it up.

                     Dear *Name*,
                     Bill the Burglar has escaped from prison.
                     He'll steal anything.
                     Be on your guard.
                     Yours sincerely,
                     A Well Wisher
                     PS I enclose a Wanted Poster.

Pull out Wanted poster and stick it up.

CD1.1   That's Bill the Burglar.
                     Yup, he looks very dangerous—I'll keep an eye out for him.

Pull forward a chair and the prop box and sit down to go through the props. Ad lib the following, depending on what you've got.

                     This is obviously going to be a very exciting Advent—I'll just get the props sorted out for the next few weeks—ah a Bible, and a donkey, and a star—I wonder who'll want them? A lamb, a crown, goodness, a present—oh, it says not to be opened until Christmas Day—a candlestick...
                     Nice amount of stuff we've got here.
                     I'll have to watch out.
                     I'll put it all out.

Spread it on the floor.

                     And make a list—and, um, keep an eye on it.

Settle down in the chair.

                     If anyone sees anyone like that character...

Indicate poster.

                     Just tell me will you?

Nod off....
Enter the Burglar, who flourishes his/her loot bag and steals a couple of props. The kids will go berserk—the Burglar hides behind the chair—
Run the "Look behind you!" pantomime gag.

> What Burglar?
> Behind me?
> I can't see anything.
> I shall just settle down again and have a nice nap...

Eventually the Burglar steals the last prop, takes the Wanted poster—and only then does the Leader realize that something is amiss.

> Hey! Where's all our Christmas stuff gone?
> It's been stolen!
> Why didn't you tell me? (**Uproar!**)
> Oh, did you? Well, okay—we'd better get moving.
> Time for the Gospel.

Look in the prop box.

> Good Heavens, the Bible has been stolen too.
> Fortunately I always carry a spare.

Pull out the pocket Bible, open it and quickly scan the Gospel—then collapse.

> Oh no!

Leader 1   I think I'd better see what the Gospel says.

Take it from slumped Leader 2.

Leader 1   Ah, yes, it's a pity we didn't read this before...

THE GOSPEL *Matthew 24:42-44*

Jesus said,
"Stay awake! For you do not know when I shall come back. If a householder had known when a thief was about to break in, he'd have stayed up to catch him. You don't know when I am coming, any more than you know when a thief is about to strike. So be ready for me—stay awake and watch out!"

AFTER THE GOSPEL

Leader   What does Jesus tell us to do this Advent? (**Watch out!**)
Exactly, watch out. That's something we need to practice.

OPTIONAL ADVENT WATCH GAMES

What's the Time, Mr. Wolf?

The children advance on the wolf (who has his back to them), chanting: "What's the time, Mr. Wolf?" The wolf says: "3 o'clock," and they move three steps towards him, "8 o'clock," and they move eight steps and so on. They have to be hyper alert because when he says "Supper-time!" they run back to base before he catches them. Canny wolves let them get quite close. (Any child who manages to touch Mr. Wolf, before the dreaded "Suppertime," becomes the Wolf in his stead. It doesn't normally happen.)

Pick a Key

Blindfold a kid and put a bunch of keys just beside her: the others try to creep forward to get them, and the kid points in the direction of the sound she hears. Any child pointed at is out.

REHEARSAL

Practice your presentation for when you go back to church (see below).

FINAL **PRAYER**	God our Father, Help us this Advent To watch out for your Son So that when He comes at Christmas He may find us ready to welcome Him. *Amen.*

BACK IN CHURCH

The children line up at the front.

Leader   The Children's Church has been thinking about Advent this morning, and have come back with a special message for the church . . .

Give them a cue.

Kids   **Watch out!!**

(CD1.1)

Script 2 "Repent!"

Advent 2

Matthew 3:1-6

THEME

Today the Church hears the message of John the Baptist and his call to repentance. The Bible uses "repent" to translate a Greek word "metanoia" which means "turn round." If you've done something wrong, go back and start again. It's a wonderfully simple idea and fits into practically any adventure story you can think of. This morning we'll be using it in the next thrilling episode of Bill the Burglar.

SET UP

- The liturgical color is Purple or Blue.
- An Advent Wreath (see Advent 1).
- Empty box.
- Burglar kit: a party mask (preferably black), a striped shirt and a floppy bag or sack (like a laundry bag) labelled "loot" (see Advent 1).
- The loot bag should be full of stolen property: a Bible plus some Christmas props, anything feasible will do—a toy crown, a lamb, some candlesticks if you're stuck, even a figure from a nativity set.
- Somebody prepared to dress up as the burglar—a grown-up or an older child.
- Pictures from the CD-ROM.
- Large colored marker.

WELCOME *the children and start the session with one Leader saying:*

Leader	Okay, we have a special message for today, it is...
All Leaders	Repent!

Lead the children in **The Sign of the Cross + (p. xxxvi).**

INTRODUCTION

Remind the children about Advent

Leader	The color in church is purple or blue—that always means we're getting ready for something. What would that be? (**Christmas!**)
	Exactly! We're getting ready to welcome Jesus when He comes at Christmas.
	One way to do that is to clear away all the things we did wrong last week.
	What was that special message again...?
All Leaders	**Repent!**
	Let's do that now.
THE KYRIE	Lord Jesus, you came on earth to tell us how much God loves us, Lord have mercy.
	Lord have mercy.
	Lord Jesus, you came on earth to help us say sorry, Christ have mercy.
	Christ have mercy.
	Lord Jesus, you came on earth to forgive us, Lord have mercy.
	Lord have mercy.

Ask the children to repeat **The Prayer for Forgiveness** *after you* (**p. xxxvi**).

THE ADVENT WREATH

Ask two kids forward. One to light the purple or blue candle for the first Sunday of Advent, the other to light another purple or blue candle for the second Sunday

OPENING PRAYER	God our Father, Thank you for Advent.
	Help us this Advent to open our hearts
	So that we can welcome Jesus when He comes
	With love and joy. *Amen.*

BEFORE THE GOSPEL

Leader *(with empty box)*

Last week I started Advent by sorting out the stuff we'll need for Christmas. But something happened...

Turn the box upside down.

Can anyone remember?

The children will presumably remember Bill the Burglar—let them tell you last week's story and establish that Bill stole all their stuff.

Well, I had a very exciting week.

I set off after Bill—and I had my cell phone with me, so I could take loads of pictures—just in case I caught him. They'll come in handy for evidence.

Go through the story sticking up the "photos" as you go: ad lib the following as much as possible—the pictures will cue you in.

CD2.1   I picked up his trail at once... *(footprints)*

CD2.2   And I followed them right out of town, out into the country, down a little road until I came to a turning... *(T-intersection showing Right Way and Wrong Way)*

I could see the footprints going that way, so I just peered round the corner when I heard...

Draw a huge ROAR! in the balloon on picture **CD2.2.**

Hmm, I thought—that sounds dangerous.

I wonder which way I should go?

What do you think?

(**The children should urge you to go the Right Way.**)

Ah, but it may be a trick...

Put in a GROWL next to the ROAR!

Yup, I think I'll go this way.

Point to the Wrong Way.

CD2.3   Well, I hadn't gone a minute before I fell into a swamp...

It was awful—my feet got stuck, I couldn't move, I tried to get my feet out and my hands got covered with mud and eventually I

CD2.4   shouted...

What do you think I shouted?

Take any answer—end up putting HELP! in the balloon.

CD2.5   And this strange man appeared... *(The picture is clearly of John the Baptist, but don't name him.)*

He had a long beard and was dressed in animal skins—and he carried a bucket of water.

He pulled me out of the swamp, and swooshed water all over me and gave me something to eat. It was ghastly...

CD2.6   Locust sandwiches and fizzy honey.

CD2.7	Then he said to me... *(Write REPENT in the balloon.)*
	"Repent? What does that mean?" I asked.
CD2.8	"Oh, turn round." *(Write TURN ROUND in the balloon.)*
	"What! Go back the way I came?"
	And I thought, it's really scary, but I've obviously gone wrong, so I walked back—very slowly—in fact I'm going back to that intersection now...

Turn round, reach the signpost, hesitate—enter Bill the Burglar.

| Bill | Hello I'm glad I've met you—I can give you this stuff back... |

He hands over the bag.

Leader	That's my stuff! Thanks! Why have you done that?
Bill	Well, I met this funny guy—long beard, hairy jacket—and he told me to repent.
Leader	That's just who I met! Who is he?
	Perhaps it will tell us in the Bible...

Pull the Bible out of the loot bag and hand it to another Leader.

THE GOSPEL *Matthew 3:1-6*

At that time John the Baptist appeared in the Wilderness and began to preach. "Repent of your sins!" he said, "for the Kingdom of God is at hand!"

John's clothes were made of camel hair, he wore a leather belt round his waist and he lived on locusts and wild honey.

People came from the country all around to listen, and they confessed their sins and were baptized by him in the River Jordan.

AFTER THE GOSPEL

Leader	So who was the bearded man? (**John the Baptist**)
	John was sent by God to prepare the way for Jesus.
	Can you remember his message? (**Repent!**)
	What does repent mean? (**turn round**)
	Brilliant. John was saying, "if you've made a mistake, the simplest thing is to turn round and start again."
	I think we'll go back and tell the rest of the church John the Baptist's message.

REHEARSAL

Practice your presentation for when you go back to church (see p. 11).

SONG

"On Jordan's bank" *verses 1, 2 and 5 fit in well here.*

FINAL	We'll end by saying the family prayer of the Church.
PRAYER	**Our Father... (p. xxxvi).**

BACK IN CHURCH

Leader	We've been listening to John the Baptist this morning and we'd like to hand on his message:
Kids	**Repent!**

(CD2.3)

(CD2.5)

(CD2.6)

Sample cartoons for this script

Script 3   "Rejoice!"

Advent 3

Matthew 11:2-6

THEME

The third Sunday of Advent is called "Gaudete Sunday:" *Gaudete* means "Re-joice!" and comes from the Bible verse that was traditionally read out at the start of the Eucharist. The liturgical color is pink—or rather rose—but as many churches don't possess rose colored vestments, most priests will still be in purple or blue.

There's always a moment in a purple or blue season when things lighten up and this is it. The mood of the session should be very cheerful—easy to do given the joyful fulfilment of prophecy in today's Gospel.

(This session does not use the word "Messiah," it's such an important idea it needs a whole introduction to itself—see Script 45, p. 229.)

SET UP

- The liturgical color is Pink—try to wear some for this session.
- Your Advent Wreath.
- Picture from CD-ROM.
- Bible with the Old Testament passage (see below) printed on a separate sheet and slid into its pages.
- A walking stick.
- A pair of sunglasses.
- Either some toy handcuffs or a piece of rope.
- Choose three kids to be lame (plus stick), blind (put on sunglasses), and a prisoner (handcuffs, or secure his/her wrists with a rope).
- A large ball for one of the games (see below).

WELCOME *the children and start the session with one Leader saying:*

Leader	Okay, we have a special message for today—it is...
All Leaders	Cheer up!

Lead the children in **The Sign of the Cross +** (p. xxxvi).

INTRODUCTION

Remind the children about Advent.

Leader   The color in church has been purple or blue for nearly three weeks: that always means we're getting ready for something. What would that be? (**Christmas!**)
Yup, and it's getting closer all the time.
Let's get ready for Christmas, and our time in church this morning, by saying sorry for our sins:

THE KYRIE   Lord Jesus, you came on earth to tell us how much God loves us, Lord have mercy.
Lord have mercy.

Lord Jesus, you came on earth to help us say sorry, Christ have mercy.
Christ have mercy.

Lord Jesus, you came on earth to forgive us, Lord have mercy.
Lord have mercy.

Ask the children to repeat **The Prayer for Forgiveness** *after you* (**p. xxxvi**).

THE ADVENT WREATH

You'll need three children, two to light the two purple or blue candles and one to light the pink one. Try to choose a kid in pink.
Before the pink one is lit, pause...

Leader   Which candle shall we light today? I'm going to give you a clue— what color is my scarf—or tie—or what color is *Name* wearing? (**Pink**)
Exactly—it's Pink Sunday, let's light the pink candle.

OPENING   God our Father,
PRAYER   Thank you for Advent.
Thank you for sending your Son to us at Christmas.
Help us to rejoice on that day with love and joy. *Amen.*

BEFORE THE GOSPEL

CD3.1   *Put up the picture of John the Baptist.*

| Leader | We heard about this man last week—can anybody remember what he's called? (**John the Baptist**) |
| | And can you remember the job God gave him? (**Baptizing people, telling people to repent, eating locusts**) |

Take everything that comes—sum up with:

He was sent by God to prepare the way for Jesus, to get people ready for Jesus' coming.

Now the interesting thing is that John knew God was going to send His Son, but he suddenly got worried as to whether Jesus was the right man.

He spent a lot of time thinking about it and reading the Bible.

One bit he read was this...

Take out your Bible to read this:

When the Lord comes,
The blind will be able to see,
The deaf will hear,
And the lame will jump for joy.
God has sent me to heal the broken-hearted
And set the prisoners free.

Close the Bible.

Well, there were lots of people living then who needed God's help. Let's see some of them.

Enter the lame, the blind and the prisoner—set three chairs for them at the front.

John sent some of his friends to ask Jesus if He was the person he'd been expecting.

At that moment Jesus was out and about—healing the blind...

The blind kid takes off the sunglasses, leaves them on the chair, and stands to one side.

And the lame...

The lame kid gets up, leaves the stick behind.

I think you run to join your friend...

The kid does.

And freeing captives...

The prisoner gets out of the cuffs, leaves them behind and joins the other two.

So when John's friends passed by all they found were...

Pick them up.

some sunglasses, a stick and a pair of handcuffs.
AND a lot of happy people.

The children grin.

Then they found Jesus.
Let's hear what happened next in the Gospel.

THE GOSPEL *Matthew 11:2-6*

Leave out the verse about John being in prison.

AFTER THE GOSPEL

Leader   So John's friends said to Jesus—are you the person we've been expecting?
What was Jesus' answer?

Depending on their age you may have to carry on.

Jesus said,
"Look around, all the things the Bible said would happen when God's Son arrives are coming true.
The blind can see, and the lame can run and the prisoners are set free.
Work it out. Who do you think I am?"
Well, then they got it.
Of course! Jesus was doing all these things because He was God's Son.
Just think how pleased the blind and the lame and the prisoners were—they could run around again. It's one of the reasons this is such a happy Sunday. I think we should remember this by running round ourselves.

ACTIVITY

Take a view of the kids you've got, and the amount of space, and play a game.

Up, Down, Stop, Go!

If space is limited, this is a listening game that does your head in.
On "GO"—the children stop still.
On "STOP"—the children run on the spot.
On "UP"—the children sit down.
On "DOWN"—the children stand and stretch up to the ceiling.

After a couple of practice runs, if you think the little ones are up to it, catch people out, or just do it straight—little ones will find that difficult enough.

Gather the children round the Advent Wreath at the end, ask them to sit down.

Leader   I love Pink Sunday.
It's got a special name in the Church—it's called "Gaudete," that's Latin for "Rejoice!"

REHEARSAL

Practice your presentation for when you go back to church (see below).

FINAL   (*The response is:* **Rejoice in the Lord**)
PRAYER

Rejoice in God,
He has given sight to the blind:
Rejoice in the Lord.

He has set the captives free:
Rejoice in the Lord.

He has made the lame jump for joy:
Rejoice in the Lord.

Rejoice in the Lord always
Rejoice in the Lord.
Amen.

BACK IN CHURCH

Leader	This morning we lit the pink candle on our Advent Wreath, and we'd like to give you a message for this Pink Sunday.
Kids	**Gaudete!**
Leader	*(To the children)* I'm not sure the grown-ups understand Latin. Shall we try English?
Kids	**Cheer up!**

(CD3.1)

Script 4   Joseph

Advent 4

Matthew 1:18-21

THEME

A chance to talk about Joseph: a great saint who stays out of the limelight. We're so used to seeing him at the crib, we forget how he got there. This session sees Christmas from his point of view.

SET UP

- The liturgical color is Purple or Blue.
- The Advent Wreath.
- Pictures from the CD-ROM.
- A large sheet of paper.
- Glue or tape.
- Pens for the children.

WELCOME *the children and lead them in* **The Sign of the Cross + (p. xxxvi).**

INTRODUCTION

It's the last Sunday of Advent—that must mean it's nearly... (**Christmas**)
When is Christmas? (**The children will tell you.**)
Really? And I haven't wrapped my presents yet!
There's so much to do before Christmas—and one of the really important things is to say sorry for anything we've done wrong.
Let's start with that.

THE KYRIE   Lord Jesus, you came on earth to tell us how much God loves us,
Lord have mercy.
Lord have mercy.

Lord Jesus, you came on earth to help us say sorry,
Christ have mercy.
Christ have mercy.

Lord Jesus, you came on earth to forgive us,
Lord have mercy.
Lord have mercy.

Ask the children to repeat **The Prayer for Forgiveness** *after you* (**p. xxxvi**).

THE ADVENT WREATH

This is the countdown moment. Have four children lined up and ask the children to count each candle as it gets lit.

1, 2, 3, 4!
We're nearly there!

OPENING	God our Father,
PRAYER	Thank you for Advent.
	Fill our hearts with your love
	So that we will be ready to greet your Son on Christmas Day.
	Amen.

BEFORE THE GOSPEL

	Well, we might be rushing around getting ready for Christmas but, the first Christmas, there was one man who was tearing around like a maniac. He thought Christmas was going to do his head in.
CD4.1	He was...
	Joseph.
	He had... *(stick these pictures up randomly)*
CD4.2	Forms to fill in... *(ad lib about the census)*
CD4.3	And a donkey to catch...
CD4.4	And bags to pack.
	Then he had to work out where he'd been born and how to get there
CD4.5	—and remember he didn't have a GPS.
CD4.6	And he had to close down his carpentry business.
	And then to top it all he discovered his fiancée Mary was pregnant—and they weren't even married.
	He didn't know what to do and he threw himself into bed and pulled the covers over his head...
	At which point something happened.
	Let's find out in the Gospel.

Pull out a chair and read the Gospel as if you're telling a story.

THE GOSPEL *Matthew 1:18-21*

AFTER THE GOSPEL

Go through the Gospel.

Leader   What was really worrying Joseph? *(the fact that Mary was going to have a baby)*
                  And what happened? *(An Angel told him that the baby had come from God.)*
                  And after that Joseph found everything got easier.
                  Let's give him a hand.

ACTIVITY

Pass out the census form to a kid to fill in.
Get another child to find Bethlehem on the map and circle it.
Two children fill the suitcases (they are transparent) with the sort of things Mary and Joseph will want for their journey.
Another writes "Closed" on the sign on Joseph's door.
Another child gets the donkey and colors it in.
One child draws Mary, looking as if she's on the donkey.
Another draws Joseph as if he's leading the donkey.

The rest gather around a table on which a paper is laid and fill in a path that wiggles from top to bottom (trace it in for them beforehand).
One kid writes "Nazareth" at the top.
Another draws the town of Bethlehem at the bottom.
The others draw in trees, cacti, rocks, anything that they think suitable, around the edge of the picture.
CD4.7   *Then make a collage—put the census form, Joseph's shop, the baggage, etc. at the top of the paper, Mary, Joseph and the donkey at the bottom. Stick everything down and admire it.*

Leader	Where are Mary and Joseph going? **(Bethlehem)**—*(Write it in.)* And when will they get there? **(on Christmas Day)**—*(But get the day of the week out of them.)* Yup, next Saturday—*(or whenever the day falls)*—let's make sure we're in church to greet them.

REHEARSAL

Practice your presentation for when you go back to church (see below).

FINAL PRAYER	Looking at Mary and Joseph on their journey, I think we should remember them in our prayers:
	God our Father, We thank you for Mary and Joseph. Help us to follow the example of their courage, patience and love, And bring us to the manger to greet them, and the Christ Child, on Christmas Day. *Amen.*

BACK IN CHURCH

Bring the picture into church. Two children hold it up.
Either the priest goes through it with the kids, or a Leader points out some of its highlights.
End with:

Leader	Mary and Joseph are on their way to Bethlehem now, they'll be at the manger by Christmas Day. And so will we—but of course we'll all be sitting in the pews. So while we're together, all the children would like to take this opportunity of wishing you a...
Kids	**Merry Christmas!**

Script 5 The Word

Christmas 1

John 1:1-18
Optional Genesis 1:1-7 for younger children

THEME

This reading couldn't be more abstract! But it's a wonderful passage, and the children can at least understand the power of the Word.

An optional section on Creation is included if your group is very young.

SET UP

- The liturgical color is White.
- Pictures from the CD-ROM.
- Or Creation pictures from the CD-ROM for a special session for younger children.
- Have a spare Bible ready.

WELCOME *the children and lead them in* **The Sign of the Cross + (p. xxxvi).**

THE KYRIE	Lord Jesus, you came on earth to tell us how much God loves us,
	Lord have mercy.
	Lord have mercy.
	Lord Jesus, you came on earth to help us say sorry,
	Christ have mercy.
	Christ have mercy.
	Lord Jesus, you came on earth to forgive us,
	Lord have mercy.
	Lord have mercy.

Ask the children to repeat **The Prayer for Forgiveness** *after you* **(p. xxxvi).**

OPENING	God our Father,
PRAYER	We thank you for bringing us here today,
	To learn together
	And hear your Word. *Amen.*

BEFORE THE GOSPEL

Leader   Okay, before we start thinking about the Gospel, I want to play a game.
It's called "Simon Says."
Does anyone know it?

Go through the rules of the game with any help you get from the children: basically they have commands thrown at them which they only obey if they're preceded by "Simon Says." After a couple of practice runs any child who gets it wrong is "out" and has to sit down. The secret is to increase the speed of the commands.

Game   Simon says stand up.
Simon says sit down.
Simon says stand up.
Sit down!

Add a few refinements—stand on one leg, turn left/right, cross your arms, etc. Congratulate the winner and get the children to sit down.

Leader	I think that's a very mysterious game.
	Watch this...
	(to another Leader:) "Bring that chair over here!" *(The other Leader does so.)*
	Sit down. *(The Leader sits.)*
	Now why did *Name* do that?
	Name's not a puppet. I didn't pull some strings to make him/her move.
	All I did was say something—and *Name* did it.
	That's what I call the power of the word.
	And if I can make something happen just by saying something—just imagine what God can do!
CD6.1	We know actually, because at the beginning of the Bible we hear that God made Heaven and Earth just by speaking.
CD6.2	He said, "Let there be light!" and there was light.

*Attach the balloon (**CD6.2**) near to God's mouth (**CD6.1**).*
It's not important for this session to go into a religion vs science debate on Creation. If the children ask you about it make the point that it doesn't matter how long God took to make the world, or how it evolved, what Christians believe is that once there was nothing (except God) and then, after God spoke, there was something.

> The Jews were very interested in God's Word: they could see how powerful it was and they began to wonder if, once the Word was spoken, it ever changed.
>
> Whether it was part of God, yet separate from Him.

Detach CD6.2 from CD6.1.

> And when Christians came to think about this, they realized that the "Word of God" was Jesus.

Put up the "Jesus as Word" picture.

CD6.3	Some people found that very weird—because you can't see a word.
	It might make vibrations in the air, but you can't see the vibrations.
	But Christians say, I know it's odd, but God's Word can be seen.
	Let's hear the first Christian ever to write about this idea, John.

THE GOSPEL PROCESSION

THE GOSPEL *John 1:1-18*

Optional version	In the beginning was the Word: the Word was with God and the Word was God.

He was with God in the beginning,
All things were made by Him,
And there was not one thing that was made, that was made without Him.
He came to this world,
The world He had made,
And the World did not know Him.
He came to His own people,
And His people did not accept Him.
And the Word was made flesh
And lived among us.
And we saw His glory,
The glory He had received from the Father,
Full of grace and truth.

AFTER THE GOSPEL

Leader   "The Word was made flesh and lived among us."
            What does "flesh" mean?

Take all answers—but establish it's the stuff we're made of, muscle and tissue and skin, pinch a bit of your arm—it's solid.

            So John tells us God's Word became a human being.
            In fact, John actually met the Human Being that the Word became.
            I'm going to read you the next sentence in today's Gospel.

Refer to the Bible.

            "And we saw His glory, the glory He had through being the only Son of the Father, full of grace and truth."
            Lucky John, he saw the Word, and he knew who He was.
            Who was He? (**Jesus**)
            Now how are we going to tell the grown-ups about this?

ACTIVITY

Get the children to suggest a Back in Church session. It should be based on demonstrating the power of the Word, but head them off from yelling commands at the entire congregation.
If the kids draw a blank—do a version of Simon Says with them and finish with the script below.

REHEARSAL

Practice your presentation for when you go back to church (see below).

FINAL   Lord Jesus,
PRAYER   Word of God,
                    Be with us this week
                    In everything we speak and do,
                    So everything may be done to the glory of God your Father. *Amen.*

BACK IN CHURCH

Demonstrate the power of the word and sum it up by saying something like:

Leader   Today we played a game.

Run a very short version of Simon Says, the last command is "sit down"

                    Did you notice that I just had to say something and the kids moved?
                    I didn't pull a string or anything.
                    Watch this...
                    (to kids:) Stand up! *(They do.)*
                    There you are, it's happened again.
                    And we realized that if our words had so much power, how incredibly
                    powerful the Word of God must be.

ALTERNATIVE SESSION

Start this session after

                    ". . . just imagine what God can do!" on page 24.
Leader   Actually, we know what God can do, because at the beginning of the
                    Bible...

Pick up the Bible and go to the beginning.

                    We hear that God made Heaven and Earth just by speaking.

THE GOSPEL *Genesis 1:1-7*

Put up the pictures for the six days of creation as you read

In the beginning God created the Heavens and the Earth:
CD6.4   And God said, "Let there be light!" and He separated the light from the
darkness and made the Day and the Night.
That was the first day.
CD6.5   On the second day God said: "Let there be sky and sea!" And they appeared.

CD6.6   On the third day God spoke and made the dry land, and He caused plants and trees to grow out of the Earth.

CD6.7   On the fourth day God spoke and made the Sun and the Moon and the Stars and set them in the sky to give light to the Earth.

CD6.8   On the fifth day God spoke and made the fish and the great sea monsters to live in the water, and birds to fly in the air.

CD6.9   On the sixth day God spoke and made all the animals that live on the land, and when He'd finished making them He said, "Let us make human beings, and let us give them the whole world to live in, and let them rule the Earth."

So God made man and woman from the dust of the earth, and breathed into their nostrils the breath of life and they began to live. And God blessed them.

And on the seventh day God rested.

ACTIVITY

There is no drawing for the seventh day, the day God rested. Perhaps the children could supply it. How do you suppose God chills out?

SONG

"All things bright and beautiful" *is the obvious hymn, but* "All creatures of our God and King" *(based on the canticle of St. Francis) is also very good.*

FINAL	Lord Jesus,
PRAYER	Word of God,
	Be with us this week
	In everything we speak and do,
	So everything may be done to the glory of God the Father. *Amen.*

BACK IN CHURCH

Bring in the six days of Creation pictures to give a context for the children's own pictures of the seventh day.
Encourage the priest to comment on them.

(CD6.6)   (CD6.8)   (CD6.9)

Sample cartoons for this script

Script 6   The Flight into Egypt

Christmas 2

Matthew 2:13-23

THEME

Joseph and Mary take the Christ Child and hurry off to Egypt to escape King Herod. This is a session about story telling, and enjoying the game afterwards—it's still Christmas!

SET UP

- The liturgical color is White.
- Three Christmas crackers (look at the label on the back of the box to make sure they contain jokes and paper crowns).
- Download the board game for this session from the CD-ROM.
- Either buy inflatable (or bouncy) dice from a party/joke shop or make a couple of large dice by covering boxes with stiff white paper and drawing on the dots. (Hang on to these as they will come in useful throughout the year.)

WELCOME *the children and lead them in* **The Sign of the Cross + (p. xxxvi).**

THE KYRIE   Lord Jesus, you came on earth to tell us how much God loves us,
Lord have mercy.
Lord have mercy.

Lord Jesus, you came on earth to help us say sorry,
Christ have mercy.
Christ have mercy.

Lord Jesus, you came on earth to forgive us,
Lord have mercy.
Lord have mercy.

Ask the children to repeat **The Prayer for Forgiveness** *after you* **(p. xxxvi).**

OPENING	God our Father,
PRAYER	We thank you for Christmas,
	For the fun we had,
	For the food we ate,
	For the love in our homes,
	And most of all, for the birth of your Son,
	Jesus Christ. *Amen.*

BEFORE THE GOSPEL

Talk through Christmas.

Leader	Did Santa Claus arrive?
	Anybody got a new toy with them?

Enjoy the toys for a moment.

Bring out the Christmas crackers.

Did any of you get any of these?
What do you do with them? (**Pull them.**)
I thought so—can anyone help me?

Pull a cracker, gather up the bits.

Do you know why we pull crackers at Christmas?
Because they've got jokes inside.

Read it out.

And we're so happy we laugh at even the silliest joke.
And because they've got presents inside...

Ask the child who helped you to hold it up.

And that reminds us that God sent us the best present of all at Christmas—His Son Jesus.
And because they've got a crown...

Put it on the child.

And that reminds us that Baby Jesus is King of the World.
Crowns look lovely on children—but they look rather different on grown-ups.
Let's pull another cracker.

The kids pull the cracker, the Leader reads the joke.

They don't get any better do they?

Give the toy to a child, hang on to the crown.

When a grown-up wears a crown—*(crown another adult)*—it makes them a king or a queen—but you can't help looking more carefully, under the crown, at the face; is it a good king or queen?

I'm sure *Name* would be a good king/queen.

But when Baby Jesus was born one of the cruellest kings in history was on the throne. His name was King Herod—and we're going to hear about him now.

This is the first time we've used a Gospel Procession in this book (see p. xxix and run through the procedure with the children).

THE GOSPEL PROCESSION

THE GOSPEL *Matthew 2:13-23*

You might decide to leave out the massacre of the babies in Bethlehem. Most children cope with it perfectly well, they're more worried about the safety of Jesus.

Optional Paraphrase

Preamble

When the Three Kings came to visit Baby Jesus, they had visited King Herod first, to ask the way. Their news, that a Baby King had been born in Israel, frightened King Herod and he immediately decided to kill the Child. Herod asked the Three Kings to send him word when they'd found the Child, but an Angel warned the Kings to do nothing of the sort. So the three of them went home another way—and never spoke to Herod again.

Gospel

When the Kings had left, an Angel appeared to Joseph in a dream and said, "Get up! Herod is looking for the Child and wants to kill Him! Wake up Mary and Jesus and escape to Egypt."

So Joseph got up and woke Mary: they gathered up baby Jesus and crept away, at dead of night, for Egypt. There they stayed until Herod died.

But when Herod realized that the Kings had tricked him he was furious. And he sent his soldiers to Bethlehem to kill all the little boys aged two or under. But Jesus was hidden safely in Egypt.

Once Herod had died the Angel came back. "Get up," he said to Joseph, "and take Mary and the Child back to Israel. The man who tried to kill Him is dead."

So Joseph packed up again and, realizing that Herod's son was now on the throne, he took his family to Galilee—far away from the new king—and made a home for them in Nazareth.

AFTER THE GOSPEL

Leader So you see, almost the moment Jesus was born, the powers of darkness were after Him. Fortunately He had brave parents who were able to protect Him.

I wonder how good we'd be at protecting Baby Jesus? We're going to play a game to find out.

ACTIVITY

CD5.1 *Depending on numbers, either gather round the board game and let the children compete against each other or reproduce the game as large as you can, stick it up, and divide the children into teams. If you go for teams, you'll find that all the children will want to throw the huge dice, try to make sure everyone has a try.*

REHEARSAL

Practice your presentation for when you go back to church (see below).
It's about the crackers, the kids will love the opportunity to pull another one.

FINAL
PRAYER

Think about the Holy Family, how glad we are that Jesus had Mary and Joseph to look after Him.

Eternal Father,

Thank you for Mary and Joseph.

Grant that our homes will be as loving as theirs,

And help us to love our family

As much as Jesus loved His. *Amen.*

Either **Hail Mary... (p. xxxvii).**
or **Glory Be... (p. xxxvii).**

SONG

"Unto us a child is born" *has a very graphic verse describing Herod's fury.*

BACK IN CHURCH

Leader Today we've been thinking about Jesus and Mary and Joseph, and all the fun we have at Christmas.

We even pulled some crackers.

Do you know why we pull crackers at Christmas?

We're going to show you...

Two children pull a cracker, gather up the bits.

Child 1   We pull crackers because they've got jokes inside.
                     They are there because we're feeling happy.

Child 2   And they've got presents inside...
Hold them up.   They remind us that God sent us the gift of His Son Jesus.

Child 3   And they've got crowns...
Hold it up.   And that reminds us that Baby Jesus is King of the World.

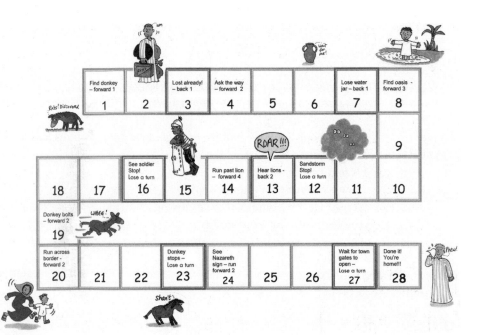

Script 7   The Baptism of Jesus

Epiphany 1

Matthew 3:1, 6, 13-17

THEME

The Baptism of Jesus. This is obviously the moment for some holy washing—and an exercise in straight story telling, with the help of a radio play.

SET UP

- The liturgical color is White.
- Holy water stoup and aspergillum (a holy water sprinkler). (If your church doesn't possess these, a bowl, some water and a sprig of rosemary, or fir tree, will work just as well.)
- Make copies of the Gospel passage to hand out to small groups of children: print it in a child friendly font (Arial or Comic Sans Serif).
- Six highlighter pens.
- Some fake microphones, made from the template on the CD-ROM (**CD7.1**), or cannibalized from any recording equipment you have. (They don't have to work.)
- Large bowl of water.
- Something to make thunder with: you can download thunder sound effects from YouTube—or just bring in a pair of saucepan lids.

WELCOME *the children and lead them in* **The Sign of the Cross + (p. xxxvi).**

INTRODUCTION

Leader   Today we are going to think about Baptism.
           Has anyone seen one? (**Hands up**)
           What does the priest use to baptize somebody? (**Water**)
           How does he do it? (**He pours it over them**)
           Why?

Take anything that comes and sum up.

           There are lots of reasons and one is that water *washes* things.
           The water in Baptism is a sign that God washes away people's sins.
           Even babies need that wash.

This is such a good idea that the church often uses water to wash older Christians as well.

THE KYRIE

Pick up the stoup.

Now, every Sunday, we say the Kyrie (the "Lord have mercy.") to say sorry for anything we might have done wrong.
Today we are going to do the Kyrie with water.
I'll say "Lord have mercy.," you repeat it and as you repeat it, I'll sprinkle you with water. (I'm going to enjoy this...)
As you feel the water splash you, make the Sign of the Cross and you'll know God has washed you and forgiven you.
But as I have to be forgiven as well, will somebody sprinkle me first?

Get a child to dip the aspergillum.

He or she says "Lord have mercy."—*(and splashes you)*
You reply "Lord have mercy."—*(and cross yourself)*

Repeat the Kyrie, sprinkling the children—remember to get the grown-ups as well.

Lord have mercy.
Lord have mercy.

Christ have mercy.
Christ have mercy.

Lord have mercy.
Lord have mercy.

Ask the children to repeat **The Prayer for Forgiveness** *after you* **(p. xxxvi).**

OPENING God our Father,
PRAYER We thank you for our Baptism.
Help us to remain faithful Christians
All our lives. *Amen.*

Go straight into:

THE GOSPEL PROCESSION

THE GOSPEL *Matthew 3:1, 6, 13-17*

Now, John the Baptist appeared in the desert, preaching that people should come to be baptized and repent of their sins.

So people came from all the country round, they confessed their sins, and were baptized by him in the River Jordan.

And Jesus came as well, from Galilee, to be baptized. John tried to stop Him and said, "I ought to be baptized by you, not the other way round!"

But Jesus said,

"Let it be so for now: this is what God wants."

So John agreed.

And as soon as Jesus was baptized, He came out of the water and the Heavens were opened and He saw the Spirit, like a dove, descending upon Him. And a Voice came from Heaven and said,

"This is my beloved Son, in whom I am well pleased."

AFTER THE GOSPEL

Leader   Okay, we're going to hear that story again.

Set the mikes in a line on a table, chairs behind, bowl and CD player in hand.

> We're going to do this as a play—not an ordinary play, that's too easy—nor a TV play, anybody can do that—but a radio play.
> Think about radio for a moment.
> How do you tell a story on radio?
> You can talk of course—but can you make faces? Why not?
> So if *Name* was on TV she could walk into the room looking like this...

Another Leader enters through the door, grinning.

> Everyone can see she was happy and I'd say, "Oh, hello *Name*..."
> But on radio...

Get behind a mic.

> We'd have to do it like this.

The other Leader knocks on the table.

> "Who's that?"

Name opens and shuts the door noisily.

> "Oh, hello *Name*, you look happy."
> You have to describe everything on radio—and you have lots of sound effects. Today we are going to do a radio play of the Gospel.

Production Meeting

Divide the children into groups, pass out a copy of the Gospel text and a highlighter pen per group and ask them to highlight the sounds in the Gospel. They might need to add some extra ones—tell them that a sound effect in the theater is just called "FX." Give them about five minutes, keep it snappy.

Choosing Sound FX

Accept what the children come up with, but push them. For example:

It might be a good idea actually to hear John—what would he be saying? (**"Repent!" "Come and be baptized!" "Jesus is coming!"**) How do we know loads of people have arrived?

Make noise like a mighty thunder of feet.

And how would the people confess their sins? (**"Sorry God!" "Lord have mercy.!" "Kyrie eleison!"**)
And what about the noise of Baptism? (**"I baptize you,"** splosh!)
How shall we do the splosh?
How will we know when Jesus has entered? (**"Cool! There's Jesus!"**)
What about the Heavens opening? *(Thunder FX)*
How on earth do we do the dove? *(A kid once suggested a dove sound effect by saying "coo coo"—personally I prefer flapping wings—but it was a good idea.)*
And the Voice from Heaven—loud or soft? near or far away?
Now how are we going to run this? Because it isn't a pantomime, it's got to sound good, no extra noises, and the Voice must come in and clinch the whole show at the end.

The Radio Play

Allocate parts, Q (cue) them into the script.
Allocate the kids who are doing sound FX, Q them into the script.
Write up flash cards for the moments when all the kids are running on the spot or saying something as a crowd (a possible script is attached to the end of this session). The Leader takes on the Floor Manager's job and Qs everyone in. Rehearse the children, then run it.

FINAL
PRAYER   *End with a* **Glory Be...** (p. xxxvii).

BACK IN CHURCH

Leader or Competent Child	Today we worked out a radio play on the Baptism of Jesus. When we did it we realized the most important moment was when the Voice said...

Person who plays the Voice

This is my beloved Son, in whom I am well pleased.

RADIO PLAY SCRIPT

Narrator	Now, John the Baptist appeared in the desert, preaching that people should come to be baptized and repent of their sins.
John	Repent! Come and be baptized! Hurry up!
Narrator	So people came from all the country round...
Q Sound FX	*Running feet*
Narrator	They confessed their sins...
Q Crowd	Sorry God!
	I repent!
	Lord have mercy.!
Narrator	And they were baptized by John in the River Jordan.
John	I baptize you...
Q Sound FX	*Splosh!*
John	I baptize you...
Q Sound FX	*Splosh!*
John	I baptize you...
Q Sound FX	*Splosh!*
Narrator	And Jesus came as well, from Galilee, to be baptized.
Q Crowd	Wow! There's Jesus!
Narrator	John tried to stop Him and said,
John	I ought to be baptized by you, not the other way round!
Narrator	But Jesus said,
Jesus	Let it be so for now: this is what God wants.
Narrator	So John agreed.
	And as soon as Jesus was baptized, He came out of the water and the Heavens were opened...
Q Sound FX	*Thunder*
Narrator	And He saw the Spirit, like a dove, descending upon Him.
Q Sound FX	*Dove noise or flapping*
Narrator	And a Voice came from Heaven and said...
Voice	This is my beloved Son, in whom I am well pleased.

Script 8 Behold the Lamb of God

Epiphany 2

John 1:29-42

THEME

It's a long Gospel passage today but, as we covered Jesus' Baptism last week, this session will focus on John the Baptist's description of Jesus as the "Lamb of God."

There is so much to unpack in this idea that I'm going for the lamb as "scape-goat" (you may remember that the Jews could take their lambs either "from the sheep or the goats"—but don't confuse the children with this bit of information). Of course, Jesus is also, not to say pre-eminently, the Passover Lamb, but that's something to think about in Lent and Holy Week.

SET UP

- The liturgical color is Green.
- Pictures from CD-ROM.
- A couple of black markers.
- A toy lamb.
- Download some images of St. John and the Lamb. Searching on the following painters will bring up some excellent pictures: Geertgen (van Haarlem), Titian or Grunewald (zoom in on St. John if you use this picture and cut off the graphic crucifixion). The Wilton Diptych has an excellent St. John, with his lamb, on the left panel.

WELCOME *the children and lead them in* **The Sign of the Cross + (p. xxxvi).**

INTRODUCTION TO THE KYRIE

Leader	Think over the past week:
	How did it go?
	Anything we wished we hadn't done?
	Anything we forgot?
	Let's put that right now...

THE KYRIE   Lord Jesus, we are sorry for the times we forgot you,
Lord have mercy.
Lord have mercy.

Lord Jesus, we are sorry for the times we were unkind,
Christ have mercy.
Christ have mercy.

Lord Jesus, we thank you for always listening to us, and forgiving us,
Lord have mercy.
Lord have mercy.

Ask the children to repeat **The Prayer for Forgiveness** *after you* (**p. xxxvi**).

OPENING PRAYER *from Psalm 39*

(*The response is:* **I come to do your will**)

Here I am, Lord.
I come to do your will.

I waited for the Lord, and He knelt down to me.
Here I am, Lord.
I come to do your will.

He put a new song in my mouth.
Here I am, Lord.
I come to do your will.

God does not ask for sacrifices and offerings;
Instead, here am I.
Here I am, Lord.
I come to do your will.

BEFORE THE GOSPEL

Leader   Today we're going to talk about lambs.
Let's draw some first.

Drawing sheep is easy, use the templates (**CD8.1, CD8.2**) *from the CD-ROM, and ask some children to give you a hand. Pause for a minute to admire the flock.*

I've got one here...

Produce the toy sheep.

Why does everyone like lambs?

Take all answers, something on the lines of being small and woolly, they look as though they could be cuddled, and they spring up in the air when they're feeling cheerful.

Chance for a Lamb Story

If you haven't got one, see if any of the children have held a lamb, or seen one skipping about. This is the lamb story I use:

The only lamb I ever met was the little one we used for the *St. John Passion* at our church. He was cute but extremely smelly (not being house trained) and our Stage Manager—who knew about lambs—refused to have the lamb's pen anywhere near her office. Near the end of the show one of the singers had to walk on to the stage holding the lamb, and he'd always glare at the animal beforehand: "One noise from you," he'd say, "and you're lamb chops!" The lamb never took any notice, and as the singer came to the most beautiful bit of his music, it would look sweetly round at the audience and say "Baa!" (It always got a clap.)
The point is, lambs are cute.

THE GOSPEL PROCESSION

THE GOSPEL *from John Chapter 1*

One day John saw Jesus walking towards him and John said to his friends, "Do you see that Man? He is the Lamb of God!"
"God told me to baptize people in the River Jordan. I knew that one of them would turn out to be the Messiah, but I didn't know which. And then Jesus came to be baptized, and I saw the Holy Spirit come down like a dove from Heaven and hover over Him, and I realized who He was."
"I'm telling you the truth," said John, "Jesus is God's Chosen One."
The next day John was standing talking to his disciples and Jesus went past again. "Behold the Lamb of God!" said John.
And the two disciples left John and followed Jesus.

AFTER THE GOSPEL

Talk about the story very briefly—and the big question.

Leader   Why did John call Jesus a "lamb?"

Pick up the toy lamb again.

Well, it wasn't because Jesus was cute.
Let's think about lambs in Jesus' time.
People liked them then, just as much as we do. Jesus talks about

holding little lambs close to His chest.

But of course people ate lambs then, just like us, and they did something else—they sacrificed them...

Turn the toy lamb graphically upside down. The kids never seem to mind.

Sacrifice

All ancient peoples sacrificed animals. They built an altar—very like the altar we have in church—and they killed an animal and cooked it.

They thought that the gods could smell the delicious smell of roast meat that went up to into the sky.

Then they ate the rest of the animal themselves.

Well, the Jewish people didn't think that God wanted to smell roast meat.

But they sacrificed lambs anyway.

They did it at their great feast of Passover and when they wanted to say "sorry."

They felt they could pile up all their sins on the lamb's back and kill the whole thing—all the sins, all their guilt—and, of course, the lamb.

And John realized, that's just what Jesus was going to do.

He'd be everybody's Lamb; innocent, nice and good.

And He'd carry our sins on His back, get killed—and take them away.

That's why we still call Jesus "the Lamb of God." We do it at every Eucharist.

Let's learn that bit of the Eucharist now.

FINAL PRAYER

Bring the children into a prayer circle and pass the toy lamb round.

Leader   Just hold the lamb for a minute and pass it to your neighbor.
It's nice, isn't it?
You know, the Jews always felt sorry for lambs, even when they sacrificed them.
Jesus knew He was the Lamb of God.
He knew He'd be sacrificed.
But that was okay—He loved us so much, He was prepared to accept that.
People have never forgotten that John the Baptist called Jesus the "Lamb of God."

If you've got some pictures of St. John, this is the moment to show them.
At the end focus everyone's attention either on an image of the Lamb of God, or on a large candle, which you light and place in the middle.
Remind the children of the words of the Agnus Dei, and pray together.

O Lamb of God, that takes away the sins of the world,
Have mercy upon us.

O Lamb of God, that takes away the sins of the world,
Have mercy upon us.

O Lamb of God, that takes away the sins of the world,
Grant us peace.

BACK IN CHURCH

Bring in the toy lamb.

Leader   Today we heard John the Baptist call Jesus the "Lamb of God."

A child holds up the lamb, the right way up.

And we learned that he called Him that not because lambs are sweet and good...
But because they were sacrificed.

The child turns the lamb upside down.

It made us realize how much Jesus loved us.

(CD8.1)

Script 9 Fishers of Men

Epiphany 3

Matthew 4:18-24

THEME

Vocation. This is a difficult one as God's call is often presented as either too specific, for example: "Do you want to be a doctor?" Or impossibly vague: "Jesus wants you for a sunbeam." This session suggests that vocation follows your natural bent: God likes the differences between us, and offers us jobs that suit us.

SET UP

- The liturgical color is Green.
- Picture of fisherman and disciples from CD-ROM, plus the templates of the drawings you're going to add.
- Marker.
- Magnetic fish game—either ready made from a toy shop, or constructed by you.
- Templates for fish and tank are provided **(CD9.1)**. (You'll need at least two magnets (from any toy shop or via a website—<u>www.first4magnets.com</u> has a good range).
- Two dowels and some string.
- Attach paper clips to the pictures of fish and people on the CD-ROM, put them in the tank and there you are.

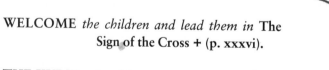

WELCOME *the children and lead them in* **The Sign of the Cross + (p. xxxvi).**

THE KYRIE Lord Jesus, you came to earth to tell us how much God loves us, Lord have mercy.
Lord have mercy.

Lord Jesus, you came to earth to help us,

Christ have mercy.
Christ have mercy.

Lord Jesus, you came to earth to forgive us,
Lord have mercy.
Lord have mercy.

Ask the children to repeat **The Prayer for Forgiveness** *after you* (**p. xxxvi**).

BEFORE THE OPENING PRAYER

Look round the room and ad lib into what a mixed bag of people we are: start with age.

Leader   We're all different ages.
                   Hands up, is anyone five? How about ten?

And so on. You'll probably have to let the toddlers get their various ages off their chest. Include the grown-ups.

                   What about these guys?
To a Leader   How old are you? *(The answer to this is always 21.)*
                   What about the food we like?
                   Anyone here like pasta? hamburgers? French fries? lovely delicious cabbage...

Find out some of the things the children are good at, just a show of hands.

                   Anyone here good at football? drawing? math?
                   We're all different.
                   God likes us to be different. He's interested in what we like and what we do.
                   Let's think about that as we pray.

OPENING   God our Father,
PRAYER   Thank you for bringing us here today.
                   Thank you for making us so different.
                   Thank you for the people who can run, and draw, and kick goals and do math.
                   Help us to use all the things we're good at to show how much we love you,
                   Through Jesus Christ our Lord. *Amen.*

BEFORE THE GOSPEL

Ad lib on fishermen if you know any: how they sit on muddy river banks all day, under umbrellas, watching the float on their fishing line. They love it.

CD9.2   *Put up the Fisherman picture.*

> What is this guy doing? (**fishing**)
> What do you suppose he thinks about all day?

CD9.3   *Draw thought bubble.*

CD9.4   (**fish**)—*(Draw fish in thought bubble.)*
> Jesus knew some fishermen. They were called... ?
> Does anybody know?

CD9.5   *Put up the Disciples pictures and write in their names: Peter, Andrew, James and John.*

> These guys were real fishermen.
CD9.6   They had fish for breakfast...
CD9.7   They had fish and fries for lunch...
> What do you suppose their favorite movie was?

Give a heavy hint—most people can have a stab at the theme tune.

CD9.8   Yes, *Jaws.*
CD9.9   And if they had a birthday, they had a fish cake...
CD9.10   And a nice jelly fish...
> They liked fish.
> Jesus liked these men, and He thought they had a very useful skill.
> "Fishing," He thought. "Hmm, I could use that..."
> Let's hear about that in the Gospel.

THE GOSPEL PROCESSION

THE GOSPEL *Matthew 4:18-24*

AFTER THE GOSPEL

Quick Q and A session:

Leader   Whom did Jesus meet? (**Peter, Andrew, James and John**)
> What were they doing? (**fishing**)
> What did He ask the fishermen to do?

Accept all answers and sum them up.

> He said, "Follow me, and I will make you fishers of men."
> Did Andrew and Peter and James and John follow Jesus? (**yes**)

God likes to give people jobs, but He always makes sure it's something they can do.

Fishermen can catch things, so He said, "Right, go and catch things for me—

not fish—but people."

I think this would be a good thing for us to practice.

The Fishing Game

We need a fish pond... *(Put box on table.)*

And some fish... *(Throw them in.)*

And some fishing rods... *(Produce the magnetized rods.)*

Give the kids a chance to see how the rods work. You can run a game, how many fish can they catch against the clock? You might need to split them into teams if there are too many, with a few kids fishing for their team.

Okay, so you're good at catching fish.

CD9.11   *Once the fish have all been caught, stealthily slide the little man into the "pool."*

But Jesus wanted His disciples to practice hard and learn to catch . . .

Get one kid forward for this—he or she pulls out the little man on the fishing rod.

People!

Practice the script below if you're going to make a presentation in church.

FINAL PRAYER   Andrew, Peter, James and John turned out to be so good at catching people that they helped Jesus found the Church. We're going to remember them in our final prayer and ask them to pray for us:

Lord Jesus,

Thank you for calling the fishermen, Peter and Andrew, James and John, to follow you.

Help us to follow you and do whatever job you think we'd be good at.

Hear our prayer, and those of your friends, the fishermen, as we ask them to pray for us:

Holy Andrew, **Pray for us.**

Holy Peter, **Pray for us.**

Holy James, **Pray for us.**

Holy John, **Pray for us.** *Amen.*

BACK IN CHURCH

Put one fish and the little man in the box. Set it fairly high—on a stool or the top step up to the altar. Two kids flank the box, with rods. A Leader or a child with a nice emphatic delivery reads the script.

Leader   Jesus made friends with Andrew, Peter, James and John.
They were fishermen, and were very good at catching...

One child catches the fish

Fish! *(Child holds it up.)*
Jesus said to the fishermen, "Follow me, and I will make you fishers of..."

The other child catches the man.

People! *(Child holds the little man up.)*

(CD9.2)

(CD9.7)

(CD9.8)

(CD9.9)

(CD9.5)

Sample cartoons for this script

Script 10 Wedding at Cana

The story is not in the Revised Common Lectionary but is included here

John 2:1-11

THEME

This is, of course, Jesus' first miracle, and is a good moment to think about miracles generally. They are emphatically not magic but manifestations of the normal way in which God works—healing, creating, transforming—only (in this case) speeding things up.

Go for a straight re-telling of the story. The kids love the moment the water turns into wine, even when they know it's a trick.

SET UP

- The liturgical color is Green.
- Glass or transparent cup, in a plastic holder to conceal the spot of red food coloring on the bottom. (If you can't find a plastic holder, hold the glass by its base with the napkin round it when you pick it up.)
- Large clear glass pitcher of water.
- A waiter's napkin.
- Pictures from the CD-ROM.

WELCOME *the children and lead them in* **The Sign of the Cross +** (p. xxxvi).

THE KYRIE Lord Jesus, you always forgive those who admit they've done wrong,
Lord have mercy.
Lord have mercy.

Lord Jesus, we are sorry for the times we have been unkind,
Christ have mercy.
Christ have mercy.

Lord Jesus, we thank you for always listening to us, and forgiving us,
Lord have mercy.
Lord have mercy.

Ask the children to repeat **The Prayer for Forgiveness** *after you* (**p. xxxvi**).

BEFORE THE GOSPEL

Leader	Today we are going to think a bit about how the world works. It's got rules of course, but they're rather odd.

Ad lib on the Law of Gravity.

CD10.1   *See the picture of two mountains and the routes taken by a fast skier and a slow skier. They are very easy to draw.*

If you go straight down a mountain you go very fast.
If you make turns it slows you up a bit—why's that?

Children always seem to know about gravity.
Give an impressive demonstration of the Law of Gravity.

Anyone can jump off a chair—easy peasy...
Jumping back on to it, however, is not so simple...

(You might have to do this yourself if you're worried about safety.)

Who made the world? (**God**)
And the rules? (**God**)
Yes, He did, so if the world is a bit strange, it must be because He likes it like that.
Let's think about the weird way in which things change in our world.
Things are always becoming other things...

CD10.2–10.7   *Ad lib through the pictures of caterpillar/butterfly, acorn/oak tree, baby/teenager, etc.*

So in our world, things can become other things—though it's usually a long process. Today we are going to think about water turning into wine.
What does wine come from? (**grapes, vines**)

CD10.8   Right, I am going to draw a very small grape plant, a vine, in the ground...
And God sends the Sun... and the Rain... *(Draw them.)*
and the vine grows—and it has tiny little bumps all over it...

Draw a larger plant with a few dots to represent the infant grapes.

You won't get much wine out of these grapes—so God sends more rain... *(Draw rain.)*
And they plump up... *(Draw a bunch of grapes.)*
And they ripen in the sun...

And then we come along, and pick them, and squash them, and eventually we get—*(draw a bottle and label it)*—wine.

It's a long process, but it's the way God works.

Except sometimes He works faster...

THE GOSPEL PROCESSION

THE GOSPEL *John 2:1-11*

Read the Gospel freely, it's a very good story. Have the "fixed" glass ready and a large pitcher of water, pour the water in (from an immense height) at verse 8.

He said to them, "Now pour it out..."

Add the line: The water had become wine.

If you make sure the "servant" doing the pouring flourishes the napkin over his arm, the children are so fascinated by the napkin they don't inspect the glass.

AFTER THE GOSPEL

Hold up the glass.

Leader	Do you think this really is wine? (**No!**)
	No, it's a trick.
	But when Jesus turned water into wine, it wasn't a trick—it was...
	(**miracle**).
	A miracle is something that only God can do.
	God is always changing things:
	Acorns to oak trees...
	Caterpillars to butterflies...
	Babies to grown-ups...

Hold up your beaker of "wine."

Water into wine and...
Bad people into good.

Q for SONG   The people who gave that party at Cana were very poor—that's why the wine ran out. Jesus gave them 40 gallons of extra wine and I bet they broke out into song. Let's sing something really cheerful.

Sing any of the children's favorites or "Give me joy in my heart."

Two traditional hymns work well here—"All people that on earth do dwell" *or* "All things bright and beautiful."

FINAL PRAYER   *End with a* **Glory Be... (p. xxxvii).**

BACK IN CHURCH

Set up three kids, one to read, one to hold the "fixed" glass, one to pour the water.

Reader   Today we learned how Jesus turned water...

Kid holds up water pitcher.

Into wine...

Kid pours the water into the glass.

We learned that God can change things:
Water into wine;
Bad people into good.

Script 11   The Beatitudes

Epiphany 4

Matthew 5:1-12

THEME

A quiet session today about the kind of people God can get through to.

You'll see that the version of the Gospel below uses the word "blessed" rather than "happy"—"Blessed are the peacemakers," for example. "Blessed" and "happy" are not identical as "blessed" suggests that the person described is not only fortunate but approved by God.

The children will hear the word "blessed" a lot in this session, teach them to pronounce it with two syllables—bless-ed—especially in the psalm.

As this is quite a difficult session for the very young I've added an alternative script, a story of one of the gentle Desert Saints, at the very end, which you could do instead.

SET UP

- The liturgical color is Green.
- Letter from St. Paul in an envelope (see text below). (Give the letter to another Leader or a child, who waits outside and enters on cue.)
- Small radio.
- Some sheets of paper (see below).
- Marker pens, some colored.
- Pictures from the CD-ROM.

WELCOME *the children and lead them in* **The Sign of the Cross + (p. xxxvi).**

THE KYRIE   Lord Jesus, you came to earth to tell us how much God loves us,
Lord have mercy.
Lord have mercy.

Lord Jesus, you came to earth to help us,
Christ have mercy.
Christ have mercy.

Lord Jesus, you came to earth to forgive us,
Lord have mercy.
Lord have mercy.

Ask the children to repeat **The Prayer for Forgiveness** *after you* (**p. xxxvi**).

Leader	I'm going to start with a Jewish prayer, it's very short and I'd like you to say it after me.

OPENING PRAYER	Blessed be God, King of the Universe. **Blessed be God, King of the Universe.** Blessed be God for ever. **Blessed be God for ever.** *Amen.*

BEFORE THE GOSPEL

Leader	"Blessed be God..." That word "blessed" is quite odd. What does it mean?

(This will probably turn out to be rhetorical.)

I think it means Holy, if a priest "blesses" something he or she makes it holy.
Now God of course is Holy.
But what about people? Are they "blessed"?
Saints are, but what about ordinary people?

This is the cue for a loud knock on the door.

Hello! What's that?

Enter a messenger—hands over a special delivery.

Ah, a letter—*(opens it)*—from St. Paul!
Okay, what's he got to say...?

Epistle	A reading from the letter of St. Paul to... *(Put in your own city or town name.)* My friends, I'd like you to think about yourselves for a moment. How many of you are wise? or successful? or come from good families? And yet we are the people God chose. God bless you, PAUL

After the Epistle

Talk through the letter.

> St. Paul obviously thinks the Church is full of ordinary people—
> he's right, isn't he?
> If you look around our church, or down main street, or anywhere,
> you'll see loads of people. Not always successful, or clever, just
> ordinary.
> That's the way the human race is. God loves it like that.
> And St. Paul says it's the ones that look useless that are the ones God
> loves most.
> Let's think about that.

Line up some kids as though they were in a pew.

> Look, here's a pew full of Christians:

Have a couple sitting;
one praying,
one with head in hands,
and a few looking very alert.

> Some of these may be obviously serving God.
> *Name—(call a kid out)*—might be a server.
> Or *Name—(call another kid out)*—may be in the Children's Church
> School.
> But in the Gospel today Jesus highlights these people:

Touch the shoulder of each kid as you describe the sort of person they are.

> The quiet ones.
> The unhappy.
> The people who pray in their heart.
> Of course, God loves the happy energetic ones too...

Indicate the energetic kids.

> But the other people have a stillness about them, God can talk to
> them.

A Radio Moment

Get the kids to sit down again. Produce the radio.

> Look, if I want to hear a station, I have to get the right frequency.

Twiddle the knobs—make sure you get interference.

If the radio starts to buzz, I can't hear the program.

That noise is called "interference"—and that's what some human beings are like.

They talk too much, they buzz around.

God finds it very difficult to get through to them.

If I get the right station... *(Make sure you do!)*

I hear something.

It's like that in church.

The people who don't *look* as though they're paying attention can be very close to God, because God is close to them.

Of course we need energetic people to run things, but they're not necessarily the holy ones—the holy people are often the quiet ones in the pews.

Let's listen to Jesus talking about the people whom He thought were specially blessed by God.

THE GOSPEL PROCESSION

THE GOSPEL *Matthew 5:1-12*

Seeing the crowds, Jesus sat down, and began to teach them.

This is what He said:

"Blessed are the poor in spirit, for theirs is the Kingdom of Heaven.

Blessed are those who mourn, for they shall be comforted.

Blessed are the gentle, for they shall inherit the earth.

Blessed are the merciful, for they shall obtain mercy.

Blessed are the pure in heart, for they shall see God.

Blessed are the peacemakers, for they shall be called the children of God."

ACTIVITY

Depending on the number of children, divide the phrase "Blessed are the Peacemakers" over a set of sheets of paper. Tape the sheets together.

Turn the banner over and write the word "SSSSHHHH!" on the back in a bold color. When the children go back to church they hold up the banner and then, on cue, turn it around.

REHEARSAL

Practice your presentation for when you go back to church (see below).

FINAL PRAYER

Gather the children around a prayer candle. Ask them to put their hands together, shut their eyes, listen to the quiet,

> "Be still, for I am with you," said the Lord.
> "Be still, for I am listening to you.
> Be still, let me give you my peace."

SONG

"Be still for the presence of the Lord" *works well here.*

Or play some quiet music on a CD player—Handel's Pastoral Symphony from "Messiah" is very good. Play just a couple of minutes.

End with: Jesus said to His friends:
"Peace be with you."
Let's go back to church and share His peace.

BACK IN CHURCH

Line the children up.

Leader   Today we thought about the Beatitudes.
Particularly this one.

Q the children to hold up "Blessed are the Peacemakers."
Read it out (the people at the back won't see it).

We realized that God was especially close to quiet, gentle people, so
we thought the Gospel is asking us to be...

Q the children to turn the banner round.

Very quiet.

ALTERNATIVE SCRIPT FOR YOUNG CHILDREN

SET UP

• The liturgical color is Green.
• Pictures for the hermit story—see CD-ROM.

Go straight through the **Welcome, The Kyrie, The Prayer for Forgiveness** *and the*
Opening Prayer, *as above, and then talk to the children about the word "Blessed."*

Leader   "Blessed be God..."
That word "blessed" is quite odd.
What does it mean?

(This will probably turn out to be rhetorical.)

I think it means "holy:" if a priest "blesses" something he or she
makes it holy.
Jesus thought some people were very holy, very blessed indeed, let's
hear what He said.

THE GOSPEL PROCESSION

THE GOSPEL *from Matthew Chapter 5*

Seeing the crowds, Jesus sat down, and began to teach them.
This is what He said:
"Blessed are the gentle, for they shall inherit the earth.
Blessed are the merciful, for they shall obtain mercy.

Blessed are the pure in heart, for they shall see God.

Blessed are the peacemakers, for they shall be called the children of God."

AFTER THE GOSPEL

Talk through the Gospel.

What sort of people did Jesus think were especially "blessed"?

(Quiet people—gentle people, people who don't quarrel, peacemakers)

Lots of Christians have been like that.

Some of them were great saints—and some we hardly know anything about—not even their names.

I'm going to tell you the story of one of them.

He was a hermit.

CD11.1, 11.2   *Stick the picture of the hermit on his background picture. Go through it with the children—point out the cave, the garden and the Bible.*

A hermit is a man who wants to live quietly, far away in a lonely spot, and spends his time praying.

And though this hermit obviously had a name, nobody who met him ever remembered it—though they always remembered what a gentle man he was.

He was gentle with everyone, with sinners who came to confess, and with young monks who came to learn, and with animals—even wild animals.

And, although this man was a hermit he loved it when guests arrived, and always did his best to feed them.

CD11.3   One day, two monks turned up... and he welcomed them with open arms.

But, of course, he was very poor.

He only had his cave for shelter, and some lentils for supper—and no extra bedding at all.

So he gave one monk his bed.

CD11.4   And the other monk his cloak.

And he settled down on the floor in nothing but his underwear.

The monks were too polite to refuse the cloak or the bed, but it was a cold night and they couldn't sleep for worrying about the old man. Would he die of cold?

And then, just as it got really cold, they heard a noise outside, a scuffling noise, then a scratching noise, and then something panting in the darkness.

"A wild beast!" they thought. "Help!" And they hid their heads under their covers.

But the hermit said, "Is that you, Brother Lion?"

CD11.5   The monks risked one look, and sure enough, there was a lion in the cave! The lion rushed up to the hermit—and lay down beside him, then he put his paws round him, and kept him warm all night.

The next morning the lion had gone and, as the hermit said nothing about it, the monks thought they'd better not mention it either.

But they never forgot that lion, and they realized that when somebody is very gentle and loving they are truly blessed—and even wild animals love them too.

ACTIVITY

The pictures are in black and white, so the children can color them in.
You might ask them to think up a name for the hermit.
He's undoubtedly in Heaven and would be very pleased to get a new name from them.

(CD11.3)

(CD11.2)

Sample cartoons for this script

(CD11.4)   (CD11.5)

Script 12   Lights and Bushels

Epiphany 5

Matthew 5:14-16

> **THEME**
>
> A session on lamps, candles and bushels—all showing that light is there to be seen, and it's no use being a Christian if people don't know you are.

SET UP

- The liturgical color is Green.
- Matches, tapers.
- A large flashlight.
- Somebody ready to turn off lights.
- Votive candles, some Leaders ready with lighted tapers for the Kyrie.
- An overcoat, set outside, by the door.
- One pot with a flat base (earthenware would look very authentic).
- A Roman lamp, otherwise a votive candle.
- Christian posters—Red Cross, Christian Aid, Heifer Project, Bread for the World, anything you can find at the back of the church, in church newspapers, or download from the internet.

Start the session in a semi-darkened room with all the blinds and curtains drawn and the lights on low.

WELCOME *the children, and lead them in* **The Sign of the Cross + (p. xxxvi).**

Leader	It's dark in here, isn't it?
	I'm glad I brought my flashlight. *(Switch it on.)*
	Now I can see who is here. *(Spotlight a few kids.)*
	Anybody here own a flashlight? (**Hands up...**)
	I like flashlights, they're nice things to have.
	When is it really useful to have a flashlight?

Take all answers, but establish the fact that flashlights come into their own when it is dark.

Anyone here not like the dark?

Make sure a couple of adults put up their hand.

Being in the dark can be quite scary.
Sometimes when you're unhappy you can feel as if you are in the dark. Then it's a good idea to ask God to help you.
He can get us out of the dark.
God's like a flashlight.
Let's think about that as we say the **Kyrie.**

This week the Leaders say the Kyrie, at each response light a votive candle.

God our Father,
Every time we forget you, we walk into the dark,
Lord have mercy.
Lord have mercy. *(Light a candle.)*

Lord Jesus,
Every time we say sorry, you bring us into the light,
Christ have mercy.
Christ have mercy. *(Light a candle.)*

Holy Spirit,
Fill us with God's light and forgiveness,
Lord have mercy.
Lord have mercy. *(Light a candle.)*

Ask the children to repeat **The Prayer for Forgiveness** *after you* **(p. xxxvi).**

OPENING	*Ask the children to repeat this prayer after you.*
PRAYER	**Lord Jesus,**
	You are the Light of the World.
	Thank you for taking the darkness away. *Amen.*

BEFORE THE GOSPEL

Leader	Right, just before we give ourselves some more light, I'd like to show you something.
	Do you remember my flashlight?
	Well, we're going to turn all the lights off now, and I'm going to be really helpful and keep some light in the room with my flashlight.
	I'll start outside...

Exit and put on overcoat as another Leader turns the lights off.

Enter with the flashlight under the overcoat.

Can you see me?
Really—why not?
Oh, the coat! *(Remove it.)*
Is that better?
Jesus was rather good on light: He obviously liked it.
Let's look at the sort of light He'd have been used to at night.

Pull out the Roman lamp (still with flashlight), pour in oil, add wick, light it.
Or bring forward one of the votive candles still lit from the Kyrie.

It's not very bright, is it?
But if we did this to it...

Cover with the earthenware pot.

It would be even more useless.
The old word for a pot like this
was a "bushel." You still hear
people saying it's silly "to hide
your light under a bushel'—what
you should do is this...

Put the lamp on the upturned pot.

That way you get as much light as
possible.
Well, let's put the lights on and see why Jesus was so interested in
light.

THE GOSPEL PROCESSION

THE GOSPEL *Matthew 5:14-16*

USE THE WORD "BUSHEL" INSTEAD OF "BOWL" OR "TUB:" THE
CHILDREN WOULD PROBABLY LIKE TO KNOW WHERE THE PHRASE
"HIDING YOUR LIGHT UNDER A BUSHEL" COMES FROM.

AFTER THE GOSPEL

Leader   So Jesus said it was silly to put a lamp under a bushel.
Where did He say you should put it? (**On a lamp stand**)
Then He says, "In the same way, your light should shine before
people."

Jesus didn't want any of His followers hiding themselves under bushels.

Look at this...

Pull out the publicity material you've acquired from the relief agency. Talk about the logo. Many have crosses as part of their logo.

These charities are carrying out Jesus' commands to help the poor, and to show that the help they give comes in Jesus' Name, they've got the word "Christian" in their title, or they use the sign of the "Cross."

They are being Lights in the World,

And so must we.

FINAL Lord Jesus Christ,
PRAYER You have called us to be lights in the world.

Grant that we may so shine,

That people may see the good we do,

And praise Almighty God. *Amen.*

BACK IN CHURCH

Ad lib a skilled demonstration, with the flashlight and overcoat, as to what you do with a light, and what you don't.

The children sum it up.

Child 1 Jesus told us to be "lights in the world."
Child 2 He didn't want us to hide our light.
Child 3 It's no use being a Christian if people don't know you are one.

Script 13   Staying Good

Epiphany 6

Matthew 5:29-30

THEME

This is a very alarming Gospel, but it's a good one to tackle as it forces us to stop taking the Bible at face value and attend to what it actually means.

Jesus had no problem with exaggeration. He'd say anything to make people wake up—for example: "Guys, you have as much chance of getting to Heaven as a camel has of getting through the eye of a needle," or, "Listen, if you had a drop of faith this big, you could get that mountain over there to move." None of this was intended to be taken literally and nor is this Gospel.

(The session reintroduces Bill the Burglar from Advents 1 and 2.)

SET UP

- The liturgical color is Green.
- Burglar kit—striped shirt, loot bag and mask.
- The bag should contain some stuff Bill has already stolen: cell phones, candy, jewelry, wallets, anything.
- Have a couple of tempting things for the burglar to steal in front—candlesticks are fine.
- A large wastepaper basket.
- A cup of water at the front.
- At the start of the liturgy, Bill is out of sight.
- Different colored hula-hoops or color-coded shallow boxes (printer paper box lids are ideal) and different colored bean bags or soft balls.

WELCOME *the children and lead them in* **The Sign of the Cross +** (p. xxxvi).

THE KYRIE   Lord Jesus, we are sorry for the times we forgot to talk to you last week,
Lord have mercy.
Lord have mercy.

Lord Jesus, we are sorry for the times we were unkind,
Christ have mercy.
Christ have mercy.

Lord Jesus, we thank you for always listening to us, and forgiving us, whenever we do wrong,
Lord have mercy.
Lord have mercy.

Ask the children to repeat **The Prayer for Forgiveness** *after you* (**p. xxxvi**).

BEFORE THE GOSPEL

Leader   *Repeat the third petition again.*
"Lord Jesus, we thank you for always listening to us, and forgiving us, whenever we do wrong."
Jesus loves us, listens to us and forgives us—but wouldn't it be great if we didn't do anything wrong in the first place!
Jesus would really like that.
I've got a friend, actually, a really nice person—but he's always getting into trouble. He wears a striped shirt and a mask and he's got a big bag on his back labelled "loot."
What do you suppose his job is? (**burglar!**)
Yes, I'm afraid it is.
He said he'd come along this morning. Tell me if you see him.

Ad lib for a bit as the burglar sneaks in...
Uproar from kids, get the burglar down to the front and shake hands.

            Hi Bill, good to see you!
            Put your bag down—gosh that's heavy, what's in it?
Look inside.   Oh no!
            What's all this?
Bill   Well, I was just doing a bit of work before I came here...
Leader   Work, eh?

Go through the loot, ad libbing freely. End by saying:

            Look, do you want to get to Heaven or not?

Bill nods vigorously.

> Well, you're going to have to throw all this stuff out. Nothing bad gets into Heaven, and that includes stolen goods. Okay, let's get rid of this...

Put all the loot in the wastepaper basket, item by item, then shake the loot bag upside down.

> There, now you can walk into Heaven with your head held high.

Turn to the children and ad lib as...
Bill swipes the goodies from the altar.
End by saying:

> So you see, my friend the burglar has now got a clean conscience, and an empty bag... *(Burglar holds it up.)*

Looks inside   Oh, no!
Listen, friend.
If a cell phone stops you getting to Heaven—throw it away... *(Throw it away.)*
If a wallet stops you getting to Heaven—throw it away... *(Throw it away.)*

Bill   Okay, okay, the problem is, it's not so much me as this thieving arm of mine, I can't seem to stop it...

Starts to pick the Leader's pocket, but the Leader grabs the arm.

Leader   And if your arm stops you getting to Heaven—throw that away too!
Bill   *(taking his arm out of the Leader's grip)*
Okay, okay, I get the point!
Leader   *(to the children:)*
Do you think I really meant that Bill should throw his arm away? **(no)**
No, I didn't, but sometimes you have to say something really scary to get people to listen.
Jesus used to get really worried about the people around Him.
He could see them cluttering themselves up with things that were stopping them getting to Heaven. Bad habits, bad feelings, sins—loads of stuff, getting in their way.
Let's hear what He said:

Have Bill the Burglar prominently come to the front. He puts his hand up to ring one of the Gospel bells, rings one and listens attentively to the Gospel.

THE GOSPEL PROCESSION

THE GOSPEL *Matthew 5:29-30*

> Jesus said:
> "If your hand causes you to sin, cut it off!
> It is better for you to go to Heaven with one hand, than be thrown out.
> And if your foot gets in your way, chop it off!
> It's better to hop into Heaven, than to be thrown out...
> And if your eye gets in your way..."

Bill	Hey, stop! I get the point! Is that the Gospel?
Leader	Yes it is.
Bill	*(Bill sits down.)* Gee, well I need a drink after that...

Get a child to offer Bill the cup of water.
Bill drinks it and thanks the kid.

Leader	The Gospel also says... *(Hold it up impressively.)* "If anybody gives just one cup of water to one of my friends, then I tell you, that person will be rewarded."
Bill	That sounds a bit better.

AFTER THE GOSPEL

Leader	The Gospel isn't really frightening— but sometimes Jesus wants to wake us up. He loves us so much that doing even a tiny amount of good, like giving somebody a cup of water, will get us to Heaven.

ACTIVITY

Leader	It might seem easy for Bill here to give up stealing—but actually being good and staying good is exhausting.

Smuggling Bean Bags

Scatter the hoops or box lids round the room, split the children into two teams—the goodies and the baddies.
The goodies have a 30-second head start to place the bean bags in their corresponding colored hoop. On the word "Go!" the baddies "steal" the bean bags from their correct hoops and place them in the wrong ones.
The goodies have to race round trying to put things back.

If you have loads of kids you may have to do this in groups: 12 is the maximum number for comfort.
Let the little kids play the game all by themselves.
On the word "Stop!" everyone sits down.

Sum up

Look around and assess how well the goodies did—congratulate them on keeping going at all.

Leader	You couldn't do that all day could you?
	Being good can be like that, just when you think you've got it sorted, another bad thing comes up and knocks you down.
	I think we ought to tell the grown-ups how hard it is to stay good.

REHEARSAL

Practice your presentation for when you go back to church (see below).

FINAL PRAYER	Jesus wants us to try, but we can only ever try to be good with God's help. Let's think about that as we say the Our Father.

Our Father... (p. xxxvi).

BACK IN CHURCH

The children stand in a line along the front.

Leader	We read the Gospel this morning and studied how important it was to be good and stay good. We've been trying for the last 30 minutes—and now...

Q the kids—they collapse.

	We're totally exhausted!
	What does that teach us, *Name*?
Child	You can only be good with God's help.

Script 14   Turning the Other Cheek

Epiphany 7

Matthew 5:38-48

THEME

This is the famous Gospel in which Jesus tells us to turn the other cheek. It begins a whole string of extravagant commands which Jesus used to startle His disciples ("Does somebody want your shirt? Give him your jacket too!"). And of course He's quite serious. Not perhaps about whipping off your shirt, but about how to deal with outrageous demands and people.

Jesus wants us to get out of the whole tit-for-tat mentality and dare to be generous. It's asking a lot of people, but it can be life changing, as the story of St. Philip and St. Peregrine demonstrates.

SET UP

- The liturgical color is green.
- Pictures from the CD-ROM. (You'll see that both Philip and Peregrine start off with a set of clothes which you cut out and place over the basic picture of the saint.)
- The Peregrine picture has a detached arm which you should stick to his shoulder with paper fastener. Make sure it can swivel.
- If you know anyone who can show you a bit of basic fencing or karate—invite them!

WELCOME *the children and lead them in* **The Sign of the Cross + (p. xxxvi).**

Ask the children to think back through the week—was there anything we did we wished we hadn't? or something we should have done? Let's ask God to forgive us.

THE KYRIE   Lord God, you always forgive those who say they are sorry,
Lord have mercy.
Lord have mercy.

Lord Jesus, we are sorry for the times we have been selfish or unkind,
Christ have mercy.
Christ have mercy.

Lord God, help us to try to serve you in the coming week,
Lord have mercy.
Lord have mercy.

Ask the children to repeat **The Prayer for Forgiveness** *after you* (**p. xxxvi**).

OPENING PRAYER *from Psalm 102*

(The response is: **God our Father loves us**)

The Lord is compassion and love,
Slow to anger and rich in mercy,
God our Father loves us.

As far as the east is from the west,
So far does He remove our sins,
God our Father loves us.

As a Father loves His children,
So the Lord loves those who fear Him,
God our Father loves us.

BEFORE THE GOSPEL—on fighting

Leader   We're going to start this morning by talking about fighting.
A lot of fighting is just fun.
Fencers fight for sport in the Olympics—but they make sure they cover themselves with visors and body armor first.
Some kids learn karate—but they practice on mats and obey the karate rules.
Actors fight on stage—but they practice for weeks beforehand to make sure it looks good but they don't hurt each other.

Can you demonstrate any of this? If you can't call on a talented fencer or Black Belt, get a couple of toy swords and work out an easy fight routine. Show the kids how carefully an actor prepares as you go through the moves.

We cross swords at the top, then at the bottom, then I take a swipe at so-and-so—and they jump—then they take a swipe at me—and I jump.

Then we meet and clinch our swords, and the other person pushes my sword down and wins. Then we do it a bit faster—but we never ever alter the moves.

But, of course, all this is pretend fighting.

In real life it's rather different.

When Jesus was here on Earth His country was ruled by the Romans...

CD14.1 *Put up the picture of a Roman soldier.*

They were very good fighters indeed...

Point out the armor, the sword, the grim look.

And you didn't mess with them.

If a Roman hit you—you let him.

If he wanted something you were wearing—you gave it to him.

If he asked you to carry something—you carried it.

There was nothing else you could do—until Jesus came along.

He suggested a very strange way to deal with the Romans: let's hear it now.

THE GOSPEL PROCESSION

THE GOSPEL *Matthew 5:38-48*

Jesus said,

"Don't take revenge on someone who wrongs you.

If somebody slaps your right cheek, turn your face and let him slap your left cheek too.

If somebody wants your shirt—give him your jacket.

And if a soldier tells you to carry his pack one mile, carry it two miles.

When someone asks you for something, give it to them, and if someone wants to borrow something, lend it."

AFTER THE GOSPEL

Leader   What a weird set of instructions!

I'm not sure that Jesus meant us to take our jackets and shirts and jeans off every time someone asked for them (but I wouldn't count on it).

What I think He was saying was: "Listen, Romans are people—and you've got to love them just as much as you love your friends. In fact

you've got to love them more, because they've got to notice you love them. That might mean carrying a soldier's pack an extra mile—or not whacking a bully just because he's whacked you."
Love is so important that you even have to love your enemies.
It's the only way to live.
Do you think it would work?
Well, I'm going to tell you a story about one guy who tried it.
It's the story of a saint.

Philip and Peregrine

The story happens way back in the Middle Ages when a young Italian called Philip Benizi (**CD14.2, 14.3**) became a student at the university of Padua.
He got his degree but he loved God so much that he turned his back on a brilliant career and became a friar (**CD14.3**)—*(take off the robes, St. Philip is a friar underneath)*—and went to work in the friar's monastery garden.

CD14.4   *Give Philip a spade and a bag of compost.*

There he is, working quietly away.
Well, eventually the other friars realized how clever Philip was, and they gave him all sorts of jobs to do—teaching young friars, (**CD14.5**)
CD14.6   keeping the peace between the friars,

Ad lib it's astonishing how argumentative really holy people can be.

And eventually he was made head of his order.
One awful day Philip heard there was even an idea he should be the next pope—and he ran off and hid in the hills until they found somebody else.
We're talking about a very humble, quiet man. In fact the only thing that got Philip excited was people not loving each other. He couldn't bear it.
Friars arguing, people arguing, soldiers fighting—he hated all these things, and did his best to stop it.
That didn't go down too well at the time, as the Italians were at war with each other.
CD14.7–14.9   But Philip insisted on preaching to the huge hairy Italian leaders,
telling them to throw down their weapons and love one another for the sake of Jesus.
And one of them, a man called Peregrine Laziosi, got so fed up with Philip that he slapped him in the face.

Swivel Peregrine's movable arm...

Philip took the blow quietly—and went on preaching peace.
And Peregrine was so astounded that he gave up being a soldier, and became a friar.
Remove Peregrine's armor.
CD14.10   There he is, looking just like Philip. *(Have a cut-out halo ready.)*

I've forgotten to give the saint his halo—can somebody do it for me?

Get a kid to put it on—it doesn't matter which saint is chosen, adapt as necessary.

Actually it's this one, St. Peregrine. He spent the rest of his life caring for others and was made a saint—but of course St. Philip was made a saint too.

Sum up

Leader	It can be very difficult loving people—they might think you're a wimp and push you around.
	But St. Philip didn't care about being pushed around, he just hung in there and loved people anyway.
	That's what changed Peregrine's life:
	he slapped Philip,
	Philip turned the other cheek,
	and Peregrine realized it was braver to love than to fight.
	We'll think about those two saints in our last prayer.
FINAL PRAYER	Lord Jesus,
	We thank you for St. Philip and St. Peregrine.
	Help us to follow their example,
	And obey your command to love other people.
	Amen.

SONG

The hymn "We are one in the Spirit" *with its refrain* "They'll know we are Christians by our love" *ends the session very well.*

BACK IN CHURCH

Put Peregrine back in his armor and re-play the moment when he hits Philip.

Today we heard Jesus' command that we should love people, even if they are cruel to us. We thought it was an odd thing to say.

Then we heard the story of St. Philip and St. Peregrine:

St. Philip—*(hold up his picture)*—was trying to get two armies to stop fighting and a soldier called Peregrine—*(hold up Peregrine's picture)*—hit him.

But St. Philip didn't fight back. He went on preaching peace and Peregrine was so impressed that he took off his armor. *(Take it off.)*

And became a friar, and a saint.

So loving people really can work.

Script 15   Trusting in God

Epiphany 8

Matthew 6:24-34

THEME

This is the famous passage where Jesus tells us to "consider the lilies of the field."
He is asking us to trust God to look after us. In this session we think about trust:
how essential it is in a crisis.

SET UP

- The liturgical color is Green.
- A large cushion.
- A boat (made out of chairs).

WELCOME *the children and lead them in* **The Sign of the Cross + (p. xxxvi).**

THE KYRIE   Lord, for the times we have forgotten to love you,
Lord have mercy.
Lord have mercy.

Jesus, for the times we have forgotten to love others,
Christ have mercy.
Christ have mercy.

Lord, we thank you for never forgetting to love us,
Lord have mercy.
Lord have mercy.

Ask the children to repeat **The Prayer for Forgiveness** *after you* (**p. xxxvi**).

OPENING   (*The response is* **In God I trust**)
PRAYER

In God alone is my trust.
My help comes from Him.
In God I trust.

God is my rock and my stronghold.
He is my fortress: I shall not fall.
In God I trust.

Put your trust in God alone,
For He is our hope.
In God I trust.

BEFORE THE GOSPEL

Trust

Leader   Today we're going to think about "trust."

At which point you tell a "Trust Story." Have you ever got a child, an animal, or an inexperienced climber or sailor out of a difficult situation? The story I usually tell is below, you'll probably come up with something much more exciting.

I was in the local park one day when I saw a little girl, up a tree, clinging to a branch.
She'd climbed too far and was too frightened to get down.
So I climbed up and told her not to worry.
I said, "Don't worry about the tree or your legs or the ground or anything. Just listen to me and we'll be fine."
Then I guided her feet and hands down, branch by branch, inch by inch, until we reached the ground.
She only managed it because she trusted me.
Something like that happened to the disciples once. It's a story we're going to tell together.
It's called "Stilling the Storm." Some of you probably know it—but we'll run through it, just in case.

Stilling the Storm

One day Jesus and His friends went on a journey—
How do you think they went? a bus? (**a boat!**)
It was sunny when they set out, but suddenly a storm blew up and the disciples were...
How were the disciples? (**terrified**)
And do you remember what Jesus was doing? (**He was fast asleep.**)
Well, the wind got stronger and the sea got rougher, and the disciples knew that Jesus was the only person to get them out of this mess—so they woke Him up—
Then what happened? (**Jesus stilled the storm.**)
Let's sort that out as a play.
We'll need props, and sound effects, and a cast, and some action.

Production Meeting

First we need to make a boat—out of these chairs, I think.
And there has to be a cushion for Jesus to sleep on.
Then we need to make the sound of the wind—can you do that?

Get the children to give you some wind noises.

Then we need the cast...

Choose Jesus, the Disciples and the Sea.

REHEARSAL

The really important group to rehearse is the Sea.
The children stand with their arms horizontal for a calm sea, they slightly bob the
arms for a bit of a swell, and then do co-ordinated acute angles for the storm.
Practice the cues (Qs):
Give the kids a beat to start bobbing,
another to get stormy,
and (this is the crucial one) do the theatrical gesture of "kill that" (finger across the
throat) for them to stop.
Keep practicing until they get the "kill" bang on Q.
Do the same with the wind, Q it in, and then "kill" it.
Now do the "kill" Q with Jesus stopping the wind and sea by stretching out His
hands.
The disciples will also need to practice their "Wake up Jesus!" line.
Now run the story, once as a practice, then for real.
One of the leaders is the Narrator, the other Qs people in.

Narrator	One day Jesus and His friends decided to cross the lake on a boat.

The disciples get into the boat.

Jesus was very tired.

Major acting from Jesus here.

He sat down at the front of the boat, found a pillow, and went to sleep.

He does so.   Off they went.
The sea was very gentle
And the disciples began to enjoy themselves.

Bit of waving here from the disciples, grinning.

But half way across the waves began to bob.

Q bob.   Then they bobbed some more.

Q bob a bit more.

> And then the waves went mad, the sea got rough, the rain came down and there was a horrible storm.

Q storm.   And the disciples were terrified.

Make sure they are.

> "Where's Jesus??!" said one.

Everybody looks round.

> "He's asleep!" said another.
> "Typical!" said another.
> And then all said together

Children   **"WAKE UP JESUS!"**

Narrator   One of them even shook Him.

Q the shake.   "Look at the sea!" said a disciple. "Don't you care that we are drowning?"
> And Jesus stood up.
> The wind was howling...

Q wind sound effect.

> But Jesus said to the wind:
> "Be quiet!"
> And He stretched out His hands...

Q kill the wind.

> And the wind stopped.
> Then Jesus looked at the sea,

Q storm.

> He said, "Be still!"
> And stretched out His hands...

Q kill the rough sea.

> And the sea went calm.
> Then He sat down again.
> And the disciples said to each other, "How did He do that? Who is this that even the wind and waves obey?"

And that's it. Congratulate the children and get them to sit down.

Sum up

Leader	That's one of the great stories.

That's one of the great stories.

The disciples had the fright of their lives—but they trusted Jesus to get them out of it.

I must say Jesus wasn't very pleased with the disciples: He thought they should have trusted Him even when He was asleep.

Still they trusted Him enough to wake Him up, and that was something.

Jesus likes us to trust Him.

He often looked at the people who followed Him around and thought they all worried too much in the Gospel this morning he told them to sit down, listen to Him, and calm down.

THE GOSPEL PROCESSION

THE GOSPEL *Matthew 6:24-34*

Jesus said, "Don't worry about your life, what you're going to eat or drink, or what you're going to wear. Look at the birds of the air, they don't sow, or reap, or store things in barns, and yet your Father in Heaven feeds them. Don't you think you are more valuable than the birds?

And look at the lilies growing in the fields, they don't work or spin, yet even King Solomon, in all his splendor, was never dressed so magnificently. If God clothes the flowers in the fields, don't you think He'll clothe you?

So stop worrying, don't keep thinking about tomorrow—tomorrow will take care of itself."

REHEARSAL

Practice your presentation for when you go back to church (see below).

FINAL PRAYER

Set up a prayer candle and ask the children to sit round it.
Get them to shut their eyes, and put their hands on their chests.

Can you feel how close your heart is?
That's how close God is.
Think about the week ahead—
Is anything worrying you?
Homework? Exams? Something you're not looking forward to?
Tell God about it now, ask Him to be with you—and then forget it!
You can't nag God, you have to trust Him.
He'll be there when you need Him.

Give the children time to pray.
Gather their prayers together in an
Our Father... (p. xxxvi),
or a **Song** *(the spiritual* "He's Got the Whole World in His Hands" *is good here).*

BACK IN CHURCH

Line up the children at the front, facing the congregation, their arms outstretched.

Leader   Today we thought about trusting in God
                    In unsettled weather...

Q the kids to start bobbing their arms.

                    In storms...

Q the kids to slope their arms up and down for a storm.

                    And in quiet times...

Q the kids to hold their arms horizontal.

                    And we decided that, whatever the weather, God would be with us.

Kids   *Amen!*

Script 16 The Transfiguration

Last Epiphany

Matthew 17:1-8

THEME

Jesus was really and truly Man, but He was also God—and for a moment the disciples caught a glimpse of His Heavenly glory. We explore this idea through a session on disguise.

SET UP

- The liturgical color is Green.
- Raincoat, and a hat with a brim, for an archetypal Secret Agent.
- Fake mustache.
- Get a kid to agree to be a Secret Agent for the disguise session.
- Pictures from the CD-ROM (set the "normal Jesus" over the "transfigured Jesus" so that He is hidden from view).

WELCOME *the children and lead them in* **The Sign of the Cross + (p. xxxvi).**

THE KYRIE   Lord Jesus, we are sorry for the times we have forgotten you,
Lord have mercy.
Lord have mercy.

Lord Jesus, we are sorry for the times we have been unkind,
Christ have mercy.
Christ have mercy.

Lord Jesus, thank you for always listening to us, and forgiving us,
Lord have mercy.
Lord have mercy.

Ask the children to repeat **The Prayer for Forgiveness** *after you* (**p. xxxvi**).

OPENING   Lord Jesus,
PRAYER   True God and True Man,
　　　　　　　Help us to hear you,
　　　　　　　And worship you,
　　　　　　　This morning. *Amen.*

BEFORE THE GOSPEL

Leader   Okay, today we're going to think about disguise.
　　　　　　　Now not many people know this, but *Name* here is really a
　　　　　　　Secret Agent.

Bring him/her forward.

　　　　　　　Naturally, when on a job she adopts a disguise—
　　　　　　　a raincoat...
She puts it on.　Remember to put the collar up...
She does.　　　And a hat...
She puts it on.　Remember to pull the brim down.
　　　　　　　Yup, you look just the part.
　　　　　　　Anyone else want a disguise?
　　　　　　　A really quick way is to put on a false moustache...
　　　　　　　It looks pretty impressive, doesn't it?
　　　　　　　But I wonder whether it works?
　　　　　　　Of course nobody would guess that this bearded ruffian was *Name*,
　　　　　　　or that this Secret Agent was *Name*.
　　　　　　　But do you think it's sensible to dress up as an agent?

See what they think, they usually spot the problem.

　　　　　　　Quite so.
　　　　　　　I think it's only suspicious people who have obvious disguises—
　　　　　　　good people don't need them.
　　　　　　　And yet, funnily enough, being ordinary can often look like a
　　　　　　　disguise all by itself.

A Saint or Hero Story

Do you know anybody, quiet, unassuming, whom nobody would ever have guessed was a hero—somebody who did some amazing thing, or has been famous in some way? The old people in church often turn out to have had the most astonishing lives, it's worth hearing their stories. If you haven't got time to research them this session, a couple of stories are offered below. You have pictures of them on the CD-ROM.

CD16.1   I knew an old lady, Alice Jones, who lived until she was 90. She was very frail in her last years, and loved nothing more than sitting in a chair, looking at the garden. But, when she was a young woman she drove a truck for the Air Force. A special truck with a great spotlight at the back, to guide the planes home after they'd been fighting in battles. Many of those planes were on fire, and careering about, and their pilots were wounded, or dazed or just exhausted. It was very dangerous driving just in front of a beat-up plane, but she brought hundreds of them in to safety.
She was a heroine.

CD16.2   *Add the medal to Mrs. Jones's picture.*

CD16.3   There was a priest I knew called Father Joe McGeady. He used to embarrass us all by wandering around (fill-in name of your city) in an awful grey cardigan, pushing a shopping cart, and rooting through trash bins for bottles and cans. He looked like a priestly tramp. Yet he always knew when people needed him, and he'd turn up, out of the blue—midnight, anytime—to pray with them or give them money or whatever they needed in their crisis. And he and his cans helped to finance the homeless project we now have in our town. Most of us think he was a saint...

CD16.4   *Add a halo to Fr. Joe's picture.*

You see, a very good person usually looks ordinary, it's difficult to spot the wonderful person underneath.
Jesus was like that. He looked so normal that even His family didn't always realize who He really was. But one day His friends saw Him looking completely different.

THE GOSPEL PROCESSION

THE GOSPEL *Matthew 17:1-8*

> One day Jesus took His disciples, Peter and James and John, up a high mountain to pray.

CD16.5   *Put up the picture of the normal Jesus.*

> And, as He was praying, His face shone, and His clothes became dazzling white.

CD16.6   *Remove the normal Jesus from the transfigured Jesus beneath.*

CD16.7, 16.8   And two holy men appeared beside Him, Moses and Elijah.
They had come from Heaven to talk to Jesus.
Peter didn't know what to do, but he called out,
"Lord, it's good to be here—shall we make some tents for you and
for Moses and Elijah?"
As he spoke a bright cloud overshadowed them.

CD16.9   *Place cloud picture over transfigured Jesus.*
CD16.10   *Stick speech balloon on cloud.*

And a Voice from the cloud said, "This is my beloved Son, listen to
Him!"
The Voice filled the disciples with awe—and they fell flat on their
faces. But Jesus came down to them, touched them and said,
"Don't be afraid, get up."
And Peter, James and John looked up, and found that everything had
gone back to normal.

Remove Cloud, Voice, Elijah and Moses.

Put the ordinary Jesus back over the transfigured Jesus.

And they were alone with Jesus on the mountain top.

AFTER THE GOSPEL

Leader   Talk through the story with the children.
Whom did Jesus take up the mountain?
(Peter, James and John)
What happened to His face? And His clothes?
(His face shone, and His clothes became dazzling white.)
Who do you think the Voice was? **(God)**

Sum up

Leader   Just for a moment Peter, James and John saw Jesus as He really was:
His face shining with the light of Heaven, His clothes bright with
glory—talking to holy people who died ages ago—God the Father's
Voice all around them.

FINAL	Remembering who Jesus really is, let's praise Him in the
PRAYER	**Glory Be... (p. xxxvii).**

FINAL PRAYER   Remembering who Jesus really is, let's praise Him in the Glory Be... (p. xxxvii).

BACK IN CHURCH

Show a picture of the transfigured Lord with the normal Jesus on top.
Prime one child to hold picture, one to whip off the normal Jesus and one to read.
Hold up picture.

Leader   When Jesus lived on earth, He looked like an ordinary man, but one day His friends saw that He was something else as well...

Whip off normal Jesus to reveal the transfigured Lord.

His face shone.
His clothes were bright.
And His friends realized that He was the Son of God.

(CD16.5)   (CD16.6)   (CD16.7)   (CD16.8)

Sample cartoons for this script

Script 17   Jesus in the Desert

Lent 1

Matthew 4:1-11

> **THEME**
>
> The start of Lent: we mark the penitential mood of the Church by replacing our bells and candles with a mini desert.
>
> Today's Gospel is about Jesus' experiences in the desert and the Devil makes an unwelcome appearance. Given the prevalence of Satan in popular culture it's helpful to tell the Gospel straight and give the children a Christian take on this worrying, but ultimately ridiculous, character.

SET UP

- The liturgical color is Purple.
- Try to wear some purple —even if it's only a scarf.
- Place the candles and bells for the Gospel Procession on the table at the front.
- Have materials on hand to make a "desert" which will be used in all the Lent sessions. You'll need:
    - A deep baking tray filled with sand.
    - Some rocks or large stones.
    - Mini cacti, or candle cacti from a florist.
    - And any suitable extras—like a toy camel.
    - Plus a large candle, that will stand by itself in the sand, to represent Jesus.

- Ash (optional)—either see if there is any left from Ash Wednesday, or make some by burning the charcoal used for incense (it'll take a good 15 minutes). Cool it down with some water (you'll need a spot of water anyway to add to the ash and make it stick). This is optional—check it out with your priest beforehand.
- A large box for the candles and bells, covered in purple wrapping paper if you've got the time.
- Picture from CD-ROM.
- Hallowe'en horns or a plastic pitchfork, if you've got them. They make excellent devil props and there's a lot to be said for following the medieval tradition and turning him into a comic figure.

WELCOME *the children and lead them in* **The Sign of the Cross + (p. xxxvi).**

Leader	Did anybody notice the color in church today? (**purple**)
	What color are my socks? (**purple**)
	We're in Purple time—
	Does anyone know what Purple means in church?

Take all answers, but end up by establishing:

Purple is a dark, serious color, and the Church always goes into purple when we're about to get ready for something.
What are we getting ready for? *(Give some hints.)* (**Easter**)
Absolutely. Easter—but it's ages away, not for another six weeks.
But Easter is so important, that we start getting ready six weeks before.
Those six weeks have a special name—does anyone know it? (**Lent**)

OPTIONAL ASHING

Check this out with your priest.

Leader	Lent started last Wednesday and people came to church to be receive ashes.
	We start Lent by putting a cross on our foreheads.
	It's made of ash. *(Show them the ash.)*
	We do this to show:
	this is Lent.
	We're sorry for the things we've done wrong.
	We're going to return to God.
	Every time we look in the mirror today, we'll see the ash, and remember it's Lent.
	This is how you ash somebody.

Another Leader ashes you with these words.

>Return to God. *Amen.*

Ash the children.

>Return to God. *Amen.*

End with the **Kyrie.**

If you haven't ashed the kids introduce the **Kyrie** *by saying:*

>As we start the holy season of Lent, let us call to mind the things we've done wrong and ask God to forgive us:

THE KYRIE   Lord Jesus, you came to call us back to God,
Lord have mercy.
Lord have mercy.

Lord Jesus, you fasted in the desert,
Christ have mercy.
Christ have mercy.

Lord Jesus, you told sinners how much God loves them,
Lord have mercy.
Lord have mercy.

Ask the children to repeat **The Prayer for Forgiveness** *after you* **(p. xxxvi).**

Leader   Well, Lent is such a serious season we get rid of some of the fun things we do in church. So this morning we're going to bury our bells and candles in that box over there.

Somebody holds up the box at the other end of the room.
Pass out the bells and candles and practice stopping the bell sound.
Q the children in and bring in the "kill that" Q (finger across throat)—of course, you give the "kill" Q bang in the middle of a ding.
Set up a procession of kids to take the bells and candles from the front.

LENT PROCESSION

Children hold the candles high.
Ring the bells.
Everything goes silent as they go into the box.

Leader   Right, now we're ready for Lent.
Jesus understands about getting ready.
Before He began His ministry, He got ready Himself
Let's hear how He did it.

One child brings the Gospel Book up from the back.

THE GOSPEL *Matthew 4:1-11*

Gospel for Narrator and Devil

The Devil stands just behind the Narrator and insinuates his temptations in the ear of the Narrator.

Narrator	Filled with the Holy Spirit, Jesus was led into the Desert. He was there for 40 days and ate nothing. And when the 40 days were up, He was hungry. Suddenly, the Devil spoke to Him:
Devil	If you are the Son of God, do some magic, command this stone to become bread.
Narrator	Jesus answered him, "It is written, 'Man does not live by bread alone.'" Then the Devil took Jesus up and showed Him all the kingdoms of the world in a single instant, and he said:
Devil	Listen, here's the whole world. I can give it all to you—if you fall down and worship *me*.
Narrator	Jesus said to him in reply, "It is written, 'You shall worship the Lord, your God, and Him alone shall you serve.'" Then the Devil led Him to Jerusalem and placed Him on a parapet of the Temple, and said to Him:
Devil	Prove you're the Son of God: throw yourself down from here. God is bound to save you, it says in the Bible, "God will command His Angels to save you—lest you dash your foot against a stone."
Narrator	But Jesus said to him in reply, "It also says, 'You shall not put the Lord, your God, to the test.'" When the Devil had finished every temptation, he departed from Him—and the Angels came, and served Him.

Exit Devil with a very mad face, ad libbing.

Rats!

AFTER THE GOSPEL

Leader	That's an odd story. Jesus goes into a desert, stays there for 40 days and He gets a visitor—who was it? (**the Devil**) What's all that about?

The Desert

Well, let's look at a desert.

Bring the desert tray forward filled with sand only.

This is our desert...

Run the sand through your fingers.

It's very dry...
The only things you'd see there would be **rocks**.

Get the kids to put in the rocks.

The only things that grow would be **cacti**.

A child puts in the cactus.

The only animals that could live there would be weird things like **camels**.

In goes the camel.

It's very rocky, and lonely, and Jesus was there for 40 days.
Fasting and praying.
Now, for some of us that might give us nightmares and see stupid things that weren't there, like this...

CD17.1   *Put up Devil picture.*

Usually when people see the Devil, especially if he looks like this, they're just having a nutty moment.
But the Gospel doesn't say Jesus *saw* the Devil, it says He *heard* him—whispering things in His ear.
What sort of things?

Take any answer here—add the temptation pictures as they get it.

Sum up

The Devil suggested things that Jesus could easily have done—
CD17.2   like turn rocks into bread,
CD17.3   jump off high buildings,
CD17.4   ditch God the Father and rule the world.
For a second, it might have sounded rather a good idea. But do you think it would have helped if Jesus had worshipped the Devil, or done a stunt from the top of the Temple?

Any answer will do.

Actually it wouldn't—because another name for the Devil is The Father of Lies.
He'll say *anything* to get people to do wrong.
None of us knows what the Devil looks like—but I bet he doesn't look like that...

CD17.1   *Refer to picture.*

What we do know is that the Devil is always trying to nibble away at the good things we do.
He sidles up to us sometimes and says things like...

Get the Devil character to sidle up to somebody and say:

"You don't need to go to church this morning, you have a nice sleep-in."

Get the Devil to say to the leader:

"I know you've given up chocolate for Lent, but you deserve a little bit, go on have a candy bar."

Leader   And we have to be like Jesus...

The Leader turns on the Devil and does a grab-by-the-collar moment.

"Just a minute! It's good to go to church, it's right I should stick by my promises. Go away, Devil!"
There's only one way to deal with those sorts of temptations.

Pull the Devil picture off the flip-chart...

Crumple it up!

Get a kid to crumple up the picture and throw it in a wastepaper basket.

So, this Lent, we're going to be like Jesus.
We'll be in the desert with Him and getting ready for Easter:
By fasting—that means giving up things—
And praying.
Fortunately the desert isn't really lonely:
Jesus is there in the middle...

Place the Jesus candle in the desert.

And, as He prayed in the desert, we'll do so too.

Light the candle and ask the children to repeat after you:

God our Father,
This Lent, help us to return to you,
To pray to you,
And to love you.

Help us to see you more clearly,
To love you more dearly,
And follow you more nearly,
Day by day. *Amen.*

BACK IN CHURCH

The Leaders bring in the desert.

Child   This Lent we are going to follow Jesus into the desert.

Bring the desert tray forward.

This is our "desert."

Run the sand through your fingers.

It's very dry.
Very rocky.
Very lonely.
But Jesus is there in the middle.

Point out the Jesus candle.

(CD17.1)

(CD17.3)

(CD17.4)

Sample cartoons for this script

Script 18   Nicodemus (and Noah)

Lent 2

John 3:1-5

THEME

Nicodemus has a long and learned discussion with Jesus about New Birth. It's not very suitable for children, but it offers us a session on Baptism—and a chance to tell the story of Noah's Ark.

SET UP

- The liturgical color is Purple.
- The desert tray (see Lent 1).
- Pictures from the CD-ROM.
- A hammer or mallet.
- A dozen chairs.
- Three print-outs of the Noah's Ark script.
- Something that could feasibly be an olive branch.

WELCOME *the children and lead them in* **The Sign of the Cross + (p. xxxvi).**

Résumé on Lent, *comment on the purple drapes and vestments.*

Leader	Purple is a dark, serious color.
	The Church uses it when we're getting ready for something.
	What are we getting ready for? (**Easter**)
	Yes. And one of the ways we get ready for Easter is to think through the things we've done wrong and ask God to forgive us.
	Let's do that.

THE KYRIE   Lord Jesus, you came to call us back to God,
Lord have mercy.
Lord have mercy.

Lord Jesus, you fasted in the desert,
Christ have mercy.
Christ have mercy.

Lord Jesus, you told sinners how much God loves them,
Lord have mercy.
Lord have mercy.

Ask the children to repeat **The Prayer for Forgiveness** *after you* **(p. xxxvi).**

The Desert

Before Jesus began His ministry, He fasted in the desert.
So, every Lent we go into the desert with Him.
Here it is.

Bring the desert tray forward.

This is our desert...

Run the sand through your fingers.

Very dry.
Very rocky.
Very lonely.
But with Jesus in the middle.

Place the Jesus candle in the desert.

And, as He prayed in the desert, we'll do so too.

Light the candle and ask the children to repeat after you.

OPENING   Lord Jesus,
PRAYER   You fasted and prayed in the desert.
Help us to follow your example,
To keep our Lent promises,
And fast and pray. *Amen.*

Leader   Today we're going to go straight into the Gospel and hear a conversation Jesus had with a very clever disciple of His called Nicodemus.

THE GOSPEL *John 3:1-5*

AFTER THE GOSPEL

Leader	That's a rather strange conversation:
	Nicodemus wants to enter the Kingdom of Heaven and Jesus tells him he'll have to be born again.
	Can you be born twice? (**No**)
	What could Jesus have meant?
	One of the things I think He meant is, when you're born normally,
CD18.1	you arrive as a little baby.
	But there's a moment when your parents bring you along to church to be baptized.
CD18.2	The priest prays for the Holy Spirit to bless some water,
CD18.3	Then he pours the water over you,
	And you become a Christian.
	It's like becoming a new person—
	You're born again.
	That's what Jesus meant when he said you must be
	"born of water and the Holy Spirit."
	Nicodemus didn't really understand, but he stayed a disciple of Jesus right up to the end. He even helped to bury Him.
	So if Nicodemus tried to figure this out—so should we.
	One of the stories that helps us is this one.

Noah's Ark

CD18.4   *The kids are to be the animals in the Ark, so split them up into twos and get them to come up with the noises. Farmyard animals are easy, so are cats and dogs— how about hamsters? elephants? mice? and lions? Anything the children want—but it must have a noise.*
Write the animals down, so you can cue (Q) them in.
You must have a dove.
Run a rehearsal session. Q in the noises, in pairs, by a downward stroke and then cut them off by the "kill that" gesture (finger across throat).
One Leader is the Narrator, the other is Noah. If you've got a third ask them to be God, otherwise the narrator is God.

Narrator	Once upon a time a very long time ago there was a man called Noah.
	He was a good man and greatly loved by God.
	Unfortunately he lived in a city where the people were so horrible that God got fed up with them. "I can't stand these sinners any

longer," said God to Himself one day. "I feel like washing them down the drain."

And He began to gather His thunder clouds. Then He remembered Noah.

"Noah!" He called.

Noah	Yes, God?
God	"I want you to build a boat."
Noah	But we're miles from the sea.
God	"Just do it."
Narrator	So Noah began to build a boat.

Noah goes round with his hammer, tapping chairs and arranging them in a line. You can call on some help here, Noah had loads of children.

Narrator	When it was ready God said, "Okay, Noah, I want you to gather two of every animal in the world."
Noah	What, all of them!?
God	"Yes. Well you can leave out the ducks and the fish."
Narrator	Why did He say that? (**They can swim.**)
	So Noah started to collect the animals.
	He called the...
	and the...
	and the...
	And he put them in a line...

The kids make their animal noise as they are called, but kill it the moment they're in the line

Narrator	And when they were all ready Noah led them into his boat.
	He called it the Ark.

The kids follow Noah behind the row of chairs.

Narrator	The animals were very excited, and once they were all aboard they all began speaking at once.

Q in the kids.

Noah	Be quiet!

Q kill the noise.

Narrator	And as they stopped chattering they heard the rain begin to fall.

Q rain effect—you do this by getting everyone to click their fingers.

Narrator	The rain went on for 40 days and nights. The rivers flooded, the seas flooded and soon there was no more dry land and the Ark floated out to sea.

Q get the children to sway to the waves.

Narrator   And all the time the rain kept falling.

Q rain effect.

Narrator   Then one day...

Q kill the rain.

Narrator   The rain stopped.
                  And the Ark bumped to a halt. Watch me for the "bump" and make sure you bump too—it went *(jerk yourself suddenly, then Q it in)* like that.

Noah   We've landed.

Narrator   Everybody looked out of the window. There was nothing but water all around. Noah sent out a dove to see what the world was like... *(send out dove)*
                  She came back very fast—*(she does so)*—because there was nowhere to perch.
                  Next day Noah sent her out again... *(he does so)*
                  This time she came back with an olive branch in her beak... *(she does)*
                  She'd found a tree.
                  The next day Noah sent her out again but she never came back— obviously she'd found somewhere to live.

Noah   The world is dry again—let's get out of here.

Narrator   He opened the doors of the Ark and all the animals came out.
                  The...
                  and the...
                  and the...

Kids come out making brief animal comments as their name is called.

Narrator   And once they were out they all began to speak at once.

Q ghastly noise.

Noah   Be quiet!—*(Q kill that)*—I can hear Somebody talking...

Narrator   And Noah and the animals heard God say.
                  "I shall never flood the world again. No matter what you or your children do, Noah, I shall bless you.
                  And to show I mean what I say
                  I shall put my bow in the sky."

CD18.5   And a rainbow appeared in the sky.

Congratulate the children and ask them to sit down.

Sum up

Leader   That's a very old story. And because it's so full of water, Christians have often thought it's a good story to teach people about Baptism.

CD18.4   You see, water is very nice if you're thirsty, or need to wash your face—but it's also very dangerous. People can drown in it.

And for Noah and his family and the animals, when they were in that Ark, with water all around them, water pouring down on top of them...

Draw sheets of rain falling down on the Ark picture.

It must have felt as if they were drowning.

And when they got through it all, and stood on dry land, they must have felt as if they had come back to life.

And when people are baptized the priest tells them that they "go down into the waters of Baptism"—some priests actually dunk the whole baby at this moment—and come up through it again to new life.

It's like being born again.

REHEARSAL

Practice your presentation for when you go back to church (see below).

FINAL PRAYER

Ask the children to repeat after you:

God our Father,
This Lent, help us to return to you,
To pray to you,
and to love you.

Help us to see you more clearly,
To love you more dearly,
And follow you more nearly,
Day by day. *Amen.*

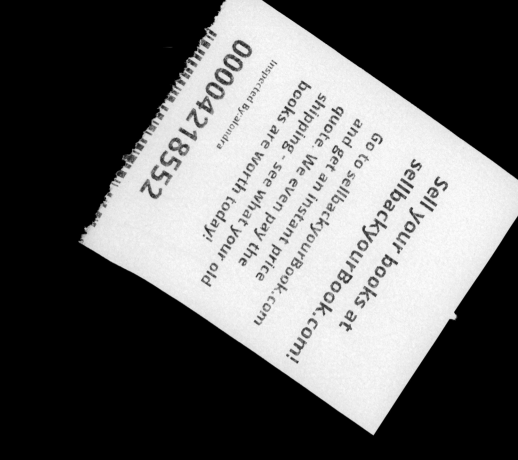

BACK IN CHURCH

Line up the children at the front—arms out horizontally.

Leader   Today we thought about Baptism.
                    We thought it was like being with Noah in his Ark:
                    Surrounded by water...

Q the children rock their arms.

                    Being rained on...

Q the children click their fingers.

                    Feeling you're being drowned...

Q the children fold their arms round their bodies as they sit down.

                    And then coming up out of the water to...

Q the children spring up.

Kids   New Life!

(CD18.1)   (CD18.2)   (CD18.3)

(CD18.4)

Cartoons for this script

Script 19   The Samaritan Woman

Lent 3

John 4:1-15

THEME

The Gospel is about Jesus' encounter with the Samaritan woman at the well. Their long and interesting conversation is not particularly suitable for children, so this session uses the story as a springboard for thinking about the well and what it tells us about the sacraments.

SET UP

- The liturgical color is Purple.
- The desert tray (see Lent 1).
- Picture from the CD-ROM.
- Bucket full of water.
- Teaspoon.
- Cup.
- Ladle.
- Holy water stoup or bowl.
- Aspergillum or sprig of rosemary or fir (with which to sprinkle someone with water).

WELCOME *the children and lead them in* **The Sign of the Cross + (p. xxxvi).**

Résumé on Lent, *comment on the purple drapes and vestments.*

Leader   Purple is a dark, serious color.
          The Church uses it when we're getting ready for something.
          What are we getting ready for? (**Easter**)
          Yes, and one of the ways we get ready for Easter is to think through the things we've done wrong and ask God to forgive us.
          Let's do that.

THE KYRIE   Lord Jesus, you came to call us back to God,
Lord have mercy.
Lord have mercy.

Lord Jesus, you fasted in the desert,
Christ have mercy.
Christ have mercy.

Lord Jesus, you told sinners how much God loves them,
Lord have mercy.
Lord have mercy.

Ask the children to repeat **The Prayer for Forgiveness** *after you* (**p. xxxvi**).

The Desert

Before Jesus began His ministry, He fasted in the desert.
So, every Lent we go into the desert with Him.
Here it is.

Bring the desert tray forward.

This is our desert...

Run the sand through your fingers.

Very dry.
Very rocky.
Very lonely.
But with Jesus in the middle

Place the Jesus candle in the desert.

And, as He prayed in the desert, we'll do so too.

Light the candle and ask the children to repeat after you.

OPENING   Lord Jesus,
PRAYER   You fasted and prayed in the desert.
Help us to follow your example,
To keep our Lent promises,
And fast and pray.
Amen.

BEFORE THE GOSPEL

Leader	Okay, today we're going to hear a story about someone Jesus met when He journeyed into Samaria.
	People who lived in Samaria were called Samaritans: the Jews couldn't bear them. Actually the Samaritans didn't like the Jews too much either.
CD19.1	Anyway, Jesus and His 12 disciples walked to Samaria and when they got there, Jesus was so tired, He just sat down by a well and sent His friends off to buy some food.
	At which point a Samaritan woman turned up.
	Let's hear about her.

THE GOSPEL *John 4:1-15*

Optional Paraphrase

Jesus travelled back to Galilee through Samaria. They got to Samaria about noon and Jesus sat down by a well. He was tired and sent His disciples off to buy some food. While they were gone, a woman arrived. She'd come to draw water from the well. Jesus said to her, "Draw me a cup of water."

She said, "Aren't you a Jew? I'm surprised you ask a Samaritan to get you some water." (Most Jews won't drink from the same cups as Samaritans.)

Jesus said, "If you knew who was asking you for a drink, you'd ask Him for a drink instead—and He would give you life-giving water."

"But you haven't got a bucket!" said the woman. "And that well is deep!"

"Anyone drinking from that well," said Jesus, "will get thirsty again. But if you drank the water I offer you, you will never be thirsty again. The water would become a spring in you and give you eternal life."

"Sir," said the woman, "give me some of that water."

AFTER THE GOSPEL

Leader	That's a very odd conversation—what sort of water can Jesus be referring to?
	Let's think about that well for a moment...

Talk about wells with the kids.

	When water is very deep, you have to pull it up with a bucket. The woman was right really, Jesus didn't have a bucket, He couldn't get any water.

It's difficult in hot countries if you can't find a well or a spring or if you don't have a faucet.

Any ideas how you get water if you're stuck? (**Wait for it to rain.**)

Introduce them to the idea of spreading out your shirt to catch the dew overnight.

Can you imagine how long that takes?

Look here's a cup,

And I'm thirsty.

There's a bucket with water in it—and all I've got to get the water out with is this teaspoon.

How long would it take to fill the cup?

Let's find out...

Line up the kids and pass the spoon along: the idea is to fill the cup. Set it a few yards away so there's some spillage. Once it's half full, call a halt and look in the cup.

Hmm, only half full—what I need is this!

Fill it with the ladle—and have a drink.

Fantastic. Now, when Jesus offered the woman water that would give her eternal life, He wasn't thinking of this sort of water at all. What do you think He was thinking of?

See if they get it—if they don't, ask them when we use water in church.

(**Holy Baptism**)

Baptism is one of the sacraments God has given us, one of the things that gives us His help and His grace.

As Jesus sat by that well He was thinking about water and Baptism, but I think He was thinking about the other Sacraments as well.

If you're thirsty you need a ladle, you can't wait for a teaspoon.

You certainly can't wait for the rain.

And if you need God's help, you'll often find God likes you to use something fast and effective.

Pick up the bucket and place it in the center of the children.

If the water in this bucket is God's grace, then this ladle is the Sacrament.

Do you want to become a Christian?

Ask the priest at the well for the Sacrament of Baptism.

Scoop water out of the bucket with the ladle and pour it back from a height.

Do you want God to forgive your sins?

Ask for forgiveness.

Same business with the ladle...

Do you want to meet Jesus in His own Body and Blood?
Ask for the Sacrament of Holy Communion.

Same business with the ladle...

Jesus had to sit by a well and wait for somebody with a bucket to get Him some water—but He offers us His grace and a ladle to scoop it up, every time we ask for His help.

REHEARSAL

Practice your presentation for when you go back to church (see below).

FINAL PRAYER

Leader   Let's thank God for the sacraments.

Ask the children to repeat after you:

**Lord God,
Thank you for the sacraments,
Thank you for our Baptism,
Help us, this Lent,
To see you more clearly,
Love you more dearly,
And follow you more nearly,
Day by day.** *Amen.*

BACK IN CHURCH

You need the holy water stoup and aspergillum (or a sprig of rosemary or fir)
Place a boy and a girl down the front, girl plus bucket, ladle and cup, boy plus holy water stoup and aspergillum.

Leader   In the Gospel today we heard that Jesus asked a Samaritan woman to draw Him some water from a well.
She gave Him some ordinary water...

The girl ladles out some water from her bucket and gives it to the boy.

In return Jesus offered her living water that would give her eternal life.

The boy sprinkles the girl from the holy water stoup.

Script 20   Jesus Heals a Blind Man

Lent 4

John 9:1a, 9:6, 9:11-12

THEME

The actual Gospel reading goes on to verse 41 and is one of John's long narratives. This session cuts out the quarrels that spring up once the blind man is healed and, focusing on the miracle itself, addresses the question—how is it that some people get cured from their illnesses and others don't?

To answer this we put the children in the "Angels' Sorting Office" and give them first hand experience at sorting out prayers. The children normally enjoy their moment of power—which is very appropriate as this is Laetare (or joyful) Sunday, one of the Pink Sundays that lightens up the serious mood of Lent.

It is also Mothering Sunday in the Anglican Church, so mothers get highlighted.

SET UP

- The liturgical color is Pink (try to wear something pink to make the point).
- The desert tray (see Lent 1).
- Five shoe boxes, four labelled as follows: "Yes," "No," "Maybe," "Hmmm, Try Again."
- The fifth is a "Thank you" box which you keep in reserve.
- Mailbag full of prayers from the CD-ROM. Watch how you stack it:
  - Four specific ones have to be at the top.
  - Two specific ones at the bottom (see below).
- Large colored markers.
- Enough blank paper for the banner below.

WELCOME *the children and lead them in* **The Sign of the Cross ✝** (p. xxxvi).

Résumé on Lent, *indicate that things have cheered up a bit today.*

Leader	What color is my tie? (**pink**)
	Yes, it's a Pink Sunday, we needn't be quite so serious today.
	Even so, we should start, as we always do, by thinking back over the

past week and telling God we're sorry for the things we have done wrong.

THE KYRIE   Lord Jesus, you came to call us back to God,
Lord have mercy.
Lord have mercy.

Lord Jesus, you fasted in the desert,
Christ have mercy.
Christ have mercy.

Lord Jesus, you told sinners how much God loves them,
Lord have mercy.
Lord have mercy.

Ask the children to repeat **The Prayer for Forgiveness** *after you* (**p. xxxvi**).

The Desert

Before Jesus began His ministry, He fasted in the desert.
So, every Lent we go into the "desert" with Him.
Here it is.

Bring the desert tray forward.

This is our desert...

Run the sand through your fingers.

Very dry.
Very rocky.
Very lonely.
But with Jesus in the middle.

Place the Jesus candle in the desert.

And, as He prayed in the desert, we'll do so too.

Light the candle and ask the children to repeat after you:

OPENING   Lord Jesus,
PRAYER   You fasted and prayed in the desert.
Help us to follow your example,
To keep our Lent promises,
And fast and pray. *Amen.*
Leader   Today we're going straight into the Gospel.

THE GOSPEL *John 9:1a, 9:6, 9:11-12*

Optional Paraphrase

As Jesus was passing He saw a beggar who had been born blind. Jesus spat on the ground and, making some mud with His spit, rubbed it on the man's eyes.

Then He said, "Go and wash yourself in the Pool of Siloam."

So the man went, washed his face, and came back able to see.

His neighbors were amazed and said, "Isn't this the blind beggar? What's happened?"

The man answered, "Jesus made some mud, rubbed it on my eyes and told me to wash myself in the Pool of Siloam. So I did—and now I can see."

AFTER THE GOSPEL

Go through the story.

Leader   A man is born blind... Jesus heals him... and he can see...
That man was very lucky to be alive at the time Jesus was on Earth.
Because it doesn't always seem to happen like that.
Has anyone here ever been ill?

Accept all answers.
Add in these sorts of questions if they seem appropriate:

Did you pray to God?
Did you get better at once?
Do you know anybody who's just stayed sick?
What do you think God thinks about illness?

Establish that God hates pain and illness, but He doesn't always zap in and remove them. There are all sorts of things He doesn't like—people bopping their little sister on the head for example—but He doesn't zoom in and stop that either.

Sometimes He removes illness, sometimes He sends someone to help you, sometimes He just waits.
One of the tough things about praying is that you don't always get the answer you expect, or the answer you want.
Let's think of the possible things God may say to our prayers.

Show the kids the four boxes.

We can't ever tell what God is going to say, but we can sometimes guess.
Supposing God heard this prayer?

Dig into the mailbag, pull the first one out and read:

"Dear God, I'm sorry, please forgive me."

Put it in the "Yes" box.

	God would say yes to that. He is always pleased to forgive people.
Next one...	What about this?
	"Dear God, help me to beat up my little brother."
	Where will that go?

In the "No" box: make sure they know why God will never help you do something bad.

Next one...	How about this?
	"Dear God, please send me a bike for my birthday."

Take any answer, I think it's a "maybe."

Next one	Or this? "Okay, God, here are your orders:
	I want Coco Pops for breakfast, and I want a nice sunny day, and I
	want my friend to come over, and then I want to go swimming.
	Get cracking! Amen."

Take all answers. Establish the kid isn't asking for anything naughty and God might well send them all these things—but what a dreadful prayer: self-centerd, ordering God about. God is always pleased when we talk to Him, but He'd expect this person to try a bit harder, so put it in the "Hmmm, Try Again" box.

The Angels' Sorting Office

CD20.1	Okay, now let's imagine we're up in Heaven. We're in the Angels' Sorting Office, the prayers are pouring in and we're trying to give God a hand by sorting them into their boxes.
	Of course we don't actually know how God is going to answer these prayers, but we're going to try.

Get the children to pull out the prayers, one by one, and decide which box each should go in.
You'll see some are fun, most are obvious and some quite difficult, like:

> "God, please make me better."

When you get to this prayer say:

	What will God do?
	He might send you a doctor, or He might help you be brave, or He might just want to be near you while you're ill and leave it at that.

The penultimate prayer is from the man born blind.

> Ah, this is from today's Gospel.
> "Dear Jesus, please let me see, Amen."
> We know the answer to that one—*(It got a "Yes.")*
> And afterwards, when the man could see, I think he said the best prayer of all...

Pull out the last prayer.

> "Thank you!"

Put it in the "Thank you" box.

> God's got a special answer to that. He says "Thank you."

ACTIVITY

Change of gear...

> Does anyone know what day it is today? Heavy hint if necessary. **(Mother's Day, Mothering Sunday)**
> So there's one prayer we really need to get in that postbag, a big thank you for our mothers and the people who look after us.
> Let's make an enormous "thank you" prayer for God.

Make a concertina style banner with 24 sheets of A4 paper.
It reads:

THANK YOU GOD FOR OUR MOTHERS

Have the letters already written in pencil—the children use large colored markers to make them bold, and add what decoration they've got time for: their own face for example, or a flower.

FINAL PRAYER   Our Father... (p. xxxvi).

BACK IN CHURCH

The children stand in a bunch, with the banner folded up. Make sure some fairly reliable ones are holding both ends of the banner.

Leader   Today we were thinking of all the prayers God gets through His letter box—and we decided to send Him an enormous prayer ourselves. It is...

The children pull out their gigantic prayer: make sure there are some kids holding it up in the middle so it doesn't sag.

Kids   **Thank you God for our mothers. Amen!**

Script 21   Lazarus

Lent 5

John 11:17, 20-27, 33-44

THEME

Lazarus's recall to life is an anticipation of Easter. We hear Jesus say, "I am the Resurrection and the Life" two weeks before the dreadful events of Good Friday, while His mighty cry "Lazarus! Come forth!" reminds us that He too will burst out of a tomb. (Lazarus is "revived"—that is, he is brought back to life: he'll have to die again one day. "Resurrection" means rising to eternal life.)
The children re-enact the story, using fabric.

SET UP

- The liturgical color is Purple.
- The desert tray (see Lent 1).
- Five lightweight drapes (or pieces of fabric), the size of a small tablecloth.

WELCOME *the children and lead them in* **The Sign of the Cross + (p. xxxvi).**

Résumé on Lent, *comment on the purple drapes and vestments*

Leader	Purple is a dark, serious color.
	The Church uses it when we're getting ready for something.
	What are we getting ready for? (**Easter**)
	Yes. And one of the ways we get ready for Easter is to think through the things we've done wrong and ask God to forgive us.
	Let's do that.
THE KYRIE	Lord Jesus, you came to call us back to God,
	Lord have mercy.
	Lord have mercy.
	Lord Jesus, you fasted in the desert,
	Christ have mercy.
	Christ have mercy.

Lord Jesus, you told sinners how much God loves them,
Lord have mercy.
Lord have mercy.

Ask the children to repeat **The Prayer for Forgiveness** *after you* **(p. xxxvi)**.

The Desert

Before Jesus began His ministry, He fasted in the desert.
So, every Lent we go into the desert with Him.
Here it is.

Bring the desert tray forward.

This is our desert...

Run the sand through your fingers.

Very dry.
Very rocky.
Very lonely.
But with Jesus in the middle . . .

Place the Jesus candle in the desert.

And, as He prayed in the desert, we'll do so too...

Light the candle and ask the children to repeat after you:

OPENING　　Lord Jesus,
PRAYER　　You fasted and prayed in the desert.
Help us to follow your example,
To keep our Lent promises,
And fast and pray. *Amen.*

Leader　　We're going to start straight away with the Gospel.

THE GOSPEL *from John 11*

Preamble

Three of Jesus' best friends were Mary, Martha and Lazarus—they were two sisters and a brother, and they lived in Bethany. One day Jesus heard that Lazarus was very ill: He started towards Bethany but when He arrived...

Then read verses 17, 20-27, 33-44.

AFTER THE GOSPEL

The Lazarus Play

Cast: Lazarus, Mary, Martha and Jesus. The rest of the children are the crowd.
The Leader is the Narrator, the other Leaders are stage managers, and Q the children in.
Write up the lines for the crowd (see below), and get somebody with a script ready to Q them in.
You are going to tell the story again using five drapes. Look through the text below and run through the drape acting and the crowd responses.
Start with Lazarus on the floor, lying on one drape (1).
Chair to one side.

Narrator   When Jesus arrived He found Lazarus dead.

A child covers Lazarus completely with the second drape (2).

Crowd   You're too late!
Narrator   He had been wrapped with grave clothes...

Pull Lazarus up, and take him over to the chair. Two kids apparently support him (he actually stands by himself) while someone else lightly wraps drape (1) round his hands and drape (2) round his feet.

Placed in a tomb...

Somebody places the chair behind Lazarus, he sits down.

And the entrance closed with a stone.
Crowd   Clonk!

Another drape (3) is hung by two people in front of Lazarus.
It should put him out from sight.

Narrator   Meanwhile his sisters Mary and Martha went to meet Jesus.

Mary and Martha enter, their heads covered with the drapes (4) and (5).
Jesus enters, Martha goes to Him.

Martha said, "If you had been here, Lord, my brother would not have died."
Jesus said, "Your brother will rise to life!"

Mary approaches Him.

Mary said, "Lord, if you had been here, my brother would not have died!"

Mary weeps into her drape.

Jesus saw her weeping, and all the people who were with her, and was deeply moved.

He said, "Where have you laid him?"

Crowd   Over here!

Narrator   Jesus went to the tomb.

He stands in front of the drape.

"Take the stone away!" said Jesus.

Crowd   No, don't!

Narrator   "Lord," said Martha, "He's been dead four days, there'll be a terrible smell!"

Martha and Mary cover their faces.

But they took the stone away...

Crowd   Crunch!

Drop the drape.

Narrator   And Jesus cried with a loud voice, "Lazarus, come forth!"
And the dead man came out.

Lazarus gets to his feet, and hobbles across.

Crowd   Help!

Narrator   His hands and his feet were wrapped in grave clothes.
"Untie him!" said Jesus, "and let him go!"

Lazarus's grave clothes are removed and he shakes hands with Jesus—then with everyone.

Leader   Did you notice with what a loud voice Jesus said: "Lazarus, come forth!" No wonder the dead man came back to life. Let's learn to obey Jesus as quickly as Lazarus.

Game

Do a version of "Simon Says" but instead of "Simon says" you naturally say "Jesus says!" The children only obey the commands of Jesus.
At the end rehearse the children in the presentation (see below).

FINAL
PRAYER

Ask the children to repeat after you:

God our Father,
Lazarus came back to life at the sound of your Son's voice.
Help us to hear Jesus,
In the Gospel,
And in our hearts.

Help us, this Lent,
To see you more clearly,
Love you more dearly,
And follow you more nearly,
Day by day. *Amen.*

BACK IN CHURCH

Start with the children at the back of the church.

Leader   This morning we heard that Jesus said with a loud voice,
"Lazarus, come forth!"
That showed us that even the dead can hear Jesus.
Live ones are pretty good at hearing Him too...

Raise your voice.

Jesus says: "Come forth!"

The children thunder forward and turn to face the congregation.

That's how powerful Jesus' words can be!

Script 22   Palm Sunday

Matthew 21:1-3, 6-11

THEME

Palm Sunday and the whole of Holy Week is one enormous narrative on the death and resurrection of Jesus.

This session ends by telling the kids that Palm Sunday is just the beginning of Holy Week which finishes next Sunday on Easter Day.

You will obviously have to fit round whatever your church does on Palm Sunday: the priest will probably bless and distribute palms at the beginning of the service and there might be a procession.

The session contains an English folktale, *The Little Dunk Foal*, but with only a few of the dialect words retained.

SET UP

- The liturgical color is Red—wear something red yourself.
- The desert tray minus the candle (see Lent 1).
- White or purple cloth to lay on top of the desert (see below). If you have other devotional objects in the hall, try to cover them up too with white or purple cloths.
- Toy donkey.
- If you have time make a story-telling folder: stick the picture of the donkey (**CD22.1**) from the CD-ROM on the front of a folder—or any donkey picture you've found yourself—and put the "Dunk" story (see below) inside.
- Palm crosses.

WELCOME *the children and lead them in* **The Sign of the Cross ✛ (p. xxxvi).**

THE KYRIE   Lord Jesus,
This week you allowed your enemies to capture you,
Lord have mercy.
Lord have mercy.

Lord Jesus,
This week you carried your Cross,
Christ have mercy.
Christ have mercy.

Lord Jesus,
This week you died on the Cross for us,
Lord have mercy.
Lord have mercy.

Ask the children to repeat **The Prayer for Forgiveness** *after you* **(p. xxxvi).**

OPENING	Lord Jesus,
PRAYER	Today you entered Jerusalem on a donkey
	as the Jewish children sang your praises.
	Help us to follow their example
	and sing your praises this morning. **Amen**

BEFORE THE GOSPEL

Leader	Here we are at the end of Lent—and everything has changed.
	The color in church has changed, did you spot what the new color
	is?

Give them a hint:

What color is my sweatshirt? **(red)**
Red, that's the color we normally use when we remember Christians
who have died for their faith.
Today we use it to remember Jesus Himself.
Because today is the day Jesus came to Jerusalem for what He knew
would be the last week of His life.
That last week is called Holy Week, and at the beginning of Holy
Week the Church goes into mourning. We cover up all our pictures,
and crucifixes and statues, so we can concentrate on Jesus Himself.
Which means we'd better cover up our desert.
Here it is—with its rocks and sand and cactuses.
Can anyone see what's missing? **(the Jesus candle)**
Yes, the candle we put there to show that Jesus was in the desert.
He's gone—and we'd better follow Him.
Let's put the desert away...

Ask a child forward to lay the cloth over the desert.
Put the desert away.

Now, where did Jesus go today?

Probably a rhetorical question...

Let's find out in the Gospel.

THE GOSPEL *Matthew 21:1-3, 6-11*

AFTER THE GOSPEL

Leader　　　　What a fantastic Gospel!

Jesus rides into Jerusalem, with everyone cheering, and waving palm branches and throwing down their coats in front of Him.

The disciples must have been so happy—at last everyone loves Jesus. I'm sure Jesus was pleased too, but He knew this was just the beginning of His last week.

It starts with happiness, it ends in joy—but there's a lot of sorrow in between. Let's think what's ahead of Jesus this week.

Can you remember what Jesus rode on? (**A donkey**)

How many donkeys were there? (**One, two, don't know**—*check it out in the Gospel*)

There were two:

The donkey Jesus rode and its foal, following on behind.

A foal is a baby donkey...

Pull out the toy donkey, show it round.

Jesus knew all about donkeys, we think there was one in the stable when He was born, Mary and Joseph probably used one, and today Jesus uses one to ride into Jerusalem.

Donkeys are odd creatures—and strange stories are told about them.

I'm going to tell you one now. It comes from England, so there are a few British words in the story—they're really easy to understand.

Sit on a chair among the children, show them your story-telling folder, open it and begin.

This is a story of a little donkey. He was called the Little Small Dunk Foal—a "dunk" is just an English word for a donkey.

The Little Small Dunk Foal

Once upon a time there was a little small dunk foal and he wanted to have a look round, so one day, when his Mother wasn't looking, he trit-trotted off on his wonky little legs.

First thing he met was a witch.

"I'll have you!" she said, but when she touched him she got burned. "Drat!" she said. "You were born on a Sunday, I'll be bound!"

"All little dunks are born on Sunday, or so my Mother says," said the little small dunk foal, and he went on.

Then he met Bogeyman.

"I'll have you!" said the Bogeyman, but when he grabbed him, his fists fried. "Yow!" say Bogey. "You've got a criss-cross on your back! You keep away from me!"

"All little dunks have a criss-cross on their backs, or so my Mother says," said the little small dunk foal, and he went on, until he came to a fairy ring.

"Get off out of there!" said the pixies. "We can't ride you, and now you come treading in our ring—and you just seven days old!"

"All little dunks were seven days old once, or so my Mother says," said the little small dunk foal.

But all the pixies said to that was, "Go away! Quick now!"

So he trit-trotted back to his Mother. And first she kicked him, for running away, then she gave him his dinner.

Sum up

Leader	Well, what did you think of that?
	Do you think it's true? (**No!**)
	Quite right, it's a fairy story.
	But bits are true:
	Are all little dunks born on a Sunday? (**probably not**)
	But I think most little dunks get to be seven days old,
	and all little dunks do have a criss-cross on their back.

Show them the picture on the cover—or any donkey picture you've got.

There's the criss-cross—that's just an old word for a cross.
When Jesus rode His donkey into Jerusalem, He'd have known He was sitting on a cross.

Show the children a palm cross.

Christians wave palm leaves today—just like the Jews did when they welcomed Jesus all those years ago—but our palm leaves are made into the shape of a cross.

Jesus rode into Jerusalem today, watching the palms, listening to the cheers, but knowing all the time that the Cross was ahead of Him.

Depending what your church does, tell the children about the services they can attend in Holy Week, on Good Friday and Easter Sunday

FINAL PRAYER

Gather the children into a circle and give all of them a palm cross
Put the Jesus candle from the desert in the middle

Jesus is with us.
And today He rode into Jerusalem.

Ask the kids to feel their palm crosses

They're shiny.
And dry.
But they are real leaves.
And come from palm trees that grow in the Holy Land.

Ask the children to repeat after you

Lord Jesus,
By your Holy Cross
You have saved us all. Amen

Let's finish by making the **Sign of the Cross +**
In the Name of the Father, and of the Son, and of the Holy Spirit.
Amen

BACK IN CHURCH

The children line up down the front with their palm crosses

Leader   Today we thought about our palm crosses.
They're real leaves, just like the ones people waved at Jesus on the first Palm Sunday.
But our palm leaves have been turned into crosses.
We'd like to share a prayer with you.

The children hold up their crosses as one of them says

Child   Lord Jesus,
By your Holy Cross
You have saved us all. **Amen**

(CD22.1)

Script 23   Easter Sunday

Matthew 28:1-10 or John 20:1-9

THEME

The Empty Tomb: there are lots of Resurrection stories to come, but the breaking news—first thing on Easter Sunday—is that the Tomb is empty! You'll notice that in the John passage the "other" disciple who runs to the Tomb (traditionally thought to be John himself) only has to see the emptiness to believe.

SET UP

- The liturgical color is White or Gold.
- You'll need a Hot Cross Bun.
- A large hollow chocolate Easter Egg, as fancy as possible: lots of packaging, a ribbon round the egg (you might have to supply that) and covered in foil. (Make absolutely sure it's hollow.)
- An Easter Garden (a tray filled with moss and flowers with a little Tomb constructed out of stone).
- Or a mock-up of the Tomb—some bricks making a rude shelter, with a slab of rock in front.

- Place a small piece of folded cloth inside your Tomb, and place it at the back of the room.
- You can add refinements, like three little wooden crosses in the background, some small flowers in pots and even a "Risen Jesus."

WELCOME *the children and lead them in* **The Sign of the Cross + (p. xxxvi).**

THE KYRIE   Lord Jesus, when you rose from the dead, you defeated evil,
Lord have mercy.
Lord have mercy.

Lord Jesus, when you rose from the dead, you washed away our sins,
Christ have mercy.
Christ have mercy.

Lord Jesus, when you rose from the dead, you set us free,
Lord have mercy.
Lord have mercy.

Ask the children to repeat **The Prayer for Forgiveness** *after you* **(p. xxxvi).**

THE EASTER GREETING

Teach the children the Easter Greeting:

Leader   Alleluia! Christ is risen!
Children   **He is risen indeed! Alleluia!**
Leader   The news this Sunday is so amazing, we're going to hear it right now in the Gospel:

THE GOSPEL PROCESSION

THE GOSPEL *either Matthew 28:1-10 or John 20:1-9*

AFTER THE GOSPEL

Leader   Okay, this is the greatest and happiest morning that has ever been!
Let's think about it—
I'm going to start with this...

Hold up the Hot Cross Bun.

When do we eat buns like this? (**Good Friday**)
And what's this marking on the top? (**a cross**)
Why's it there? (**Jesus died on the Cross on Good Friday.**)
Quite right, but today we eat something different.

Hold up the Egg.

What's this? (**an Easter Egg**)

Looking at it carefully.

You're quite right, so it is!
What's it made of? (**Chocolate!**)
Are you sure about that? (**Yes!**)
Anyone here eaten an Easter Egg before?

Go with the reaction—something like.

Goodness, all of you...
Well, I'm sure you're right, but I think that's rather odd:
What's so important about a chocolate egg?
I think we ought to look at this egg.
I wonder what the important bit is?
Is it the wrapping?

A rhetorical question really...

Well, it's very nice.

Say something about the casing.

But I think I'll rip it off.
Is it the ribbon? (**no**)
Okay, we'll get rid of that.

Remove it.   Is it the foil? (**no**)
Really? It's very nice and shiny—but okay we'll get rid of that too.

Remove it.   Now then, we're down to the chocolate.
Is *that* the important bit? (**yes**)
Nope, you're wrong, it isn't.
We need to get rid of some of this chocolate—anyone want to help me?

Break off about a third of the egg.

This is the one day of the year when eating chocolate is a spiritual act.

Hold up half the egg, it should look absolutely hollow.

Ah, now we're getting somewhere—*(look inside)*
What's there? (**nothing**)
Exactly! It's hollow.
That's what is so great about an Easter Egg—it's empty.
Hang on to that, and let's think about the Gospel today.
Because it was the nice empty space that cheered everyone up on the first Easter morning—
Not an empty egg, but an empty tomb!
We've all remembered that Jesus died on the Cross on Good Friday?
Well, His friends laid His dead body in a tomb and, early on Sunday morning, they went down to the tomb and found...
What did they find?

Send a couple of kids down with Leaders to investigate the tomb in the Easter Garden.

Leader 1	Have you found the tomb?
Kids	Yes!
Leader 1	What does it look like?
Leader 2 *(or any kid she can Q)*	
	Well, the stone in front of the tomb has been rolled away...
Leader 1	So, what's in the tomb?
Kids	Nothing!

They'll probably mention the little napkin.

Leader 1	But where's Jesus?
Kids	He isn't there...

If they spot Him among the garden plants add:

So He's not in the Tomb? (**no**)
Fantastic!
Jesus has gone, He's burst out of the Tomb, He isn't dead any more.
That empty Tomb is one of the happiest things we'll ever see.
Easter is the happiest day of the year and when you eat your eggs today remember why we're so happy.
Find that empty space in the middle of your egg, and remember Jesus' empty Tomb.

FINAL	Can you remember the special shout Christians do on this day?
PRAYER	Watch this:
Leader 1	Alleluia, Christ is risen!
Leader 2 and kids with her	
	He is risen indeed! Alleluia!
Leader 1 *(to the kids at the front of the group)*	
	Now you try, turn to the kids behind you...
Kids at the front	
	Alleluia, Christ is risen!
Kids at the back	
	He is risen indeed! Alleluia!

ACTIVITY

Practice the presentation below for when you go back to church.

BACK IN CHURCH—*Go back in with the Easter Egg*

Leader *(holding up the egg)*	
	Today we demolished an Easter Egg.
	We got through the packaging,
	and the foil,
	and the chocolate,
	and found that inside the egg was...?
Kids	Empty!
Leader	Then we looked at our Easter Tomb and discovered that it was...?
Kids	Empty!
Leader	We think this is the best news that we've ever heard, and we've got a special acclamation for you.
Kids	Alleluia! Christ is risen!
Congregation	**He is risen indeed! Alleluia!**

Script 24   Doubting Thomas

Easter 2

John 20:19-29

THEME

The Risen Jesus isn't a ghost. He came back with His real Body.

SET UP

- The liturgical color is White.
- If the kids know *Ghostbusters*, or any movie like it, download a logo or an image from the internet.
- Pictures and "check list" from the CD-ROM.
- Photocopy the ghost picture (**CD24.1**) twice onto paper.
- Doctor both copies of the ghost picture by cutting a vertical slit through its middle.
- Have the second doctored ghost picture ready for your presentation in church.
- Large red marker.
- A couple of very small Easter Eggs or tiny chocolate sweets, like M&Ms or Kisses

WELCOME *the children and lead them in* **The Sign of the Cross + (p. xxxvi).**

THE KYRIE   Lord Jesus, when you rose from the dead,
                         you defeated evil,
                         Lord have mercy.
                         Lord have mercy.

                         Lord Jesus, when you rose from the dead,
                         you washed away our sins,
                         Christ have mercy.
                         Christ have mercy.

                         Lord Jesus, when you rose from the dead,
                         you set us free,
                         Lord have mercy.
                         Lord have mercy.

Ask the children to repeat **The Prayer for Forgiveness** *after you* **(p. xxxvi).**

THE EASTER GREETING

Talk through the white and gold vestments in church.

Leader   Easter goes on for 50 days, "The Great 50 Days." It's a happy time
                    and pretty noisy. Especially the next prayer.

Teach the children the Easter Greeting:

> Alleluia! Christ is risen!
> **He is risen indeed! Alleluia!**

Then run it three times: softly, louder, very loud indeed.

BEFORE THE GOSPEL

Ghosts

CD24.1   *Start off by sticking up the picture of a ghost.*

Leader   What's this? (**a ghost**)
                    Yes.

Pull up a chair and sit down.

                    Well, today I'm going to tell you a ghost story...

*If you know a ghost story, this is the moment to tell it. It doesn't matter how strange
it is, the kids will love the fact that it actually happened.*
*This is the sort of story I use, feel free to use it—but dig around the collective memories
of the grown-ups first, somebody will have a weird story.*

The Coliseum Ghost

In the theater where I work we have 17 ghosts. Our favorite is the one that haunts
the balcony. He's dressed as a soldier, in khaki, with a leather belt over his chest and
we think he must have been in a war a very long time ago. (He doesn't speak, so we
don't know.)
Anyway, his particular trick is to turn up just before the show starts. He goes to his
favorite seat, G8, just as the lights are going down and he looks so real that everybody in row G gets up to let him in. Along the row he goes—G1, 2, 3... until he gets
to 8. At which point the person sitting in G8 gets a big shock. "Help!" they think. "A
soldier is about to sit on me!" But just before the soldier actually lands on the seat,
he disappears...
Does that sound scary?
It isn't really, because a ghost isn't real.

Pick up something from the story, the ghost doesn't talk, some people can't see it, etc.

You can't talk to a ghost, or shake its hand—
There's nothing there.
They're seen sometimes, but they're not real people.

Our Ghost

Somebody brings the ghost picture over to you.

If I tried to shake hands with this ghost... *(Do so.)*
...my hand would go through. *(It does.)*

If I tried to give him some chocolate, the chocolate would go through. *(It does.)*
And if I tried to talk to him... "Hi Mr. Ghost!"
... *(listen)* ...nothing would happen.
Now if I talk to a real person, it's all quite different:
If I talk to one of you—"Hi *Name*!"—I get a reply: "Hi!"
If I shake hands with *Name (shake hands with another child),* they shake hands back.
And if I offer a chocolate to, say, *Name (another child),* goodness me, it's gone!
Let's have a check list on this.

Ghostbuster Check List

CD24.2   *Stick up the checklist from the CD-ROM.*
Run through the test for a ghost, putting crosses in as you establish it can't speak etc.
Use a large red marker.

It's very important that we know the difference between ghosts and real people at Easter time, because Jesus wasn't a ghost.
All this ghost stuff is nonsense.

Give the ghost picture to a kid to scrunch up.

Let's hear something real in the Gospel.

THE GOSPEL PROCESSION

THE GOSPEL *John 20:19-29*

AFTER THE GOSPEL

Leader   In the Gospel today, we heard that the real live Jesus came into the Upper Room.

CD24.3   *Put up Jesus picture.*

There He was, in His real body, you can see the scars of the nails. Jesus spoke to His friends.

CD24.4   *Add speech balloon, "Peace be with you."*

And they felt His breath as He breathed on them.

CD24.5   *Put in "puff" drawing.*

But one of the disciples wasn't there: who was that? (**Thomas**)
He didn't believe a word of it.
All these stories about Jesus coming back from the dead, and His body coming through locked doors sounded very fishy to him, and he refused to believe Jesus had a real Body at all.
But eight days later Jesus was back. What happened?

Take all answers, but establish that Jesus came in again, called Thomas forward and offered His Body for inspection. Thomas could touch Him.

CD24.6   *Add Thomas picture.*

In Luke's version of this story we hear something else: Jesus ate a piece of grilled fish.

CD24.7   *Add the fish picture.*

Let's run these stories against the list.

Do so, putting ticks in as you describe how...

Jesus could be touched.
He could speak.
And He could eat.
Well, that's pretty clear.
Jesus came back from the dead in His proper Body—He wasn't a ghost.

You might want to add more, if the children are old enough to have picked it up, that even so Jesus' Body was rather mysterious: it could do all the normal things—but it also came and went through closed doors, and it could disappear. This was probably because it was a Risen Body. None of us knows how a Risen Body works.

Can you remember what Thomas said when he realized that Jesus wasn't a ghost? Let's look it up.

Consult the Gospel.

> He said, "My Lord and my God!"
> That's a fantastic short prayer.
> We should be grateful to Thomas for giving us that prayer.
> Let's ask for Thomas to pray for us now.

FINAL
PRAYER

> Holy Thomas, Friend of Jesus,
> Pray for us.
> When we feel doubtful,
> Pray for us.
> When we come to Church,
> Pray for us.
> When we receive Communion,
> Pray for us.
> Holy Thomas, may we say with you,
> "My Lord and my God." *Amen.*

End with a **Glory Be... (p. xxxvii).**

BACK IN CHURCH

Go in with the duplicate ghost and Jesus pictures (**CD24.1, CD24.3**).
Hold up the ghost picture.

Leader 1

> Today we investigated ghosts.
> We discovered that you couldn't
> touch a ghost,
> or speak to it,
> or give it anything to eat.

Hold up the Jesus picture.

Leader 2

> But when Jesus came back from the dead,
> we discovered that
> He could speak,
> He could eat,
> and that His friends could touch Him.
> We decided that...

All the Kids   **Jesus isn't a ghost!**

Script 25   The Walk to Emmaus

Easter 3

Luke 24:13-35

> **THEME**
>
> The Walk to Emmaus is full of wonderful themes: this session highlights the disciples' recognition of Jesus in "the breaking of the bread."

SET UP

- The liturgical color is White.
- Two pieces of pita bread.
- A small table set with one piece of pita bread, a couple of plates and cups, and three chairs.
- Two children prepared to be Cleophas and his wife Mary (you'll be Q-ing them in, so they don't need to practice).
- Another Leader plays Jesus—I'm assuming he'll have had time to read the script.
- Large hat for Jesus, Indiana Jones style, or a Panama hat.
- Label one end of the room "Jerusalem," the other "Emmaus."
- A large (unconsecrated) communion wafer.

WELCOME *the children and lead them in* **The Sign of the Cross + (p. xxxvi).**

THE KYRIE   Lord Jesus, when you rose from the dead, you defeated evil,
Lord have mercy.
Lord have mercy.

Lord Jesus, when you rose from the dead, you washed away our sins,
Christ have mercy.
Christ have mercy.

Lord Jesus, when you rose from the dead, you set us free,
Lord have mercy.
Lord have mercy.

Ask the children to repeat **The Prayer for Forgiveness** *after you* (**p. xxxvi**)

THE EASTER GREETING

Practice this once, then say it three times, quietly, loud, very loud indeed:

Leader   Alleluia! Christ is risen!
Children   **He is risen indeed! Alleluia!**

BEFORE THE GOSPEL

People Spotting

Leader   This morning I'd like to think how we recognize people.
                  Sometimes it's the way they look:
                  Whom do we know who...

Describe a distinctive member of the church—the priest is always fair game.

                  But you don't always have to see a person to know they're around.
                  Think about home.
                  Do you know anyone who thunders up and down the stairs?
                  Or plays loud music?

Let the children run with this for a moment.

                  Some people always do the same things, like rubbing their hands...
                  (do it) ...or jingling money in their pocket.
                  And what about this, who do you see doing this?

Hold up the pita formally and break it.
Take the children's answers, but don't comment.

                  Okay, well, Jesus' friends knew Him very well.
                  They knew the way He talked and the sort of things He did—but
                  after Jesus had risen from the dead, they found it wasn't so easy to
                  recognize Him.
                  His Body looked the same, but now it wasn't a matter of just *seeing*
                  Jesus, you had to *discern* Him.
                  "Discern" means feeling something in your heart as well as seeing it
                  with your eyes.
                  Let's see how it works in today's Gospel.

THE GOSPEL PROCESSION

THE GOSPEL *adapted from Luke 24:13-35*

Leader as
Narrator   On the first Easter Sunday two of Jesus' disciples walked from Jerusalem back to their home at Emmaus. One was called Cleophas—we think the other disciple was his wife, Mary.
Let's see them at Jerusalem.

The two kids go to "Jerusalem."

Emmaus was about seven miles away, and Mary and Cleophas took it slowly. They'd lived through the most ghastly three days—Jesus had been arrested and beaten up and crucified—and they walked home talking about it, and getting sadder and sadder.
They had their arms folded and their heads down as they walked.

Set the children off.

And they were so sad they didn't notice a Stranger coming up behind them.

Enter Jesus.   They didn't recognize Him.

Jesus pulls his hat down.

And, when He asked them what was troubling them, they just stood still and shook their heads.

They do so.   They told Him all the terrible things that had happened.
The Stranger listened and walked along with them, explaining how everything that happened to Jesus had been foretold in the Bible.

Jesus walks between the disciples, one hand on each shoulder.
They get to "Emmaus."

When they got to Emmaus, the Stranger looked as though He was travelling on.

Jesus raises his hat, as if in farewell.

But it was getting dark, and the disciples asked Him to stay with them. The Stranger agreed and they all sat down to supper.

The three of them sit down.

Then the Stranger took the bread
blessed it
broke it
and gave it to them.

Jesus takes off his hat and does all these actions as you say them.

And suddenly Cleophas and Mary realized who He was—they jumped up.

Jump up.	But the Stranger had disappeared.
Exit Jesus.	The disciples were so excited that they punched the air...
Go for it!	And ran all the way back to Jerusalem to tell the others.
	Let's see them go.
Whoosh!	

Terrific. Suddenly seven miles didn't seem such a long way after all. And they rushed round to the house where the other disciples were staying and cried:

"Jesus is alive!"

Let's hear that, here we all are—what have you got to tell us?

Have a grown-up ready in case of stage fright.

Cleophas and Mary

Jesus is alive!

Let's give them a hand—what did they say?

All the children Jesus is alive!

Give the actors a clap.

AFTER THE GOSPEL

Leader   So who was the mysterious Stranger? (**Jesus**)

And how *did* the disciples recognize Him? (**When He broke the bread.**)

That supper at Emmaus showed Jesus' friends that Jesus would always be there when they broke bread together.

What's happening here?

Pick up the communion wafer solemnly, hold it up and break it.

Accept all answers, and establish that:

This is what the priest does at the Eucharist:

Jesus is still here—

He's present at the Altar and in the Bread and the Wine of Holy Communion.

ACTIVITY

Everybody tells the story. Get the children down the Jerusalem end.

Right, we're all on the road to Emmaus, walking very slowly. We're fed up, arms crossed, sigh, life is just not worth living...
Jesus walks with us.
We get to Emmaus, sit down, just on the floor is fine.
Then we look up as the Stranger takes bread,
And blesses and breaks it.
Wow!
Jump up, fist pump the air, it's Jesus!
Let's tell the others.
Run all the way back to Jerusalem.
Stop! *(They normally crash into the wall.)*
Tell the other disciples...

Everybody   **Jesus is alive!**

FINAL   *Ask the children to repeat after you:*
PRAYER   **Lord Jesus,**
Risen Lord,
We thank you for coming back to us.
We thank you for being with us.
Help us to recognize you
In the Breaking of the Bread. *Amen.*

I think we ought to go back to church now to tell the other disciples the news.

BACK IN CHURCH

If your church can stand it, have the children ranged up (with a Leader) at the back
Another Leader goes to the front to say:

We've just heard some amazing news, in fact the children have run all the way from Emmaus to tell us about it.
Here they come...

The children run down to the front.
They turn to face the congregation and, on Q, shout.

Children   **Jesus is alive!**

Script 26 "I am the Gate"

Easter 4

John 10:1, 7-15

THEME

God loves us as a shepherd loves his sheep.
The actual Gospel reading only takes us to verse 10, but as it seems better for
the children to have concrete images of sheep, wolves and shepherds (rather than
wonder who the "false shepherds" are) we've skipped a couple of verses and
gone on to verse 15.

SET UP

- The liturgical color is White or Gold.
- Cut out little sheep pictures from the CD-ROM (**CD26.1–26.5**) and hide them
  round the room (sticking them under chairs works well, and along baseboards).
- Shallow box.
- Old-fashioned walking stick to act as crook.
- Chairs at the front to make a sheepfold.
- Cast some characters for the sheep drama (see below).
- Searching for "Good Shepherd icon" on Google Images produces lots of images of
  Jesus the Good Shepherd which you may be able to download.
- Ask the clergy if one of them could ask the question on pagey 138 during the pres-
  entation in the church.

WELCOME *the children and lead them in* **The Sign of the Cross + (p. xxxvi).**

THE KYRIE   Lord Jesus, you are the Good Shepherd,
                 Look for us when we get lost,
                 Lord have mercy.
                 Lord have mercy.

                 Lord Jesus, you are the Good Shepherd,
                 Guard us from danger,
                 Christ have mercy.
                 Christ have mercy.

Lord Jesus, you are the Good Shepherd,
Bring us safely back to your sheepfold,
Lord have mercy.
Lord have mercy.

Ask the children to repeat **The Prayer for Forgiveness** *after you* (**p. xxxvi**).

THE EASTER GREETING

Practice this once, then say it three times, quietly, loud, very loud indeed:

Leader   Alleluia! Christ is risen!
Children   **He is risen indeed! Alleluia!**

BEFORE THE GOSPEL

Leader 1   Today we're thinking about sheep—and the people who look after
them.
Does anyone know what they are called? (**Shepherds**)
Brilliant. In the country Jesus lived in, being a shepherd was a very
important job. You see, there were no grassy fields with hedges in
Palestine where you could leave the sheep all day. So a shepherd had
to take his flock up the bare hillsides to find food, it was terribly
difficult to keep them together.
In fact there's a load of sheep in this room—trying to eat the carpet
and the chairs—and they seem to have wandered off.
Can you help me find them?

Off the children go on a **Sheep Hunt.**
*As they find the sheep put them in your shallow box. (Sometimes a timid child likes
to stand by the box with the crook.)*

Leader 2   Okay, we've got our sheep back, and they're safely in this sheepfold.
Now a real sheepfold was made of great chunks of stone, and looked
a bit like this.

Start to make a pen out of chairs, closed in completely with no opening.

The shepherd used to drive the sheep in there for the night.
Of course he needed a gate—
Not a wooden gate, there wasn't enough wood to spare in Palestine,
so he'd make a hole in the wall... *(remove a chair)*
...and sleep in the gap all night.
That way no sheep could wander out, and no wolf or thief could
sneak in.
Let's see how it worked.

Herd all the children who want to be sheep into the pen.
Make sure they behave like sheep, on all fours, baa-ing and so on.
Choose a couple of sensible types to be "escaping sheep," plus another couple to be the wolf and the thief.

> Right, I'm the shepherd, I've got my crook and I'm going to lie down in this gate, and try to go to sleep.
> Stop baa-ing all of you—go to sleep!

The shepherd goes to sleep in the gap.
A sheep tries to escape, it steps on the shepherd and is shooed back inside.
Another one tries.
The wolf prowls around (the little ones will probably alert you to this) and stupidly growls as it tries to get in.
The shepherd shoos it off and barely gets back to sleep before a thief tries to climb in over the chairs.
The thief makes such a racket that the shepherd copes with that emergency as well.

Shepherd   Phew! Morning at last! What a night...

Leader 1   So you see, the shepherd had to be very brave—and he had to love his sheep; it's very uncomfortable sleeping outside, and frightening off wolves and thieves all night, but the shepherd thought it was worth doing.
Jesus knew all about shepherds and when He tried to explain who He was, He did so by talking about sheep and shepherds and gates. Let's hear Him in the Gospel.

THE GOSPEL PROCESSION

THE GOSPEL *John 10:1, 7-15 (Keep it moving.)*

Optional Paraphrase
Jesus said, "I want you to listen to this.
Anyone who climbs over the wall of a sheepfold, and doesn't go in through the gate, is a thief and a robber. The real shepherd is the one that goes through the gate.
I am the gate of the sheepfold.
Anyone who enters through me will be safe.
I am the good shepherd who is ready to die for his sheep. A person who doesn't *know* the sheep doesn't look after them properly—he runs away the moment a wolf appears.
But I am the good shepherd, I know my sheep and my sheep know me.
And I am willing to die for them."

AFTER THE GOSPEL

Go through the reading:

Leader	Jesus compared Himself to two things, can you guess? (**a gate and a shepherd**)
	I think Jesus was saying that the sheepfold was Heaven.
	You can only get in through Him.
	And the sheep—who did He think the sheep were? (**us**)
	Yup, His sheep.
	And He said that, like a good shepherd, He was prepared to die for us.

ACTIVITY

Ask the children to choose a sheep from the box, write their name on it and stick it on their chest, ready for the presentation (see below).

SONG—*Some traditional hymns are worth learning here.*

"The Lord's my shepherd," "The King of Love my Shepherd is," *or* "Loving Shepherd of thy sheep." *This last one has the simplest vocabulary.*

FINAL PRAYER

If you have a picture of Jesus the Good Shepherd, this is the moment to produce it.

> Jesus said,
> "I am the Good Shepherd,
> I know my sheep and my own know me."
> Lord, help us to know you, and follow you,
> And bring us at last, safely home, to Heaven. *Amen.*

BACK IN CHURCH

Line the children up in front—holding their sheep.
See if you can prime the priest to ask:

> "Why have so many sheep come back into church?"

Child 1	Because today we learned that Jesus is the Good Shepherd.
Child 2	And we are His flock!

Script 27   Mansions

Easter 5

John 14:1-14

> **THEME**
>
> It's sometimes difficult to make Heaven sound attractive. This session uses Jesus"
> description of His Father's House having many rooms ("mansions" in the trad-
> itional translation) to suggest that Heaven is going to be both interesting and
> surprising.

SET UP

- The liturgical color is White.
- "Door" pictures from the CD-ROM. (You'll find that most of the illustrations are
  "doors," with a companion picture showing what's inside. Stick the door over its
  interior.)
- The Heaven door needs its Cross shape cut out, so you can see through to Heaven
  beyond.
- Colored pencils, scissors and glue if you've got time for a craft.
- Ask the clergy if one of them could go through some of the pictures during the
  presentation in the church.

WELCOME *the children and lead them in* **The Sign of the Cross + (p. xxxvi).**

THE KYRIE   Lord Jesus, when you rose from the dead,
you defeated evil,
Lord have mercy.
Lord have mercy.

Lord Jesus, when you rose from the dead,
you washed away our sins,
Christ have mercy.
Christ have mercy.

Lord Jesus, when you rose from the dead,
you set us free,
Lord have mercy.
Lord have mercy.

Ask the children to repeat **The Prayer for Forgiveness** *after you* (**p. xxxvi**).

Remind the children we're still in "The Great 50 Days of Easter" as you say:

THE EASTER GREETING

Practice it once, then say it three times quietly, loud, and very loud indeed.

Leader	Alleluia! Christ is risen!
Children	**He is risen indeed! Alleluia!**

BEFORE THE GOSPEL

Leader   We're going to think about doors today.

Point to the street door.

That one over there, for instance—where does it go?
Or that one?

Point to a cabinet.

What's in that?

With a bit of luck the children won't know and you'll have to find out.

Even ordinary doors can be mysterious—when they're shut.
You can't help wondering what's on the other side.

Have you got a story of opening an unpromising door and finding there was something interesting on the other side?
This is the story I use—but two sentences from anyone in the team about a door that bothered them as a child would be much better.

A Door Story

Someone once took some small children to the Royal Opera House in England. They were in the dark corridor behind the boxes in the balcony and the children were too scared to open a box door. "Shall I try one?" she said.
"NO!" they said.
She knocked at a door anyway, "Is anyone there?"
No answer.
"That's odd, oh well I'm going in..." The children thought she was crazy, and quickly got behind her. She opened the door—and there, through the opening, they saw the beautiful red and gold of the great Opera House auditorium. The children loved it, they rushed into the box and the next minute they were everywhere, all round the balcony, knocking at doors and shouting, "Is anybody there? I'm coming in!"
Let's look at some doors.

Go through the door pictures.

CD27.1a and b   The Tardis door (a time machine).
CD27.2a and b   Narnia wardrobe doors.
CD27.3a and b   The Fat Lady door from Harry Potter.

See if the kids know the stories and can tell you where the doors lead to; get them up to open the doors—amplifying as necessary.
Make the point that the doors open up on somewhere extraordinary—the Tardis, Narnia, and a dormitory in Hogwarts.

There's another odd thing about these doors.
They're all quite small, but the places inside are huge.
Are these doors real? (**Nope, they're all in stories.**)
They're imaginary doors, the sort of things we'd like to find.
Now some of the things Jesus told us about sound like stories—you know, exciting things, that we'd like to happen, but which don't seem to.
But actually Jesus meant what He said, and when He said that life would get really exciting once we got to Heaven He knew what He was talking about.
Of course we have to go through a door to get to Heaven—but Jesus went through it ahead of us: He went through this...

CD27.4a and b   *Show the kids the Heaven door.*

You can just see through this door to the other side.
Can you see the shape cut into the door? (**It's a Cross.**)
Jesus went through that door to open Heaven for us, and after He'd been through He left it open.
Let's hear Jesus talk about Heaven in the Gospel.

THE GOSPEL PROCESSION

THE GOSPEL *John 14:1-7*

Jesus said,
"Do not be frightened. Believe in God, and believe in me. In my Father's house there are many mansions.
I am going ahead to prepare a place for you, so that where I am, you will be too. You know where I am going."
Thomas said, "Lord, we *don't* know where you are going, so how will we find the way?"
Jesus said, "I am the way, the truth and the life. Nobody comes to the Father except through me."

AFTER THE GOSPEL

Leader	Heaven isn't easy to understand.
	One of the disciples couldn't understand what Jesus was talking about.
	Who was that? (**Thomas**)

Rerun that bit of dialogue if necessary.

Thomas is such a super disciple, he always says the sort of things we'd like to ask. "Where is Heaven?" "What are you talking about?" And Jesus told him that *He* was the way into Heaven; if we followed Him we'll find the path and get there safely.

Now, what will we find when we get there?

CD27.5a and b   *Pull out House of God picture.*

Well, Jesus described Heaven in lots of different ways, but in the Gospel today He said it was like a House—except when you opened the door...

Open the door on the House of God picture.

You'll find there are lots of different houses inside. They're called "mansions" in the Bible.

Heaven is bigger on the inside than the outside.

It's obviously going to be a very surprising place, but not scary; Jesus said He was going ahead to prepare a place for us there—so we know we're going to like it.

You'll see the House of God has loads of little blank mansions all over it.
Either discuss what the kids would like to find in Heaven when they get there, and write them in or, if numbers allow, ask the children to produce little pictures and fill up the blanks at super speed.
They should represent some of the things the children would like to find in Heaven. (One small boy who did this filled up his blank space with piles of presents and said they were "surprises.")

FINAL PRAYER	Jesus said:
	"In my Father's house there are many mansions.
	I am going ahead to prepare a place for you."
	Lord Jesus,
	Thank you for going before us.
	Help us to follow you,
	And come safely to Heaven,
	And the place you have prepared. *Amen.*

BACK IN CHURCH

Go in with your completed House of God.

Leader or competent child   Today we thought about Heaven, and the different mansions that Jesus has gone ahead to get ready for us.

Invite the priest to go through some of the pictures/ideas in the mansions.

(CD27.1a)

(CD27.1b)

(CD27.3a)

(CD27.3b)

Sample cartoons for this script

(CD27.4a)

(CD27.4b)

Script 28   Jesus Packs Up

Easter 6

John 14:15-21

THEME

This Sunday prepares the children for Jesus' Ascension on Thursday. Jesus gets ready to go home and pulls out His backpack...

The idea behind this session is that when God the Son goes back to Heaven, He takes a fair amount of stuff with Him—His Body, of course, but also experiences and memories that mean a great deal to Him.

He also leaves things behind—these will help His friends find Him while they're still on earth.

SET UP

- The liturgical color is White.
- A backpack—two compartments inside is very useful.
- Photo/postcard of a cute scene, any vacation photo is fine. (If you happen to have one that looks like Palestine, so much the better.)
- Any picture/postcard/icon of the Virgin Mary.
- A wooden toy.
- An alb from the sacristy, or a robe—anything that Jesus could feasibly have worn.
- A Bible.
- A large communion wafer—ask your altar guild to find you one of the uncon-secrated priests' wafers.
- A "Present:" a large empty box, wrapped up in nice glitzy paper with a gift label: "To Jesus' friends—not to be opened until Pentecost."
- The "Packing Worksheet" on the CD-ROM (**CD28.1**), either photocopied for eve-rybody or enlarged for the flip-chart.
- The present, wafer and Bible are in the backpack—the alb, postcard, toy and pic-ture are not.

WELCOME *the children and lead them in* **The Sign of the Cross + (p. xxxvi).**

THE KYRIE   Lord Jesus, when you rose from the dead,
You defeated evil,
Lord have mercy.
Lord have mercy.

Lord Jesus, when you rose from the dead,
You washed away our sins,
Christ have mercy.
Christ have mercy.

Lord Jesus, when you rose from the dead,
You set us free,
Lord have mercy.
Lord have mercy.

Ask the children to repeat **The Prayer for Forgiveness** *after you* **(p. xxxvi).**

THE EASTER GREETING

Practice it once, then say it three times, quietly, loud and very loud.

Leader   Alleluia, Christ is risen!
Children   **He is risen indeed! Alleluia!**

BEFORE THE GOSPEL

Packing

Hand out the worksheets or have a group session around a large version, stuck on a flipchart.

Leader   This Sunday we are going to be thinking about journeys, really long
ones.
It's very difficult to pack for a long journey, and if we are going to
be away for ages we might decide to leave something behind, so our
family can remember us.

Look at the worksheet. Ask the children to check the things they'd like to take with them, cross out the things there's no way they're going to pack, and circle anything their families might like to remember them by.
They can suggest or draw in their own objects, of course. Keep things moving.
Talk through a couple of the children's ideas, and then produce the backpack. Go to the other end of the room if the kids have been sitting around, it'll give them a chance to move about.

| Leader | After Jesus had risen from the dead He was with His disciples for 50 days. But all the time He knew He'd have to go home to Heaven. So when He was ready, He began to pack. |

Ad lib the following as you pack up.

He packed some **clothes**—*comment on the white alb*—people really did dress like this.

Some **postcards** of Palestine: Jesus wanted to remember what a lovely place the Earth was.

A **picture of His Mother**—Jesus was going to miss her, especially her cooking—*(chicken soup, I should think)*

A **little wooden toy** His Dad, Joseph, had made for Him ages ago.

And all the time His disciples watched Him.

They felt very sad, and remembered how Jesus had once told them He wasn't going to stay on Earth for ever.

Let's hear what He said in the Gospel.

THE GOSPEL PROCESSION

THE GOSPEL *John 14:15-21*

This is a very long Gospel, you might like to shorten it as follows:

At the Last Supper Jesus talked for a long time with His disciples and at the end He said,

"If you love me, you will obey my commandments. I will ask my Father to send something to help you—the Holy Spirit, to stay with you for ever.

So when I go, you will not be left all alone.

In a little while the world will see me no more—but you will see me."

AFTER THE GOSPEL

| Leader | Did anyone spot the moment when Jesus said He was leaving? |

Ad lib the relevant verses.

So when I go, you will not be left all alone.

Where was Jesus going? (**Back home, to Heaven**)

Review the Gospel briefly and establish that:

Jesus was going

and that His Father was going to send something to help them.

Let's go back to our story about Jesus packing up.

Bring out the backpack.

>Because just before Jesus closed up the backpack He took some
>things out.
>"I am going to take my voice up to Heaven," He said,
>"But I am going to leave you my voice in the—**Bible**."

Pull out the Bible.

>"I am going to take my *Body* to Heaven,
>But I shall leave you my Body in the—**Bread**."

Pull out the bread.

>"I am going to take my *heart* up to Heaven, but I shall leave you my
>peace in your hearts'—and He shook hands with them.

Shake hands with a couple of kids.

>"I am going home, but I want you to be like me, here on Earth—and
>to help you, my Father is going to send you a **present**."

Pull out the present—get somebody to read the label.

>"To Jesus' friends—not to be opened until Pentecost."
>Oh right, we'll have to wait until Pentecost—that's the week after
>next!
>Did Jesus really pack a backpack? (**No!**)
>You're right, it's not in the Bible, that was just a story.
>But He did go back to Heaven. Next Thursday is Ascension Day—
>the day Jesus left.
>He went up, just as He was, and He really did leave all these things
>behind: His voice, His Body and His peace.
>We can hear His voice in the Bible. *(Pick it up.)*
>We can touch His Body in the bread. *(Pick it up.)*
>We can feel His peace in our hearts. *(Put your hand on your heart.)*
>What else did He leave? (**the Present!**) *(Pick that up.)*
>Yup, we've got a present as well, but we can't open it yet; we'll have
>to wait for... ? (**Pentecost**)
>Okay, so here we are, just like the disciples, still on earth. But
>remember we've got Jesus' peace in our hearts, and I think it would
>be a good idea to share it now. We can't shake hands with Jesus
>Himself, but we can shake hands with His friends. He'd like that.

| FINAL | Jesus said, "Peace I leave with you, my peace I give to you." |
| PRAYER | Let us offer each other the Sign of Peace. |

Start the ball rolling by shaking hands with a child, saying:

Peace be with you.

Everybody then shakes hands with their neighbors, saying:

Peace be with you.

Optional Final Prayer *(adapted from one by St. Teresa of Avila)*

> Jesus has no body in the world now, but ours:
> Ours are the hands that must bless His people;
> Ours are the feet that must run to do His will;
> Ours are the tongues that must proclaim His Word;
> Ours are the hearts that must glow with His love.
> Lord Jesus, use us, live in us, bless us. *Amen.*

REHEARSAL

Practice the presentation for when you go back to church (see below).
Some children should be ready to pack things, others to take them out. Encourage them to answer the Leader as they review the script—for example:

| Leader | First Jesus put in... |
| Child | Some clothes... |

BACK IN CHURCH

Take in the backpack and review the script above as you go through what Jesus packed up, and what He took out.
End with the "Present:" perhaps you could ask the priest to hang on to it until Pentecost?

(CD28.1)

Script 29   Staying Together

Easter 7

John 17:1, 6, 11

THEME

Jesus' long prayer at the Last Supper included the petition that His Church may be one, just as He and the Father were one.

This session uses a couple of games to show the disastrous results of disunity on one hand, and what fun it is to work as a team on the other.

SET UP

- The liturgical color is White.
- Two bananas.
- A knife.
- Glue.
- Tape.
- Masking tape.
- Ribbon.
- Scissors.
- Toothpicks.
- A plate.

WELCOME *the children and lead them in* **The Sign of the Cross + (p. xxxvi).**

THE KYRIE   Lord Jesus, when you rose from the dead, you defeated evil,
Lord have mercy.
Lord have mercy.

Lord Jesus, when you rose from the dead, you washed away our sins,
Christ have mercy.
Christ have mercy.

Lord Jesus, when you rose from the dead, you set us free,
Lord have mercy.
Lord have mercy.

Ask the children to repeat **The Prayer for Forgiveness** *after you* **(p. xxxvi).**

OPENING	God our Father,
PRAYER	Your Son Jesus Christ
	Ascended into Heaven and returned to you.
	May we lift our hearts to Heaven
	And look forward to the time when we shall see Him there
	Face to face. *Amen.*

BEFORE THE GOSPEL

> Today, I'm going to do an experiment.
> I'll need a banana. *(Hold it up.)*
> And a load of equipment. *(Indicate the tape, etc.)*
> The first thing I'm going to do is peel this banana. *(Peel a banana.)*
> And then cut it up. *(Chop it into four pieces.)*
> Right, so this banana... *(hold up the one you haven't chopped)* ...is a whole one, it's "united."
> Whereas this one... *(hold up the plate with the chopped banana)* ...is a chopped one, it's "disunited."

Look at the bits of banana.

> Hmm, I wish I hadn't done that.
> I want a "united" banana—
> I know, I'll stick it together again.

Try using the useless adhesives first, take advice from the children—the thing that usually works is toothpicks.
Hold up the result.

> Well, it's sort of united—
> but it doesn't look as good as it did before I chopped it up.
> I think my experiment shows that if you divide something, it's not always easy to unite it. And it doesn't look the same.
> Jesus knew that, and when He prayed for His friends at the Last Supper He was very anxious that the group should be united—they should stay together.
> Let's hear that prayer.

THE GOSPEL PROCESSION

THE GOSPEL *John 17:1, 6, 11*

Optional Paraphrase

At the Last Supper, Jesus looked up to Heaven and said, "Father, the hour has come: glorify your Son so your Son may glorify you.

I have made you known to my friends: they were yours, and you gave them to me. Now I am going back to you: I shall not be in the world any longer—but they will be. Holy Father, keep them safe! So that they may be one, just as you and I are one."

AFTER THE GOSPEL

Leader   When Jesus was praying for His friends, He was praying for His Church—that's us—so He was praying for us as well.

He wants us to be one, to be united.

Now I'll tell you something about Christians—they quarrel.

I don't know why, it's very sad, but Christians started quarrelling right from the beginning. It's always been terribly difficult to keep them together.

But Jesus *wants* us to be together. He wants us to work together, pray together and love each other.

So I think we'd better start practicing.

ACTIVITY

Back to Back

This is a game in which two people sit back to back on the floor and then get to their feet, together, without using their hands.

Once they've managed it, add another person, starting from the floor again. Eventually you are not so much back to back, but squashed into a mass of heaving backs and shoulders. Even so, our record is ten (some churches say they've have managed twenty). See how you do. You might allow a bit of judicious cheating with small children.

Once you've found the optimum number that can be guaranteed to stand up successfully, choose them as the team you'll take back into church.

FINAL PRAYER

Ask the children to form a gigantic circle.

Leader   We are now going to pray the **Our Father**, the family prayer of the Church.
We raise our hands like this as we pray...
Then, when we get to,
"For thine is the Kingdom"—we **hold** hands and on the "Amen"—we **raise our linked hands.**

Show how to do this with the people on each side of you.

I think our Heavenly Father will be very pleased to see how united we are.
Our Father... (p. xxxvi).

SONG

"We are one in the Spirit" *or* "Abba, Father" *among the modern hymns, or a classic like* "Thy hand O Lord has guided" *(verses 1, 2 and the last)*

BACK IN CHURCH (1)

If there is enough space, the children gather at the front.

Leader   Today we heard how Jesus prayed that His Church should be one.
So we thought we'd better practice our teamwork.
We started by helping each other to get up in pairs...

Some children demonstrate this.

Then we tried to see how many people could do that together...

The team now demonstrate their amazing skill.

We think that's pretty good for a first effort!

BACK IN CHURCH (2)

If there's no space for a gymnastic demonstration, the children come to the front, plus the bananas.

Leader   Today we took a banana, chopped it up, and then tried to put it back together again. It ended up looking like this...

Child holds up the repaired banana.

We think the whole banana looked better...

Another child holds up the complete banana.

Which just goes to show that, once something is broken, it never looks the same again. It made us realize why Jesus prayed that His Church should stay united.

Script 30   Detecting the Ascension

(Ascension Day)

Luke 24:50-51, Acts of the Apostles 1:7-12

> **THEME**
>
> This is the last chapter of Jesus' earthly life and one that adult Christians get nervous about. Fortunately children are totally unembarrassed at the idea that Jesus went "up," or that He ascended bodily. This session gives the kids a chance to think about Jesus' direction as He left, and celebrates the fact that He truly ascended to Heaven, Body and all.

SET UP

- The liturgical color is white.
- *Either* a thurible, charcoal (get it lit before the liturgy), incense boat and thurible stand (remember to open the windows).
- *Or* an ordinary balloon and a hydrogen balloon (the word "Jesus" is written on the latter with a black marker).
- Pictures from the CD-ROM.
- Flip-chart.
- Large black marker.

WELCOME *the children and lead them in* **The Sign of the Cross +** (p. xxxvi).

THE KYRIE   Lord Jesus, you were sent down to earth to save us from our sins,
Lord have mercy.
Lord have mercy.

Lord Jesus, you ascended into Heaven to pray for us to the Father,
Christ have mercy.
Christ have mercy.

Lord Jesus, you sent the Holy Spirit to be with us for ever,
Lord have mercy.
Lord have mercy.

Ask the children to repeat **The Prayer for Forgiveness** *after you* (p. xxxvi).

ASCENSION

Leader   Today is Ascension Day.
            Anyone know what "Ascension" means?

Establish that it means "going up."

            The Church is always asking us to look up, especially when we use
            incense.
            Let's see that in action.

Incense

*Show the kids the glowing charcoal in the incense bowl. Get a kid to add incense
from the boat.*

            Right, now let's watch that incense.
            Yup, it's going up.
            We use incense in church because it smells nice, and because we can
            see the smoke going up to God.
            There it goes—just like our prayers to Heaven.

Balloons

For non-incense churches produce the balloons.

            Right, let's look at these balloons—this is an ordinary one. I can bat
            it around... *(do so)* ...but eventually it just bumps along the floor.

            But this is a Jesus balloon, and if I let go of it... *(do so!)* ...it ascends—
            just like our prayers to Heaven.

            Let's think about that as we pray.

OPENING   God our Father,
PRAYER   We thank you for Jesus' Ascension.
            Lift our hearts and minds to the place where He went,
            To Heaven, where He lives and reigns with you, and the Holy Spirit,
            for ever. *Amen.*

BEFORE THE GOSPEL

Detective work

CD30.1	*Introduce the kids to Sherlock Levy.*
Leader	He lived at the time of Jesus—but he was kind of different from the other people.
CD30.2	He wore a special hat.
CD30.3	He smoked a pipe.
CD30.4	And his favorite possession was a magnifying glass.
	What do you suppose he liked doing best? (**Detecting!**)
	Yup. But he didn't have much to detect.

CD30.5 *Set up Sherlock's amazing solution of the Case of the Missing Fish with the picture from the CD-ROM.*
Get the kids' help on the clues: the empty plate, cat paw prints, the skeleton of the fish, more paw prints leading to—the cat asleep in its basket.

> But one day Sherlock came across a real mystery
> twelve men passed his house: there was one man in the middle, who the others obviously liked, and yet two hours later, when they came back, Sherlock noticed that the popular man had gone. Now there were only eleven of them.
> Strange, thought Sherlock, and he got his magnifying glass and began to follow their tracks.
> Yup, twelve men had gone up the hill.

CD30.6 *Picture of the hill and footsteps....*

> One man had stood at the top of the hill.

Draw in Jesus' footprints.

> But only eleven men had come down.

Point out footprints on the other side.

> What had happened to the twelfth man?
> Had he gone off on a donkey? (**No, no tracks**)
> Or a bicycle? (**Nope, not invented yet**)
> Or sprouted wings? (**Surely not!**)
> Well, it was very odd, he was obviously real—look at the tracks—but he'd simply disappeared.
> Sherlock went home very puzzled, because real bodies don't just disappear, they leave tracks. He never discovered what had happened. But *we* know, let's hear it now.
> Put some more incense in the thurible and set up the Gospel Procession

GOSPEL PROCESSION

The leader (or a server if one of the kids happens to be one) blesses the Gospel Book with incense.

THE GOSPEL *Luke 24:50-51, Acts of the Apostles 1:7-12*

Jesus led His disciples out to the a place near Bethany, and He lifted up His hands and blessed them.

And said to them,

"You will receive power when the Holy Spirit comes upon you, and you will be my witnesses in Jerusalem, and in all Israel, and to the ends of the earth."

After He said this, He was taken up before their very eyes, and a cloud hid Him from their sight.

The disciples stared up into the sky as He went, when suddenly two men in white robes stood beside them.

"Men of Galilee," they said. "Why are you looking up into the sky? This Jesus, who has been taken from you into Heaven, will come back in the very same way you saw Him go."

And the disciples went back to Jerusalem full of joy, and went to the Temple every day to thank God.

AFTER THE GOSPEL

Leader	So who was the twelfth man Sherlock had seen? (**Jesus**)
	And what *had* happened? (**He'd ascended, gone up, gone back to Heaven**)
	Yup, even so, Sherlock *had* discovered something, in fact it's very important.
Point out Jesus' footprints.	
	You see Jesus really did come back from the dead, and He had a real body: He was solid and heavy and He left real prints.
	And He went back to Heaven in that Body.
	Jesus didn't pretend to be a human being, He became one.
	But of course He was also God the Son.
	That's an astonishing thing to think about: God the Son went back to heaven with a human body.
	After the Ascension, Jesus' friends knew that that Jesus really was True God and True Man. For ever.

FINAL PRAYER

Run a truncated version of the Divine Praises, ask the children to repeat each phrase after you:

> **Blessed be God**
> **Blessed be His Holy name**
> **Blessed be Jesus, True God and True Man**
> **Blessed be the Holy Spirit**
> **Blessed be God for ever.**

BACK IN CHURCH

Go in with the Hill/Footprints drawing.
Ask designated children to lay out the footprints as you read the script.

Leader   Today we detected the Ascension.
                We looked at the footprints and worked out that twelve men had
                gone up a hill.
                That one had stood at the top.
                And that eleven men had come down.
                Then we read the Gospel and realized that the twelfth man was Jesus
                and that He had ascended from the hill, back to Heaven.

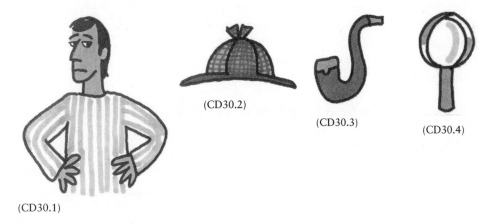

(CD30.2)

(CD30.3)

(CD30.4)

(CD30.1)

Sample cartoons for this script

Script 31 Pentecost

John 20:19-23, Acts of the Apostles 2:1-21

> **THEME The Holy Spirit**
>
> **One of the rare Sundays when we can think about the Holy Spirit, this session concentrates on Him appearing as a "mighty rushing wind." The Spirit makes us live and move.**

SET UP

- The liturgical color is Red. Try to wear something red, even if it's only a scarf.
- A couple of uninflated balloons, but blow them up a couple of times beforehand, so they inflate easily when you need them to.
- Holy Spirit pictures from the CD-ROM.
- Small mirror for the "Casualty session," and any toy stethoscopes or doctor's kit you can lay your hands on.
- The wrapped Present, plus label ("To Jesus' friends—not to be opened until Pentecost"), from the Sunday before Ascension (Easter 6, Script 28)—it now contains a cake with 12 birthday candles. (If you have to wrap it all over again, don't worry, I've never known children notice the difference.)
- Co-opt a kid to become a Casualty victim before the session.

WELCOME *the children and lead them in* **The Sign of the Cross + (p. xxxvi).**

THE COLOR OF THE DAY

Leader   As we start our service we remember in whose Name we are gathered.

See if the children have noticed the change of color in church—use your scarf as a hint.

Today we're in Red.
Red is used for special occasions, for Palm Sunday, for saints who've been martyred, and for a day like today, when we think about the Holy Spirit.

We use red for the Holy Spirit, because sometimes it appears on earth as tongues of fire.

CD31.1   *Put up picture*

Let's pray to the Holy Spirit as we say the **Kyrie.**

THE KYRIE   Holy Spirit,
You help us to know when we have done wrong,
Lord have mercy.
Lord have mercy.

Holy Spirit,
You help us to say sorry,
Christ have mercy.
Christ have mercy.

Holy Spirit,
You fill us with the love and forgiveness of God,
Lord have mercy.
Lord have mercy.

Ask the children to repeat **The Prayer for Forgiveness** *after you* (**p. xxxvi**).

INTRODUCTION

Leader   We're going to start this morning with a balloon. *(Show it.)*
I haven't blown it up yet.
What do we blow a balloon up with? (**air, breath**)
Okay, I'll try. *(Blow up the balloon—do not secure it.)*
Right, the balloon is full of air—and if I let it go. *(Do so and watch it zoom off.)*
It does that.
Did you catch that?
Let's do it again.

Repeat with second balloon.
(This is so popular, you might decide to do it a third time.)

Air makes things move.
Air is another way in which the Holy Spirit visits the Earth.
Today is Pentecost, the day the Holy Spirit came to Jesus' friends—
as a huge gust of wind. He wanted Jesus' friends to move—just like
that balloon.
Let's think about that as we pray.

OPENING	God the Holy Spirit,
PRAYER	Breathe on us:
	Help us to move,
	Help us to do things for the Father,
	To run His errands,
	And to tell people about Jesus. *Amen.*

BEFORE THE GOSPEL

Leader	Today is "Pentecost." *(Write it up.)*
	The day the "Holy Spirit" was given to the disciples.
	The Holy Spirit is very difficult to draw. It appears in many ways.

Get somebody else to stick up the Holy Spirit pictures as you go—or ask the children to draw them for you.

CD31.2	The Holy Spirit can appear as a Dove...
CD31.1	Or as Fire...
CD31.3	Or as the Wind...
	At Pentecost it appeared as the wind—as air.
	Now the Holy Spirit appeared as air for a reason, and today we are going to find out why.
	We'll start by thinking about air.
	We use it a lot—what am I doing?—*(exaggerated breathing)* **(breathing)**
	Yup, I breathe a lot—I think it's important.
	What happens if you stop breathing? (**You die.**)
	Quite.
	I suggest you guys keep breathing too.
	Good Heavens!

The casualty victim staggers across the room and collapses
Consternation—all gather round
One grown-up takes control—the grown-up has to be completely useless

	Hi, can you hear me?—*(no response)*
	Can you see me?—*(victim remains with eyes shut)*
	Where's the pulse?

Try to feel it anywhere—in the knee, the shoes, the wrist, you can't get it.

| | What about a heart beat? |

Get out a toy stethoscope.

| | Where is the heart precisely? |

An exasperated child will probably be helping you by now.

> Dear me, no heart beat. Shall we just bury *Name* now?

Leader 2   Wait!

Another grown-up has an inspiration—and produces a mirror. Show the children how shiny it is, hold it to the victim's mouth (make sure the victim breathes on it) and lo...

> Wow! It's gone misty. *Name* is breathing—the kid's alive!
> Air not only makes you move, air makes you **live**.
> Let's hear that in the **Gospel**.

THE GOSPEL PROCESSION

THE GOSPEL *John 20:19-23*

On the evening of the day Jesus rose from the dead, He appeared to His disciples. They were sitting in a room, with the doors closed—and Jesus came and stood among them. He **breathed** on them and said,
"Receive the Holy Spirit."

Acts 2:1-2

A little later, when Jesus had gone back to Heaven, the disciples were sitting in the same room, when suddenly they heard what sounded like a powerful wind from Heaven. The noise of it filled the entire house. Then little flames of fire appeared over the head of each of the disciples, and they were all filled with the Holy Spirit.

AFTER THE GOSPEL

Leader   The disciples were "filled with the Holy Spirit."
The Spirit breathed on them like a "wind."
It filled them with new life—and they started to move—they rushed out into the street to tell people about Jesus.
And at that moment the **Church** began.
Pentecost is the birthday of the Church.
Birthdays are a good moment for presents.
Haven't we got a present somewhere?

Out comes the famous "present" from Script 28. Ask a child to read the label.

> "To Jesus' friends—not to be opened until Pentecost"
> That's right now!

Ask another child to unwrap the present.

It's a birthday cake—today is the birthday of the Church. Let's take that back into church with us.

But first let's use one of the gifts of the Spirit to pray:

FINAL
PRAYER

God the Holy Spirit,
You breathed new life into Jesus' friends.
Breathe new life into us.
Fill us with your power
And your life,
So we can work to the praise and glory
of Almighty God in the week ahead. *Amen.*

We'll say together the **Glory Be... (p. xxxvii).**

SONG

"I believe in God the Father, I believe in God the Son" *or* "Breathe on me, Breath of God" *would fit in well here.*

BACK IN CHURCH

Child 1   Today is Pentecost, the birthday of the Church.
So we've got a birthday cake.
Child 2   We're going to light the candles...

A Leader does so

They remind us that the Holy Spirit came as tongues of fire at the first Pentecost.

A Leader holds up the cake with the candles

Child 3   The Holy Spirit also came as wind, and we're going to show the other way He entered our world by...

All the kids blow on the cake

Blowing them out!

Cartoons for this script

(CD31.1)   (CD31.2)   (CD31.3)

Script 32   Trinity Sunday

Matthew 28:16-20

THEME

The Holy Trinity is a wonderful doctrine—but it isn't easy to teach. You can't explain the Holy Trinity, but you can offer some approaches to it. This session concentrates on the underlying unity of the Three Persons by suggesting that the idea of three things being one thing is not as bizarre as it sounds. Even so, the images suggested are *not* equivalents of the Trinity and you'll need to use phrases like "this reminds us of the Holy Trinity," "this is a bit like the Trinity,"—to warn the children that we haven't exactly wrapped the doctrine up.

SET UP

- A lump of ice, made by freezing some water in a balloon (don't fill the balloon too full, ice expands). (Bring the balloon to church and extract the lump in front of the children—see below.)
- Electric kettle.
- Two pitchers: one full of water and one empty.
- Marker.
- A triangular sweet, like Toblerone, sliced up and wrapped in foil, if you've got time, for the end of the service.
- Pictures from the CD-ROM.
- Optional extra: Murillo's picture of "The Two Trinities"—download from the Web Gallery of Art.

WELCOME *the children and lead them in* **The Sign of the Cross + (p. xxxvi).**

INTRODUCTION

Talk about the Sign of the Cross.

Leader   That's a prayer we use a lot and in it we call God three things, what are they?

Start "In the Name of..." if they hesitate.

> **(Father, Son, Holy Spirit)**
> We remember
> The Father—the Creator of the Universe.
> The Son, Jesus—who came down to our world.
> And the Spirit—who lives in our hearts.
> The Sign of the Cross helps us remember who's who.
> Let's do it slowly.

Start the Sign, touch your head.

> The Father is at the top—in Heaven.

Continue, bring your hand down to tummy level.

> The Son, Jesus, came down to earth

Bring your hand over to your left.

> The Spirit who lives in our hearts

Finish over on the right-hand side.

> And we finish by saying "Amen."
> There is only one God, but we know Him as three People, Father,
> Son and Spirit—we call that **The Holy Trinity**.
> Today is Trinity Sunday, let's pray to the Trinity now in the **Kyrie**.

THE KYRIE   God our Father, you forgive everybody who says they are sorry,
Lord have mercy.
Lord have mercy.

Lord Jesus, you came down to earth to tell us how much
   God loves us,
Christ have mercy.
Christ have mercy.

Holy Spirit, you fill our hearts with the love of God,
Lord have mercy.
Lord have mercy.

Ask the children to repeat **The Prayer for Forgiveness** *after you* (p. xxxvi).

BEFORE THE OPENING PRAYER

Leader   Right, the grown-ups are going to have a tough time in church this
                morning, trying to understand the Holy Trinity.
                But kids are just as bright as grown-ups, so we'll try too.
                We'll ask the Holy Trinity to help us.

OPENING   Holy Trinity,
PRAYER   Father, Son, and Spirit,
                Help us to hear you this morning,
                To love you,
                And to try and understand you. *Amen.*

BEFORE THE GOSPEL

Leader   The Holy Trinity was one of the last things Jesus taught His disciples.
                You'll hear Him speak about it in the Gospel today. Listen out, and
                put your hand up when you hear Jesus talking about the Trinity.

THE GOSPEL PROCESSION

THE GOSPEL *Matthew 28:16-20*

Optional Paraphrase
After Jesus had come back from the dead, the eleven disciples travelled to Galilee to
a mountain where Jesus said He would meet them.
And when they got there they saw Him, and they knelt down to worship Him (though
some of them hesitated).
Jesus came to them and said,
"God has made me King of Heaven and Earth.
I want you to go all over the world, and make friends for me, baptizing them in the
Name of the Father and of the Son and of the Holy Spirit.
And remember, I am with you always, even to the end of the world."

AFTER THE GOSPEL

*You'll need two Leaders for this, one to do the demonstration and talk, the other to
stick up pictures and write on the board.*

Leader   Right, so we heard Jesus talk about God as three People—who are
                they? **(Father, Son, Holy Spirit)**
                Three people—so how many Gods are there—three or one?

*Take all answers, but home in on **One God.***

How can three things be one thing?
Well, they can't. Not here on earth. But ordinary things can sometimes help us understand the Trinity.
Like water.

Get the kettle going.

Let's think about water...

Produce pitcher, pour some water from a great height into another pitcher.

A Chemistry Lesson

Take them through the idea that water is made up of oxygen and hydrogen. Write an H for hydrogen, an O for oxygen.

Water is made up of two bits of hydrogen, joined to one bit of oxygen.

Write a 2 between the H and the O.

That's what scientists call water—H_2O.

CD32.1a and b   *Stick up a cartoon*

Look, here are two guys in a desert, they're terribly thirsty. The first one calls out—*(write this in the speech bubble)*
"Water! Water!"
But the other guy is a scientist, he calls out—*(write it in)*...
"H_2O! H_2O!"
So if a scientist saw this . . .

Pour the water back into the other pitcher.

What would he call it? **(H_2O)**

CD32.2   *Put up drawing of water and write H_2O by it*

And what would he call this?

Pull out the balloon, extract the ice.
The kids will probably say ice, but if there are some clever ones who immediately say H2O, put them on hold for a moment.

Yup, it's ice.
But what is ice made of? **(water)**
So a scientist would call it... **(H_2O)**

CD32.3   *Put up drawing of ice, and write H_2O by it.*

And what about this?

Get the steam going from the kettle.

What's this?

CD32.4   *Same business, establish it's steam, it's made of water, it's still H_2O. Put up picture and label it.*

> So H_2O can be:
> a liquid... *(brandish pitcher)*,
> a solid... *(show the ice)*
> and a vapour... *(use the kettle)*.
> How many different ways does H_2O appear? (**three**)
> But what are they all made of? (**water, H_2O**)
> Yup, just one thing.
> H_2O reminds us of the Trinity.
> So do other things.

Draw a triangle.

> Three lines—one triangle.

CD32.5   *Hold up three separate parts of a clover leaf.*

> Three parts... *(put them together)*... one clover leaf.

OPTIONAL EXTRAS

Trinidad

You could tell the children about the discovery of Trinidad.

Christopher Columbus discovered Trinidad about 600 years ago. He and his Spanish crew were sailing in unknown waters when they saw three mountain peaks sticking up out of the sea. They thought they'd found three separate islands but, when they got closer, they realized the peaks were part of one island—so they named the place "Trinity" or Trinidad (which is Spanish for Trinity).

A moment with Murillo

It's very difficult to draw the Trinity, but one painter—Murillo—managed to draw two.
Let's see what he did.
Show them Murillo's picture of the "The Two Trinities" (the Holy Family and the Holy Trinity linked by the infant Jesus) .
Go through the picture with them: Father, Spirit, Jesus; then Mary, Joseph and Jesus.

REHEARSAL

Practice your presentation for when you go back to church (see below).

FINAL PRAYER	*Ask the children to repeat after you:*

> Holy and Blessed Trinity,
> Three People, One God,
> We offer you this week our work, our games, and our worship.
> Holy, Holy, Holy, is the Lord God of Hosts. Amen

BACK IN CHURCH

Leader	After the service we're going to hand out some Trinity sweets. They'll look like this.
Hold one up.	We're going to tell you why we've chosen this shape.
Child 1	Because they are triangles and triangles remind us of the Holy Trinity.
Child 2	A triangle has three sides, but it's only one triangle.
Child 3	God is Three People, but there is only One God.

(CD32.1a)

(CD32.2)

(CD32.1b)

(CD32.4)

(CD32.5)

Sample cartoons for this script

Script 33   The Two Builders

Proper 4
(The Sunday Closest to June 1)

Matthew 7:24-27

THEME

This is all about sensible building practice.

SET UP

- The liturgical color is Green.
- Anything about Bob the Builder: a book, a toy, an image off the internet—anything that will prompt the kids into telling you who he is.
- Pictures from the CD-ROM.
- A couple of packs of playing cards.
- Six potatoes.
- A box of toy bricks.
- A plumped up unstable pillow.
- Building materials of any sort—sensible (Lego) or silly (packet of jelly).
- If anyone can lay their hands on a flat slab of paving stone, this would be an excellent prop.

WELCOME *the children and lead them in* **The Sign of the Cross + (p. xxxvi).**

THE KYRIE   Lord Jesus, you came to Earth to bring us back to God,
Lord have mercy.
Lord have mercy.

Lord Jesus, you came to Earth to heal us from our sins,
Christ have mercy.
Christ have mercy.

Lord Jesus, you came on Earth to tell us how much God loves us,
Lord have mercy.
Lord have mercy.

Ask the children to repeat **The Prayer for Forgiveness** *after you* **(p. xxxvi).**

OPENING   God our Father,
PRAYER   Your love never fails.
                Bless us this morning
                And help us to hear your Word. *Amen.*

BEFORE THE GOSPEL

Identify Bob the Builder, who he is, what he does.

Leader   Anybody here ever built anything?
                How about a house—quite a small house of course...

Produce the Lego, and let them tell you what it is.

                What about the seaside—have you ever built anything there?
                (Sandcastles)

CD33.1   *Put up picture of sandcastle—flags and all.*

                How long do they last? (**About a minute, because a brother or sister usually knocks it down, or it's washed away by the tide**)
                Sand isn't very useful if you want something to last.
                I've got some other stuff here—what do you think would make good building material?

Go through the props, ask a child to build a pile of wobbly potatoes.

                What do you think? (**Useless!**)
                How about jelly? No, I think you're right.

Dismiss the jelly.

                Cards aren't bad—but they're a bit flimsy.

Demonstrate or, if you're a small group, get the kids to try.

                Ah! Bricks. They're nice and solid...

Get a child to help you build a wall.

                Even so bricks are only okay if they're on something firm.
                What a building is built on is very important—it's called its foundation.
                So if we build our wall with this pillow as a foundation... *(CRASH)*
                You see the problem.
                You need a nice solid foundation—like this table...
                Or this slab—*(if you've got such a thing)*

Build the wall again.

Jesus' dad was in the building trade. Joseph is always called a "carpenter," but in first-century Palestine that meant he had to help with building houses. Jesus knew a lot about houses, and He talks about two houses in this morning's Gospel.

THE GOSPEL PROCESSION

THE GOSPEL *Matthew 7:24-27*

AFTER THE GOSPEL

CD33.2   *Over to the flip-chart. Put up, or draw (see template) a couple of houses, with their foundations. Put in some weather—the kids could help here, you need rain, thunder clouds and lightning*

Go through the story with the drawings.

Leader   Obviously the house built on rock stays up, while the house built on sand crashes to the ground.
                     You bet it does—can you imagine anything so silly as to build on sand?
                     Why did Jesus tell this story?
                     Was He talking to a lot of little Bob the Builders? (**No**)
                     This story is a "parable."
                     It's a real story, but it's got two meanings:
                     The obvious one—don't build things on sand—
                     And a hidden one.
                     Jesus was telling people how important foundations are—not just the foundations for a house, but the sort of foundations we need, the things we build our life on.
                     You see, life can be pretty tough.
                     You can see this building is having a hard time—but so do we sometimes.

CD33.3, 33.4   *Put up the picture of a man with storm clouds round him: write in them Money, Danger, Illness, Bad Job, Sin.*

                     Now we can cope with a lot of this, and God is always there to help—but can you see how much easier it'll be to stay firm if we're standing on a good foundation?
                     Jesus says that the foundation you need for life is hearing His words and doing them.
                     So the foundation this man needs is...
                     Listening to Jesus in the Bible.

Draw a Bible under the man.

> And then doing what He asks.

Draw a block with "Good Works" on it.

> Can you remember what the one thing was that Jesus particularly
> wanted us to do? It was when He broke bread and poured out some
> wine.
> "Do this!" He said, "In memory of me."
> When do we do that? (**At Mass, the Eucharist, Holy Communion**)
> Quite right.
> Jesus wants to meet us in church for Mass/Eucharist/Holy Com-
> munion.
> Now I could draw a church for this man to stand on, but I'm going
> to draw this instead...

Draw a nice craggy solid rock under everything else.

> Because the Church is often called the "Rock of the Faith," and
> there's no better foundation than a rock.
> So I think this Christian will be able to cope with life.
> And so will we, if we get our foundations right.
> Let's ask God to help us.

FINAL PRAYER

Gather the children round a prayer candle.

> Let's think about foundations...

Hand round a potato and the packet of jelly, take it slowly...

> These are silly things to build on.
> Jesus knew we'd laugh when we heard about the house built on
> sand.

Hand round the paving slab, if you've got one, or some bricks.

> These are much more sensible things to build on:
> Jesus wants us to build our lives on really solid things.
>
> Lord Jesus,
> Thank you for the story today.
> Help us to listen to you
> And do your will
> And build our lives on the Gospel
> And the rock of the Church. *Amen.*

BACK IN CHURCH

Child 1	Today we thought about building.
Child 2	We tried building things with potatoes and jelly—they were useless.
Child 3	Then we used bricks, they were great.
Child 4	We realized that Jesus wants us to build our lives on really solid things like bricks.
Child 5	We think He meant the Bible and the Church.

(CD33.1)

(CD33.2)

(CD33.3)   *Sample cartoons for this script*

Script 34 The Call of Matthew

Proper 5
(The Sunday Closest to June 8)

Matthew 9:9-12

THEME

Tax collectors are never very popular, but they were semi-traitors in occupied Israel. They got no wages (it was assumed they'd take their cut from the taxes they raised for the Romans), they handled Roman money and dealt with Roman officials. No devout Jew would dream of doing such a job. But Jesus, who seems to have taken people as He found them, called Matthew, the tax collector, to become one of the Twelve.

God is inclusive and calls everybody to His service.

SET UP

- The liturgical color is Green.
- Make some "What's My Line?" cards (see below). They should be very bold and written on poster board, so they can be seen in church.
- "Tax demand" in a brown envelope.
- Pictures from the CD-ROM.
- Ask the clergy if one of them could discuss the robber during the presentation in the church.

WELCOME *the children and lead them in* **The Sign of the Cross + (p. xxxvi).**

THE KYRIE   God our Father, thank you for sending us the Spirit,
                forgive us when we don't listen to Him,
                Lord have mercy.
                Lord have mercy.

                Lord Jesus, thank you for promising us the Spirit,
                forgive us when we forget Him,
                Christ have mercy.
                Christ have mercy.

Holy Spirit, thank you for living in our hearts,
forgive us for the times we ignore you,
Lord have mercy.
Lord have mercy.

Ask the children to repeat **The Prayer for Forgiveness** *after you* (**p. xxxvi**).

OPENING PRAYER *from the missal*

God of all wisdom and love,
Send Your Spirit,
To teach us,
To help us,
And to guide us. *Amen.*

BEFORE THE GOSPEL

Set up a "What's My Line?" game. Produce some cards with various occupations written on them—Doctor, Postal Worker, Construction Worker, Teacher, Ballet Dancer, Priest, football player, for example. Make sure you include a Robber, a Police Officer (who could arrest the robber) and a Tax Collector.
Shuffle the cards and get a kid to take a card and act out the job: they can do them in pairs if they're shy—or you could give them a hand. You might like to do the Tax Collector yourself and deliver the dreaded brown envelope to another Leader. Make sure the children realize that, however virtuous it is to pay your taxes, a tax demand is not something you look forward to.
Write up the jobs as the other children work them out.

| Leader | There's a lot of jobs there. Some are good, some are bad—is there any job there that's really bad? |

(I trust they'll say robber.)

Is there any job there you'd like to do?
Any job you'd hate?
Right, now suppose we were starting up a new church from scratch, which of these people do you think would be really useful?

Circle the ones the children suggest.

2,000 years ago people had a lot of jobs as well.

CD34.1–34.8 *Put up the pictures of a shepherd, fisherman, priest, rabbi/teacher, tax collector, soldier, agitator ("Romans Out!" placard), robber.*

Jesus was starting His Church from scratch. He had lots of people to choose from—let's see whom He chose in the Gospel.

THE GOSPEL PROCESSION

THE GOSPEL *Matthew 9:9-12*

Jesus saw a man called Matthew sitting at the tax office; and He said to him, "Follow me." And Matthew got up and followed Him.

And as Jesus sat down to eat, many tax collectors and sinners came and sat down with Him and His disciples.

And when the Pharisees saw this, they said to His disciples,

"Why does your teacher eat with tax collectors and sinners?"

Jesus overheard them and said,

"Those who are well do not need a doctor, only those who are sick. I did not come to call the righteous, but sinners."

AFTER THE GOSPEL

Leader   So, whom did Jesus choose to help start His Church?
              A tax collector—*(circle him)*—Matthew.
              That's kind of odd.
              Does anybody know whom Matthew was collecting the taxes for?
              (the Romans)

Point out the soldier.

              Jesus' country was ruled by foreigners, by the Romans.
              Lots of Jews didn't like that, and many of them protested.

Point out the agitator.

              Tax collecting was not a job for a good Jew.
              But Jesus didn't seem to mind.
              We know some other people Jesus chose.
              Think about His twelve friends—any of their jobs come to mind?

Give some outrageous hints (what lives in an aquarium?).

              Yup, fishermen, Peter, James and John.

Circle the fisherman.

              And He chose an agitator—Simon the Zealot.
Circle him.   Jesus wasn't bothered about people's jobs.
              Well of course Jesus didn't just need people to run His Church,
              He wanted people to be in it. He still does.

Move across to the modern jobs.

              Whom do you think He welcomes into the Church?

Accept answers, but move them in the direction of including everyone, especially the robber.

Everyone is welcome at church, particularly the bad guys.

Jesus said, "It's not the healthy who need a doctor, but the sick. I didn't come just for the good people, but for the bad."

Of course loving God and coming to church means that you try to obey God's commandments. A robber is very welcome to come to church, but God would expect him to stop stealing and go straight.

ACTIVITY

The children could draw a job they'd like to do on a piece of card.

Suggest to a willing pair that they might like to go for tax collector and fisherman: add the robber picture.

Practice your presentation for when you go back to church (see below).

FINAL	God our Father,
PRAYER	Thank you for making us all different.
	Thank you for giving us different skills and different jobs.
	And thank you for welcoming every one of us into your Church.
	Amen.

SONG (optional)
"We are one in the Spirit"

BACK IN CHURCH

Pick a narrator and hand out the job cards or the pictures the children have made. The kids line up in the front and the Narrator says:

Today we thought about all the jobs people have. They can be...

Each child says what job they've got and holds up their card against their chest.

Jesus chose some of these people to help Him run the Church.
He chose Peter the fisherman.

The fisherman holds his card above his head.

And Matthew the tax collector.

The tax collector holds her card above her head.

And when Jesus thought about the people He'd like to *be* in His Church, He chose...

Everyone raises their cards above their heads.

Everybody!

The priest or one of the leaders can reflect on the robber as they see fit.

Script 35 Jesus' Twelve Friends

Proper 6
(The Sunday Closest to June 15)

Matthew 10:1-4

THEME

We're using an Old Testament story as well as the Gospel this morning to show how God knows us very well and calls us by name when He wants us to serve Him.

SET UP

- The liturgical color is Green.
- Pictures from the CD-ROM.
- Marker pen and something to write on.
- You may like to mount the Apostles' pictures on wooden dowels, so the children can hold them up as puppets at the end of the session.

WELCOME *the children and lead them in* **The Sign of the Cross +** (p. xxxvi).

THE KYRIE   Lord, for the times we have
                forgotten to love you,
                Lord have mercy.
                Lord have mercy.

Jesus, for the times we have forgotten to love others,
Christ have mercy.
Christ have mercy.

Lord, we thank you for never forgetting to love us,
Lord have mercy.
Lord have mercy.

Ask the children to repeat **The Prayer for Forgiveness** *after you* (p. xxxvi).

BEFORE THE GOSPEL

Invite a child forward—preferably one whose name you are not sure about. Try to greet her and ad lib the following...

Leader	Hi—um—do you know, I've forgotten your name—don't tell me! Let me look at you and see if I can guess...

Try out some silly names—Flosshilda, Claribel.

No? I give up, what is it? (*Name*)
That's a super name.

Greet her properly then turn the child to face the others.

Polly (*or whatever*) has a name—she knows it, but none of the rest of us does unless she tells us.

Ask another couple of kids their names.

You have to *ask* people their names. You can't just guess.
But *somebody* knows all our names without asking—
Who is that? (**God, Jesus**)
God knows all our names. He's looking around at us this morning and thinking: "Ah, there's my friend Josh, and there's my friend Joanna, and there's my friend Christopher..."
I want you to shut your eyes and think about your name. Just say it to yourself... (*Pause*)
I'd like you to say this prayer after me:

OPENING PRAYER	**God our Father,** **Thank you for my name.** **Thank you for knowing about me.** **Help me to know you.** *Amen.*

And we'll finish by making the **Sign of the Cross** again, because when we do that we remember in whose Name we are gathered:
+ In the Name of the Father... (p. xxxvi).

The Call of Samuel (from 1 Samuel 3)

One Leader reads the story, another sticks up the pictures.

Today we are going to hear the story of a little boy.

CD35.1   *Stick up Samuel picture.*

He's very little—only about three—and he lived a long time ago, in Jerusalem.

CD35.2   He lived in the great Temple there with an old priest, Eli.

Stick up Eli.   The Temple was like a church—but it was bigger—and it had rooms for the priests to eat and sleep in. Samuel had his own bedroom; it was very near Eli's bedroom, so Samuel could run in whenever he wanted.

CD35.3   It had a bed—*(bed)*

CD35.4   and a lamp—*(lamp)*

And Samuel used to sleep there every night. One night, he was fast asleep when suddenly he heard a voice, calling quietly to him in the dark:

CD35.5   "Samuel, Samuel"—*(speech bubbles)*

He sat up and looked around. Nobody there. "It must be Eli," he thought, and ran into Eli's room.

CD35.6   "Here I am!" he said. Eli sat up.

Eli in bed   "Eh?" he said.

"You called me," said Samuel.

"No I didn't," said Eli. "Go back to bed."

So Samuel went back—and the voice came again...

CD35.5   *More speech bubbles*

Run the Eli dialogue again, adding two more speech bubbles as the Voice calls

Then it happens a third time. Run it all over again—more speech bubbles—but when Samuel wakes Eli for the third time add.

Eli thought for a moment and said, "Listen, Samuel, it's not me calling you—it must be God. If He calls again, say: 'Speak, Lord, your servant is listening.'"

So Samuel went back to bed, and the voice came again, "Samuel, Samuel."

Speech bubbles   But this time Samuel said, "Speak, Lord, your servant is listening."

And then God spoke to Samuel. He gave him a message for Eli, and He blessed the little boy. Samuel grew up to be a great prophet.

Samuel never forgot that God loved him, and he never forgot something else...

Ask the children to look at all the speech bubbles.

How many times did God call him? (**eight**)
God knew Samuel's **name.**
Our Gospel today is similar to the Samuel story, see if you can figure
out why.

THE GOSPEL PROCESSION

THE GOSPEL *Matthew 10:1-4*

When you come to verse 2 it will be clearer if you read it as: "These are the names of
the twelve apostles whom Jesus called..."

AFTER THE GOSPEL

Leader   What did Jesus do today? (**He called the disciples/apostles.**)
How many were there? (**twelve**)
How did Jesus call them? (**He called them by name.**)
Jesus knew all His friends' names.
He knew...

CD35.7 *Get everyone to help you remember the twelve apostles—put up their
pictures as you go.*
Give the children some outrageous hints if they hesitate.

Who's the Simpson disciple? (**Bart/Bartholomew**)
Who's the one who was known as a tank engine? (**Thomas**)
If we have a Big James, we also have a... (**Little James**)

*Below is the list from Matthew: it substitutes Thaddeus for "Judas not Iscariot" (they
were probably the same person).*

Simon Peter,
his brother Andrew,
the brothers James the Great and John,
Philip,
Bartholomew,
Thomas,
Matthew the tax collector,
James the Less,
Judas *not* Iscariot (sometimes called Thaddeus),
Simon the Zealot, and
Judas Iscariot.
Even if we don't know all their names, Jesus did—and He knows
ours too. Let's think about that as we pray.

FINAL   *Ask the children to repeat this after you:*
PRAYER   Lord Jesus,
            Thank you for my name.
            Call me by my name,
            Call me in the Bible,
            Call me at Mass (*or* in Church),
            Call me through other people.
            Speak to my heart,
            Speak, Lord, your servant is listening. *Amen.*

ACTIVITY

You could use the pictures of the apostles (on the CD-ROM) and turn them into puppets by sticking them on dowels. Give an apostle to a child, and ask them to remember the name. The children could of course draw the apostles themselves—if they do, make the drawing session quite short.

Come on, we've got twelve apostles to get through—Ready, Steady, Draw!

Practice the presentation below for when you go back to church.

BACK IN CHURCH

The children come in with their apostle puppets and line up.

Leader   Today we heard that Jesus called His disciples by name.
            They were...

Each child says the name of his or her apostle, and holds the puppet up.
Obviously you'll have to adapt this according to numbers. If you can only muster a few, it's great fun for the first one to say "Peter" as the first apostle and then run round to join the line again as "Philip."

Jesus knows the names of all His friends. He knew the apostles' names, and He knows ours.
We've been called too—here are some more friends of Jesus...

The children call out their names one by one.
If you have a horde of children, you might have to limit this too.

We've been called too—here are twelve more friends of Jesus...

And select twelve more children to say their names, one by one.

Script 36 Shouting from the Housetops

Proper 7
(The Sunday Closest to June 22)

Matthew 10:26-31

THEME

The Gospel today is a collection of Jesus' sayings. It's a mixed bag and, on the whole, rather encouraging. A warning about persecution is paired in with the surprising news that God knows how many hairs are on our head, keeps an eye on sparrows, and expects His truth to be shouted from the housetops.

The session encourages the children to be confident about their faith, and understand that there are no secrets in Christianity, the Gospel is for everyone. We read the Gospel in two sections: Part 1 and Part 2.

SET UP

- The liturgical color is Green.
- Pictures from the CD-ROM.
- You may want to photocopy the Gospel cartoon strip for each child, or make a big version to work on as a group.

WELCOME *the children and lead them in* **The Sign of the Cross + (p. xxxvi).**

THE KYRIE   Father, we are sorry for the times we have been unloving,
Lord have mercy.
Lord have mercy.

Jesus, we are sorry for the times we have forgotten you,
Christ have mercy.
Christ have mercy.

Holy Spirit, help us to know that God still loves us and
    will forgive us,
Lord have mercy.
Lord have mercy.

Ask the children to repeat **The Prayer for Forgiveness** *after you* (**p. xxxvi**).

OPENING	God our Father,
PRAYER	Thank you for bringing us here this morning.
	Open our hearts and minds
	To hear the words of your Son
	In the Holy Gospel. *Amen.*

BEFORE THE GOSPEL

Leader	Today I want to think about the Christians in the world who are persecuted:
	Who can't come to church
	And can't tell other people about Jesus.
	How do they manage?
	Because the Good News about Jesus is so important, you sometimes feel you have to tell it or burst.
	If you want to tell your friend something at school and you're not supposed to be talking—how do you do it? (**You whisper**)
	Whispering—perhaps that's a good way to tell people things.

Chinese Whispers (a.k.a. "Telephone")

Split the children into teams and give them each a Chinese whisper
Ask the children to whisper the phrase to their neighbor, who passes it on. They can only say the phrase once—the listeners have to make sense of what they hear
Separate the little kids and do a very simple version with them: one word is often enough for a toddler
Possible whispers

> "What I say in the dark, tell in the daylight."
> "You can buy two sparrows for one penny."
> "God has counted every hair on your head."

What happened?
Sometimes the kids get the phrases right, other times the whole thing collapses
If they are having huge difficulties, send around some simple whispers, like "Five sparrows" or "Get on the roof!" to encourage them.

Well, is whispering a useful way of telling people things? (*Accept any answer.*)
Sometimes it all goes wrong—and even when it goes right, it can take for ever.
Jesus had very strong views on how He wanted His disciples to speak. Let's hear them now.

THE GOSPEL PROCESSION

THE GOSPEL *Part 1—Matthew 10:26-27*

Okay, let's stop there—how does Jesus want us to proclaim the Gospel?
Are we supposed to whisper it? (**No!**)
No, Jesus said, get on a housetop and tell it from there.
I think He was probably joking about sitting on the roof, but it's obvious He wants us to proclaim the Gospel loud and clear.
But what about the places where it's dangerous to preach the Gospel? Jesus had something to say about that as well.

THE GOSPEL *Part 2—Matthew 10:29-31*

AFTER THE GOSPEL

I think Jesus is saying, you'll just have to risk it.
You might get into trouble, but God sees everything—even sparrows when they fall out of their nests—and He'll keep a watchful eye on us.
You see our faith is not a secret faith, it's something that works best in the daylight.
The Gospel is for everyone, and it's up to us to proclaim it boldly.

ACTIVITY

CD36.1   *The Gospel is in separate cartoon squares. Either give them to the children, or work on them as a group.*
The first thing is to get them in order.
The second is to fill in the speech balloon.

> What saying of Jesus are you going to proclaim from the housetop?

Think through some of the things Jesus said—they should be quite short

> **"I am the Way" / "Love one another" / "Follow me!"/
> "Turn the other cheek"**

On the basis of what saying is chosen, practice your presentation for when you go back to church (see below).

FINAL   Lord Jesus,
PRAYER   Please bless all Christians who are persecuted for their faith.
                   Thank you for our freedom.
                   Help us to proclaim boldly your Gospel in our own land. *Amen.*

SONG

A good traditional hymn for this session is "Let All the World"—draw the children's attention to the words, "The Church with Psalms Must Shout."
If you want a hymn with a swing to it, "I the Lord of Earth and Sky" fits in well.

BACK IN CHURCH

The children go to the front.

Leader	Today we heard that Jesus expected us to proclaim His Gospel from the housetops.
	And we thought we'd better practice.
	So the part of the Gospel we'd like you to hear is...
Children	**Love one another**

(CD36.1)

Script 37   A Cup of Cold Water

Proper 8
(The Sunday Closest to June 29)

Matthew 10:40-42

THEME

The Gospel this morning picks up on a theme that will become important when we come to the feast of Christ the King: the way Jesus identifies Himself with the poor.

This morning He tells us that anyone who gives a cup of water to His humblest disciple will be rewarded as if the cup had been given to Jesus Himself. (Later on this year we will discover that all our acts of mercy are accepted by God as services done to Him.)

The story of "St. Martin and the Beggar" provides a very graphic illustration of this idea—and the children love the moment when St. Martin rips his cloak in half.

SET UP

- The liturgical color is Green.
- Large glass pitcher of water and a transparent bowl.
- St. Martin triptych from the CD-ROM. (A triptych is three pictures joined in one.) Cut your copy round the frame (see right).
- The children can make their own copies of this. If you decide to go for an art session, make copies of the grey version (see below). They too will have to be cut into the triptych shape.
- Cushions or pillows for a makeshift bed.
- Something like an old sheet to act as a cloak; put a nick in it so it'll tear in half easily. (Lining material makes a very satisfying "rip" noise.)
- Dress-up box if you've got one: a plastic sword is a must for the kid about to play St. Martin, a Roman helmet would be a popular extra.

The shape of a triptych.

↑ ↑
fold
lines

- Pens for the children.
- A small votive candle.
- Ask the clergy if one of them could participate in the presentation in the church.

Optional Picture

You may like to find a picture of "St. Martin and the Beggar" on the Internet: there's a very nice stained glass window from Cluny in Google Images.

WELCOME *the children and lead them in* **The Sign of the Cross + (p. xxxvi).**

THE KYRIE   Lord Jesus, you came to earth to tell us how much God loves us,
Lord have mercy.
Lord have mercy.

Lord Jesus, you came to earth to help us,
Christ have mercy.
Christ have mercy.

Lord Jesus, you came to earth to forgive us,
Lord have mercy.
Lord have mercy.

Ask the children to repeat **The Prayer for Forgiveness** *after you* **(p. xxxvi).**

OPENING PRAYER

Settle the children—hands together, eyes shut.

Leader   Jesus said that even when a couple of Christians were together,
He'd be there with them. He's with us now.
Let's welcome Him:

Lord Jesus,
Thank you for loving us.
Thank you for being here.
Help us to welcome you
Into our games, our worship,
And most of all,
Into our hearts. *Amen.*

BEFORE THE GOSPEL

Leader   I'm going to tell you a story.
One day Jesus was tired, and hungry, and thirsty. He'd walked a long

way under a hot sun, and He sat down by a well.

His friends went off to buy food, but Jesus couldn't move.

He was too tired to look for food, or even find some shade.

All He really wanted was a cup of cold water.

And then a woman turned up, with a bucket, and she drew Him some water from the well.

Just think how hot and dusty Jesus was, and how lovely the sound and splash of the water was.

Pour the water from your pitcher (from a great height) into the bowl.

I bet Jesus drank the whole lot.

I don't think He ever forgot it. He was talking once about the way God likes us to make people welcome—and He remembered that water.

Let's hear about it in the Gospel.

THE GOSPEL PROCESSION

THE GOSPEL *Matthew 10:40-42*

AFTER THE GOSPEL

Leader   Did you hear the cup of water? What did Jesus say?

See what the children come up with.

Jesus said God would notice the smallest kindness, even a cup of water to somebody who wants it.

He also said that any kindness you do to somebody, is a kindness you do to Him.

Jesus loves the poor so much, He's right beside them when they ask for help.

To see how this works we're going to hear a story about St. Martin—or rather we're going to act it.

Setting up

I'm going to need a St. Martin.

And a beggar—a very cold beggar.

Ask the kids to act cold and choose one of them.

Plus somebody to play Jesus.

He/she gets a line to say—hand it over on a slip of paper.
The other children help you set up the room.

> We'll need a gate—how shall we do that?

Provide a couple of chairs.

> And St. Martin will need a bed—what can we use for a bed?

Provide pillows, cushions, two chairs, anything.
Pull out the dress-up box if you've got one.

> Right, Martin was a Roman soldier—what should he have?
> A sword, obviously.
> And a helmet. *(if there is one)*
> And his Roman cloak.

Drape your material round him.

> The beggar hasn't got anything—not even any clothes.
> I don't think we'll ask *Name* to take his/her clothes off.

Suggest getting down to a T-shirt if the room is warm enough.
Place Martin one side of the gate, the beggar the other, and the bed the other side of the room.
The Leader acts as Narrator.

St. Martin and the Beggar

Narrator	This story happened way back in the fourth century.

Narrator This story happened way back in the fourth century.
A young soldier called Martin was stationed in France, in a town called Amiens.
One cold winter's day, he wrapped his cloak round him —*(Martin does so)*
And left Amiens via the city gates.
There was a beggar sitting outside, too cold to walk—*(cold acting from the beggar)*
And Martin nearly fell over him. He helped the beggar up and asked what the matter was—and the beggar said he was freezing to death.
So Martin took off his cloak...
Got out his sword...
And ripped his cloak in half—*(he might need some help)*
He gave one half to the beggar, and kept the other half for himself.
They both put their cloaks on...
And shook hands—*(they do)*
The beggar went into Amiens...—*(exit beggar)*
And Martin journeyed on until he came to an Inn. There he got a bed for the night, used his cloak for a blanket—and fell fast asleep.

While he's doing that, the beggar hands his cloak to Jesus, who puts it on.

That night Martin had a dream:
He saw Jesus, standing at the end of his bed—*(enter Jesus)*
Jesus said:

Jesus Thank you, Martin, for giving me your cloak.

Narrator And Martin saw that Jesus was wearing the cloak he'd given to the beggar.

That was really well done, let's give our actors some applause.

Sum up

Leader That story tells us how much God loves us to be kind to each other. When we do any kindness to one of His children, it's as if we've done it to Him.

St. Martin is a really good saint to copy.

ACTIVITY

Show the children the St. Martin Triptych (**CD37.1**) *from the CD-ROM. You'll see that this triptych has Jesus in the center, St. Martin one side and the beggar on the other. If you have time, hand out the grey version of the picture* (**CD37.2**), (**CD37.3**), *and* (**CD37.4**). *The children can go over the lines to make their own version, or start from scratch, using the back of the picture.*

Once they're done, show the children how to fold the triptych so it stands up.

Use one of them for the **Final Prayer.**

FINAL PRAYER

Set up one of the triptychs, put a votive light before it and help one of the children light it.

Talk about the picture—the young soldier, the poor beggar—both children of God.

Lord Jesus,
You love all your people
Young and old
Strong and weak.
Help us to follow the example of St. Martin
And love your people too. *Amen.*

SONG

The hymn "Teach me my God and King" *would end the session nicely. You might like to tell the kids that the "famous stone" in the last verse is the Philosopher's Stone: a mythical substance that was supposed to turn lead into gold. Harry Potter knew all about it.*

BACK IN CHURCH

Prime the priest as to what you are going to do.
Ask the children to take their folded triptychs back into church.

Leader   Today we heard the story of St. Martin and the beggar, and we've drawn these pictures...

The children open up their triptychs.
Ask the priest to look at a couple of them and, using the pictures, elicit the story from the children.

(CD37.1)

Sample cartoon for this script

Script 38   My Yoke is Easy

Proper 9
(The Sunday Closest to July 6)

Matthew 11:28-30

THEME

God can relieve us of our burdens.

This saying of Jesus was originally offered to Palestinian peasants, crushed by their inability to keep the Jewish Law. But down the centuries Christians have found the Gospel perfectly expresses the sheer relief of following Jesus: how wonderfully our sins, doubts and worries tumble away.

SET UP

- The liturgical color is Green.
- Backpack and some bricks, or something equally heavy (potatoes), in bags and all labelled *(see below)*.
- A copy of *The Pilgrim's Progress* if you can get one: the text you need is provided below.
- Pictures from the CD-ROM.

WELCOME *the children and lead them in* **The Sign of the Cross + (p. xxxvi).**

THE KYRIE   God our Father, you forgive everybody who says they are sorry,
Lord have mercy.
Lord have mercy.

Lord Jesus, you came to earth to tell us how much God loves us,
Christ have mercy.
Christ have mercy.

Holy Spirit, you fill our hearts with the love of God,
Lord have mercy.
Lord have mercy.

Ask the children to repeat **The Prayer for Forgiveness** *after you* (**p. xxxvi**).

BEFORE THE GOSPEL

Talk through shopping in a supermarket:

Leader	How do you get the stuff round the aisles? (**shopping cart**)
	And how do you get it home? (**the car/bus/etc.**)
	Have you ever had to lug the shopping bags home on foot?
	It's awful isn't it?
	How do you suppose they managed when Jesus was alive?
	Of course they didn't have supermarkets, but they still had to carry things.
	Some people like the Romans had **carts**.
	They were very slow and (as the roads were bumpy) very uncomfortable.
CD38.1	Some people had **donkeys**.
	That was okay, still a bit slow—and of course donkeys are famous for getting fed up and just stopping.
CD38.2	Most of the time, you had to carry things **yourself**.
	If you were very unlucky your master, or a Roman, would expect you to carry things for them.
	And **backpacks**, nice, neat and lightweight—*(show one)* — hadn't been invented.
CD38.3	But they had invented **yokes**...

The picture shows the yoke on a peasant. Draw in bundles on the rope ends.

They were still very heavy, but at least the load was evenly distributed.
All the poor people Jesus talked to knew about burdens, and yokes,
and what a business it was carrying things round for your master.
So when Jesus suggested people follow Him, and make Him their
Master, He said this:

THE GOSPEL PROCESSION

THE GOSPEL *Matthew 11:28-30*

AFTER THE GOSPEL

Leader	"My yoke is easy, my burden light."
	That's a super thing to offer poor weary overworked peasants.
	But does it mean that Christians don't work?

Take any answer, then tell the bad news that most Christians work very hard indeed.

Or that Christians don't carry things? *(Ditto)*
So what did Jesus mean? Two things, I think:
One is that Christians aren't worn down by loads and loads of religious rules. We only have two—can anybody remember what they are? (**Love God, love your neighbor**)
And the other one thing Jesus meant is this:
Let's look at the average grown-up.

Pull forward a Leader.

He doesn't look as if he's carrying much around—but actually there's a pack on his back that only God can see.

Put on his backpack.

Full of...

Toss these things in, all nicely labelled with the words in bold.

Worries, Work, Fear, and **Sins**—I'm afraid there are quite a few of these—
Anger, Greed, Selfishness, Faithlessness—and then, just to top it up, **Guilt**—*(this should be huge)*—on the top.

Leader staggers under the load.

The man can't see the pack, but he can feel it all right.
Somebody wrote a book about this once.

Show them The Pilgrim's Progress.
Talk about John Bunyan and the fact that it was written nearly 400 years ago if you feel it won't interrupt the flow.
The burdened Leader should keep the backpack on, if he can, lean or sit to ease the load.

Story

This is the story of a man called Christian...

CD38.4 *Show the picture—he'll be in two parts, make sure he starts straight backed.*

Who felt a huge burden of guilt and sin weighing on his back.

CD38.5 *Add burden, bend Christian.*

In this state he felt he had to find God, and he left his home and family and started on a pilgrimage.
The burden was a terrible nuisance, he walked long dusty roads, he lost his way, he fell into ditches, he climbed narrow rocky paths and one day he came to a road, hedged in walls and leading to a hill...

Obviously read from the book.

> "Up this way, therefore, did the burdened Christian run, but not without great difficulty, because of the load on his back. And he came to a hill and upon that place stood a Cross, and a little below, at the bottom, a tomb. And, just as Christian came to the Cross, his burden was loosed from off his shoulders, and fell off his back, and tumbled into the tomb."

Take the pack off Christian, straighten him up.

> "Then was Christian glad and lightsome, and said, with a merry heart, 'Jesus hath given me rest by His sorrow, and life by His death.'" And he gave three leaps for joy, and went on his way singing.

After the Story

> So Christian went up a hill...

Draw it in at Christian's feet.

> ...and came to what? (**a cross**)

Draw that in.   And his burden fell away...

Turn to the backpack carrier.

> What do you think of that?

Leader 2   Sounds good to me.

Drop the backpack with a crash, and stretch out your arms and shoulders.

> Yup, it feels good.

Leader 1   Anybody know why Christian's burden fell away at the foot of the Cross?

Accept all answers.

> Because the *only* Person who carries the burden and weight and weariness of sin is Jesus Himself.
> Let's thank Him for that.

FINAL   Lord Jesus Christ,
PRAYER   We thank you for calling us to your service.
We thank you for carrying the load of our sins for us.
Help us to follow you with light, happy hearts,
For your Name's sake. *Amen.*

OPTIONAL EXTRA

Leader   Can anyone remember what Christian did when he felt the load fall
                from his shoulders?

Probably a rhetorical question.

                He gave three leaps for joy and went on his way singing.
                That's a good way to pray, let's try.
                One leap
                Two
                and
                Three!

Then straight into a **SONG**

"Cast your burdens on Jesus;" "Come, my brothers, praise the Lord;" "I heard the
voice of Jesus say," *or* "O praise ye the Lord, praise Him in the height."

BACK IN CHURCH

Bring in the laden Leader.

Leader 1   Today we realized how many burdens people carry:
                Worries, Work, Fear and **Sin**...
                They're all in that backpack.
Leader 2   Then we read the Gospel.
                Jesus doesn't want us to be loaded up like this—
                We can drop them all at the foot of the Cross.

The Leader does so.

Leader 3   Jesus said: "My yoke is easy, and my burden light."

(CD38.1)   (CD38.2)   (CD38.3)
Sample cartoons for this script

Script 39 The Sower

Proper 10
(The Sunday Closest to July 13)

Matthew 13:1-9

THEME

The session is all about the difference between *hearing* and *listening*.

SET UP

- The liturgical color is Green.
- A large hand bell, a little hand bell and the smallest bell you can find.
- Invite a child to run through the mini-drama with you (see below).

WELCOME *the children and lead them in* **The Sign of the Cross + (p. xxxvi).**

THE KYRIE   Father, forgive us when we forget to love you,
Lord have mercy.
Lord have mercy.

Jesus, forgive us when we forget to listen to you,
Christ have mercy.
Christ have mercy.

Holy Spirit, help us to say sorry,
Lord have mercy.
Lord have mercy.

Ask the children to repeat **The Prayer for Forgiveness** *after you* (p. xxxvi).

BELLS

Ask the children to think about bells, when do they hear them?
At the Gospel Procession, perhaps, or in the Eucharistic prayer, or pealing from the church tower.
If you don't ring bells at all, introduce the large hand bell and explain that at Easter,

some Christians go mad and ring every bell they can find during the First Eucharist of Easter. Ask a kid to ring the large bell.

> Do you think God could hear that? (**yes**)
> What about this one?

Give another kid the smaller hand bell, same business.

> How about this one?

Pick up the little bell, get a kid to ring it.

Cup your ear   Could you do that again?
That's a very little bell, it's just for this room.
I don't think anyone outside could hear it.
Do you think God heard it? (**yes**)
God is very good at listening.
He can hear us when we all speak together.
He can hear us when we whisper.
He can even hear us when we just talk to him in our head.
Let's talk to Him now.

OPENING   God our Father,
PRAYER   Thank you for listening to us.
Help us to hear you,
In the Bible,
In Church,
And through other people. *Amen.*

BEFORE THE GOSPEL

Run through a mini-drama of a child and his mom. Place them at opposite sides of the room, the kid is sitting on a chair, absorbed in an iPad or Gameboy.
He says "Yes, Mom" every time his mother asks him to do something, but doesn't move.

Mom	*(Name)*! Run upstairs for me!
Kid	Yes Mom!
Mom	It's time to do your homework.
Kid	Yes Mom!
Mom	Hurry up and clean your bedroom.
Kid	Yes Mom!
Mom	Come and eat your supper.

Whooosh!—the kid is right beside her.

Kid	Yes Mom!
Leader	That kid could hear his mother, but he only listened to her once. When was that? (**When she said supper was ready**)
	Jesus wanted His disciples to listen to Him, and He told them a story about listening.

THE GOSPEL PROCESSION

THE GOSPEL *Matthew 13:1-9*

Optional Paraphrase *(the last sentence is a straight quote)*
One day Jesus told this story.
Once upon a time a man went out to sow corn.
He scattered it all over the field.
And some of it fell on the path—and the birds ate it.
And some fell on stony ground, where there wasn't much earth.
So, though the plants sprang up, the soil wasn't deep enough for them to take root, and when the Sun came up, the corn wilted.
And some fell among weeds, and the weeds grew, and choked it.
But some fell into good soil, and the corn grew and produced grain—30 grains, 60 grains, even 100 grains.
Jesus finished the story by saying,
"Those who have got ears to hear—let them hear!"

AFTER THE GOSPEL

Leader	The disciples listened to the story, but they didn't understand it. So Jesus said:
	The sower in my story is God, and the seeds He sows are the things He tells us.
	Some people don't listen at all, and God's word doesn't have a chance (the seed on stony ground).
	And some people listen for a bit, and then get fed up and wilt (the seed in shallow earth).
	And other people sort of listen, but then start thinking about other things—computer games perhaps, or football or TV—and all that gets in the way (the seed getting choked by weeds).
	But some people listen properly—and *then* all sorts of wonderful things happen. They find they can do things for God and for other people, 30 times more than they could do before—60 times—even 100 times.

Jesus finished the story by saying,
"Those who have got ears to hear—let them hear!"

ACTIVITY

You can turn this into a drama, using the script below as the narration in church.
Choose three readers, one for the Gospel, one for the application and one for the
moral. Choreograph the children following the directions below.
As Reader 1 mentions the birds that ate the grain he gives Q1 (cue).
The kids flap their arms as birds and swoop down to the floor.
They stay down and (on Q2) start to grow pretty fast, but as the sun comes up, the
children do some "Phew it's hot!" acting and collapse on to the floor.
On Q3 they grow again, apparently shake themselves, and collapse again.
On Q4 they spring up and—at 30 grains—they fling up one hand, opening the fingers
as it goes above the head (one semi-circular movement), and bring the hand down
again.
At Q5 (60 grains) they fling up the other hand, same business.
At Q6 (100 grains) they fling up both hands, open their fingers and wave their arms.

FINAL	*Ask the children to repeat after you:*
PRAYER	**Speak, Lord,**
	Open my ears.
	Speak, Lord,
	Your servant is listening. *Amen.*

Finish with an **Our Father...** *(p. xxxvi).*

BACK IN CHURCH

Reader 1	One day Jesus told a story about a man who went out to sow.
	Some of his grain was eaten by birds—*Q1.*
	Some of it wilted—*Q2.*
	Some of it got choked by weeds—*Q3.*
	But *some* of it grew and produced grain:
	30 grains—*Q4.*
	60 grains—*Q5.*
	Even 100 grains—*Q6.*
Reader 2	Then Jesus explained the story.
	He said the sower was God,
	And the seed He sowed were the things He told us.
	Some people didn't listen at all— *Q1.*

Some people listened for a bit, and then got fed up and wilted—Q2.
Some people sort of listened, but then started thinking about other things—Q3.
But some people listened properly—and then they found they could do things for God and for other people,
30 times more than they could do before—Q4.
60 times more—Q5.
100 times more—Q6.

Reader 3   Jesus finished the story by saying,
"Those who have got ears to hear—let them hear!"

Script 40   **Wheat and Tares**

Proper 11
(The Sunday Closest to July 20)

Matthew 13:24-30

THEME

Today we hear one of Jesus' parables, one that we apply to the Last Judgement.
It's a tough text, but one we should tackle, as the children are bound to pick up
debased versions of Hell from other sources.

The doctrine of the Final Judgement comes bristling with problems. On the one
hand we may welcome it as the moment when the world is at last freed of its sin
and pain, on the other we may find the traditional idea of Eternal Punishment
both horrifying and morally repugnant. (Added to which there is the alarming
imagery of harvest and farming and bonfires.)

One way through this difficulty is to suggest that all evil *things*, diseases, lies,
wars, etc. will be destroyed at the end of time. No evil can last for ever and that
assurance is a huge relief.

(The fact that evil might appear to be inextricably entwined round the human
heart should be reserved for fuller discussion at Confirmation.)

Language

Different translations use different words to describe the plants growing among the
farmer's wheat. They are called "weeds," "darnel" or "tares," depending on which
translation you use. I've gone for the traditional "tares."

SET UP

- The liturgical color is Green.
- Pictures of the ears of wheat and the 7 Deadly Tares (on the CD-ROM). (Tape them
  to wooden dowels.)
- A handful of seeds—anything from a jar will do: cardamom seed, mustard seed—
  and a handful of black peppercorns.
- Two bags with "SEEDS" written on them.
- A couple of pillows for the Farmer to sleep on.
- A black cloak, a mask or a large hat for the Villain.

- Plastic scythe (if you managed to get one at Halloween).
- Some children to be the Farmer's helpers, others to be the crop.

WELCOME *the children and lead them in* **The Sign of the Cross + (p. xxxvi).**

THE KYRIE   Lord Jesus, you always listen to our prayers, please forgive our sins,
Lord have mercy.
Lord have mercy.

Lord Jesus, you are always beside us, help us not to sin again,
Christ have mercy.
Christ have mercy.

Lord Jesus, you always love us, help us to love you,
Lord have mercy.
Lord have mercy.

Ask the children to repeat **The Prayer for Forgiveness** *after you* (**p. xxxvi**).

OPENING   Lord,
PRAYER   Thank you for bringing us here today.
Sow your gifts in our hearts
That we may serve you with
Faith, hope and love. *Amen.*

BEFORE THE GOSPEL

Cast Leaders for the Narrator, the Farmer and the Villain. Some children help the Farmer, other are the crop.
CD40.1 and 40.2   *Lay the pictures of the wheat and tares face downwards on the floor—a child behind each one.*
The Farmer and the Villain have their seed bags ready in their hands (the Villain's are the black peppercorns).

Narrator   Jesus told us this story about a farmer who went out to sow...

The Farmer (plus helpers) sows wheat down the front of the hall, talking as he does so

Farmer   We'll have a bit of corn here. Gee, this is hard work!—*(that sort of thing)*
Narrator   He worked very hard all day, and when he'd sown all his wheat—he fell asleep.

Farmer falls asleep on a cushion, the helpers get to sleep on the floor.

Farmer   That's quite good enough.
Narrator   While the Farmer and his servants were sleeping, an enemy...

Enter Villain, plus cloak (pantomime acting please).
The kids should break into **"Boo!"** *spontaneously. If they don't, the other Leaders should egg them on.*

> crept into his field—and began to sow as well. He didn't sow wheat but...

The Villain flourishes his weed seed bag.

> tares (that's an old-fashioned word for weeds).

The Villain plants seven seeds, one at a time very precisely.

> And, when he'd quite finished, he crept away with an evil chuckle.

Villain exits appropriately
The children by the crops hold the base of the dowels.

> And that night the wheat seeds and the tare seeds grew...

The children bring their crops up from flat to vertical, slowly getting to their knees as they do so—then standing up.

> So that when the Farmer and his servants woke up they found that the field was a terrible mess of good wheat and useless tares.

The Farmer and company wake up and are appalled—farmer does a double-take.

Farmer	What's been going on??!!
Narrator	One of the servants said,

> "Sir, I thought you sowed good wheat seed in your field—what on earth has happened?"
> And the Farmer said,
> "So I did—some enemy has done this!"
> And another servant said,
> "What shall we do—pull the tares up?"
> What did the Farmer do?
> We'll hear that in the Gospel.

THE GOSPEL PROCESSION

THE GOSPEL *Matthew 13:24-30*

AFTER THE GOSPEL

Leader   So what did the Farmer decide?

Take any answers—at the end establish that the Farmer decided to let the wheat and tares grow together until the harvest, then:

Well, let's see...

Have the kids stand up with the wheat and tares and harvest the crop with the scythe. Q the children to sit down as they are "harvested."

> The reapers gathered in the crop and sorted out the wheat from the tares.

Get the Farmer's helpers to sort out the crop, the wheat one side of the room, the tares the other.

> The tares were thrown on the bonfire (bad luck, tares!), while the wheat was put in the Farmer's barn.

Ask the children to sit down.

> Why did Jesus tell this story?

Take any answer, then continue.

> Well, He's thinking about the world, and what a mixed place it is. Jesus describes the world as a wheat field, full of the good things that God has sown, and hurt by the evil things that God's enemy has put in.
>
> What sort of evil things are there in the world?

Let the kids tell you, gather up their replies.

> **(Disease, war, death, and things we do—lies, temper, greed)**
> That's why the Seven Deadly Sins are written on the tares...

Read them off as the kids hold up the tares.

> Gluttony.
> Sloth.
> Lust.
> Anger.
> Envy.
> Greed.
> Pride.

(The children don't have to learn them by heart.)

> But what are the good things in the world?

Accept all suggestions—trees, fields, people, moms and dads, games, music—anything that seems appropriate.

> That's the good wheat—let's see it.

Then hold the wheat up.

> Jesus is telling us that evil things are allowed to grow alongside good things.

Some evil things are actually inside us, in our hearts and minds, and God wants to give us plenty of time to get rid of them. But at the end of the world, *all* evil will be zapped and only good will remain. Everything that is wrong in the world, and in us, will just fizzle away: there will be absolutely no evil, unhappy things in Heaven.

FINAL PRAYER *from Psalm 1*

(*The response is:* **Blessed be God**)
Good people love God,
Blessed be God
They are like trees planted by the waterside,
Blessed be God
They grow and bring forth fruit,
Blessed be God
Whatever they do, goes well,
Blessed be God
Wicked things are like husks—they get blown away by the wind,
Blessed be God
But all that is good is blessed,
Blessed be God

End with a **Glory Be...** (p. xxxvii).

BACK IN CHURCH

The children enter, holding the wheat and tare pictures. Mix them up.

Leader   Today we discovered that the world is full of good and bad things: Wheat...

The wheat is brandished.

And tares...
Ditto the tares.   All growing together in a terrible mix.

The children wave their wheat and tares.

But one day, they'll be sorted.

The wheat pictures jump to the right side of the sanctuary, the tares to the left.
God can sort out anything.

Script 41   Mustard Seeds

Proper 12
(The Sunday Closest to July 27)

Matthew 13:31-33, 44-46

THEME

Jesus uses the most attractive images for the Kingdom of Heaven, and there's a particularly fine group in the Gospel this morning. The Kingdom, we read, is like mustard seed; yeast; treasure and the famous "pearl of great price."

This session takes up all these images and suggests to the children that getting into the Kingdom is worth a bit of effort.

SET UP

- The liturgical color is Green.
- A jar of mustard seeds (put it in your pocket).
- Pictures including treasure map from the CD-ROM.
- Money in different denominations.
- Treasure—anything you can gather together:
  Toy crown.
  Costume jewelry.
  Tacky strings of pearls.
  Gold coin chocolate money.
- Any archaeologist/Indiana Jones gear you can come up with; spades (kid's spades are fine), compass, safari hat, sun glasses, backpack, toy gun—put all these in a box.
- Make a Treasure Trove by putting a couple of tables on their sides, block the ends with some chairs and cover the whole lot with a blanket.
- Place a piece of paper on the top with a large X on it and put all the treasure inside.
- A piece of card with "For Sale, nice field, suitable for digging" written on it should be placed near the trove, face down.

• Ingredients to make bread (if you've got the time). Plain flour and dried yeast rises quickly—and it's speed you're after.

WELCOME *the children and lead them in* **The Sign of the Cross + (p. xxxvi).**

THE KYRIE   Lord Jesus, you came to earth to tell us how much God loves us,
Lord have mercy.
Lord have mercy.

Lord Jesus, you came to earth to help us,
Christ have mercy.
Christ have mercy.

Lord Jesus, you came to earth to forgive us,
Lord have mercy.
Lord have mercy.

Ask the children to repeat **The Prayer for Forgiveness** *after you* **(p. xxxvi).**

OPENING PRAYER

Lead the children in the **Our Father . . . (p. xxxvi).** *Don't omit the doxology, "For thine is the Kingdom...*

BEFORE THE GOSPEL

Leader   How does that prayer end?

(Rhetorical question, unless a kid gets in first.)

"For thine is the Kingdom..."
I wonder what God's Kingdom is like?
Jesus knew, and He tried to get people interested in it.
But nobody really knew what He was talking about—and it's very difficult to get people interested in something they don't know anything about.
So Jesus used to say, "Well, the Kingdom of Heaven is like..."
And then He'd tell them all the interesting things it was like.

Optional Bread Making

One of them was **yeast.**

Get out the ingredients and begin to combine them.
Show the children the yeast.

It doesn't look very exciting, does it?

Yet it's a really mysterious substance.

We use it to make bread rise. If we didn't put this in, this bread would end up flat, like pita bread, but *with* yeast—well, you'll see...

Add the yeast, knead for a bit (you might accept some help) and put the dough away to rise: cover the bowl loosely with a plastic bag, and put it in the warmest place you can find without cooking it.

Okay, we'll let the yeast do its stuff, and think about some other ways Jesus described the Kingdom of Heaven.

Treasure Hunt

Turn to another Leader.

Can you remember what else Jesus compared the Kingdom to?

Leader 2   He said it was like "Treasure."

Leader 1   Great. We'll go for that.

What we'll need is some treasure hunting gear...

Put on your hat or sun glasses or tie a scarf round your neck.

And a treasure map...

CD41.1   *Produce the treasure map and examine it.*

Hmm, "Go West"... I'll need a compass.

Pull it out of the box.

"Watch out for the crocs"—Golly, I'll need a gun.

Pull that out.

"Dig"... What do I need for that? (**A spade!**)
Quite right, I'll have one of those.

Pull out a spade.

And if I find any treasure I'll need help bringing it back—
anyone like to come with me?

Assuming everyone puts their hands up.

Okay, I'll take you all!

*Any very shy child can stay with Leader 2, to do the important job at the end of the
Treasure Hunt.*
*In a large hall the kids play "Follow my Leader" round the room as the Leader
follows the directions on the map.*
*If space is a problem, do the actions on the spot—turning right or left for East and
West, counting your paces while walking on the spot, miming rock climbing and
tiptoeing as you pass the lions.*

Line up! Off we go...

*The treasure map gives you very specific instructions as you navigate the room. You'll
have to improvise the exact number of steps you need—make sure you all jump over
the deadly bogs, climb Mount Doom, have the gun ready for the crocs and so on.
Eventually you come to the trove.*

Aha! This looks like the place!
Yes!—*(hold up paper)*—X marks the
spot!
Let's start digging.

*Dig through the blankets exaggerate the care with which
you peer into the pit.*

I can see something down there.
Got it! A crown!
Can you see anything?

Let the kids excavate some of the treasure.
Try to leave the jewels to the end.

Something's glittering, wow! Jewelry—
and some of them are...?

Hold them up.   **(pearls)**
This is fantastic!
The trouble is, I don't own this field...

Leader 2 holds up the "For Sale" notice.

Wow! Look at that!
The field is for sale!

Pull out your wallet.

How much have I got? $5, $10, $25—oh hey, I'll give the owner all of it. I must buy this field!

Sum up

Leader   That's how exciting the Kingdom is.
Let's hear what Jesus has to say about it.

THE GOSPEL PROCESSION

THE GOSPEL *Matthew 13:31-33, 44-46*

AFTER THE GOSPEL

Ad lib on what Jesus compared the Kingdom to.

Leader   "Treasure," "a fabulous pearl"—and then a couple of strange things, "mustard seed" and "yeast."
Well, I've got some mustard seed in my pocket—here it is.

Pour some into your hand.

They're tiny, aren't they?
And yet one of these seeds will grow into an enormous bush and birds will perch on it.
Jesus is saying that the Kingdom is not only exciting, like treasure, but unpredictable.
You don't know what you're in for.
If you're the sort of person who's going to live in God's Kingdom, you might start this small—*(hold up a mustard seed)*—but you're likely to grow into the most amazing person.
And if you let amazing people loose in our world, they can transform it.

Optional Dough Moment

> Like that **yeast** I showed you at the beginning of this service.
> Let's see what it's done...

Pull out the bread tin (praying hard as you do so).

> Look at that! The bread has risen.

It might be advisable to have another Leader check the dough before you commit yourself: if it looks as if there's a bit of a way to go, leave the dough until the end of the Eucharist.

FINAL PRAYER

Ask the children to form a prayer circle.
Take a handful of mustard seeds, pour them into your hand—then go round the circle pouring them into the children's hands.
Don't worry about spillage (as long as you know where the dustpan and broom are kept).

> Look how small the seeds are—
> yet they'll grow into enormous plants.
> Think about God, looking down at us from Heaven—
> how small we must look.
> Yet we can become mighty Saints in His Kingdom.
>
> Lord Jesus,
> Thank you for telling us about your Father's Kingdom:
> Help us to seek for it, as if it were treasure;
> To value it as if it were a pearl;
> To grow into it—
> As if we were mustard seeds.
> So that one day, we will get there, and see you face to face. *Amen.*

SONG

"Seek ye first the Kingdom of God"

BACK IN CHURCH

The kids bring the spades, the map and the treasure.
Present the kids and their props.

Leader   Today we used this map...

Kid brandishes map.

To discover treasure in the Church Hall.
And we thought that, if the Kingdom of Heaven was as exciting as
our Treasure Hunt, then we're going to try to find God's Kingdom
too.

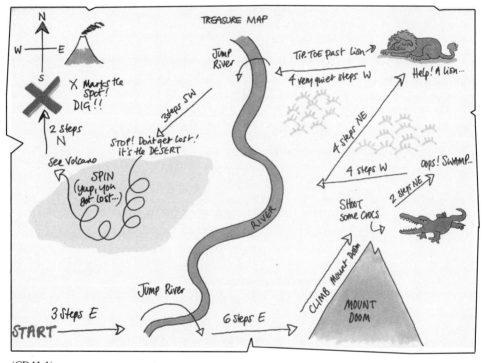

(CD41.1)

Script 42   The Feeding of the 5,000

Proper 13
(The Sunday Closest to August 3)

Matthew 14:13-21, also John 6:8

THEME

One of the great miracles: you can't do better than just tell the story.
Unfortunately Matthew's account leaves out the little boy and his picnic (he turns up in John's version) but I've included him here. I think he's crucial: the grown-ups don't think for a moment that five loaves and two fishes are enough to feed 5,000 people, but the little boy has faith and is wiser than they are.

SET UP

- The liturgical color is Green.
- Pictures from the CD-ROM.
- A deep basket with a false bottom—a dish towel would do.
- Hidden in the bottom of the basket are mini rolls and fish-shaped biscuits (if you've got time to make them).
- On top of the tea towel are five rolls and two fish-shaped biscuits, or chocolate fish. (Cut some toast into a fish shape if you're desperate, or use fish pictures from Script 9, Fishers of Men.)
- Two loaves of bread for the presentation—one to rehearse with, the other to use in church (see below).

WELCOME *the children and lead them in* **The Sign of the Cross + (p. xxxvi).**

THE KYRIE   Lord Jesus, you came to earth to tell us how much God loves us,
Lord have mercy.
Lord have mercy.

Lord Jesus, you came to earth to help us,
Christ have mercy.
Christ have mercy.

Lord Jesus, you came to earth to forgive us,
Lord have mercy.
Lord have mercy.

Ask the children to repeat **The Prayer for Forgiveness** *after you* (**p. xxxvi**).

OPENING God our Father,
PRAYER Thank you for your many gifts to us.
 Help us to offer you our gifts in return:
 Our love,
 Our faith
 And our service. *Amen.*

BEFORE THE GOSPEL

Bring forward your most impressive grown-up—a teacher perhaps, or somebody with a cool job. Stand them next to one of the children—make sure the child is very small and unassuming—no child "stars" this morning.

Leader Today I'd like us to think about how smart we are at St. *Name's (add the name of your church)*
 Here's *Name (the grown-up)*
 Can you tell us what you do?—*(bring them out)*
 Did you have to go to college to do that?
 How did you get into show business?

...or whatever seems appropriate...

 Wow, that's really impressive!
 And here's *Name—(the child)*
 What do you do most days? (**go to school**)
 Any degrees or anything yet? (**no**)
 Oh well, all to come.
 Now guys, who's the smartest of these two?

Don't wait for an answer.

 It's little *Name (the child)* without a doubt.
 I've been thinking about this a lot, and I've come to the conclusion that children are usually much brighter than grown-ups.
 It's in all the stories.
 Look at this one.

CD42.1–42.4 *Put up the Hansel, Gretel, Witch and Gingerbread Children and house pictures from the CD-ROM.*

Does anyone know this story?

Let the children tell you who everyone is and what happens.
All you need to establish is that Hansel and Gretel are lured into the Witch's gingerbread
*house (**CD42.3**) and captured by the Witch. She intends to turn them into gingerbread*
but fortunately Hansel and Gretel outwit her and slam her into her own oven
That turns the witch into gingerbread herself.

Sum up

Leader   So there's the evil Witch who turns kids into gingerbread and she
meets Hansel and Gretel.
Do we worry for a second who's going to win?
Of course not!
Kids always win in these stories, and the poor Witch hasn't got just
one to deal with but two!
No wonder she gets turned into gingerbread.

CD42.4 *Put up gingerbread Witch.*

Is *Hansel and Gretel* a true story? (**No!**)
No, it's a fairy tale.
But fairy tales often have something true about them—not the
witches and stuff, but the children.
Fairy tales are about ordinary children, who have true hearts, lots of
sense, and always come through.
I think that's very realistic.
There's a boy like that in the Gospel today, let's hear about him.

THE GOSPEL PROCESSION

THE GOSPEL *Matthew 14:13-21, also John 6:8*

Jesus heard about the death of John the Baptist and got in a boat, to
be alone. But the crowds saw Him go and ran round the lake to meet
Him when He got to the other side. And when Jesus got out of the
boat, His heart was touched with pity for them, and He healed those
who were ill.
Evening fell and His disciples said, "It's very late and this is a lonely
place. Send the people away to get food in the nearby village."
"They don't have to go," said Jesus. "You could give them something
to eat."
Andrew, Peter's brother, said: "There's a boy here with five barley
loaves and two fish—but they're not nearly enough!"
"Bring the loaves and fishes here to me," said Jesus.

Bring the basket forward—take out the five loaves and two fish, show them to the children and put them back.

> Jesus asked the people to sit on the grass, then He took the loaves and fish...

Take the basket.

> and thanked God for them. He lifted them up, broke a roll and gave it to the disciples, and the disciples began to feed the people...

Hand out rolls and "fish" by quietly sliding your hand under the false bottom in your basket: you'll have to take a view on numbers as to whether you feed the entire group.

> And the rolls and the fish kept coming, and everyone had enough to eat.
> The number of people Jesus fed was more than 5,000.

AFTER THE GOSPEL

Leader   How did *we* do that?

The children are bound to tell you.

> It was a trick—*our* basket had a fake bottom.
> But when Jesus multiplied the loaves and fishes it wasn't a trick—it was a miracle.
> But what would have happened if the little boy hadn't offered Jesus his picnic?

Accept all answers.

> I don't think anything would have happened.
> You see a miracle isn't magic. Jesus wouldn't make bread and fish out of nothing.
> He made fish out of fish, and bread out of bread—that's the natural way God makes things multiply, it's just that Jesus speeded it up a bit.
> What I like about that boy is that he was so sensible.
> There were the grown-ups looking at his picnic and thinking, "No way—that's impossible."
> But the little boy thought, "Jesus needs some food, so I'll give Him my picnic."
> He didn't worry about what was possible or not: he trusted Jesus.
> Let's think about him as we pray.

FINAL
PRAYER

God our Father,
Help us to trust you.
Help us to bring you our gifts,
Knowing that, however small they are,
You can transform them into something wonderful,
Through Jesus Christ our Lord. *Amen.*

ACTIVITY

Practice your presentation for when you go back to church.

BACK IN CHURCH

The children line up, one on the end has the loaf of bread.

Leader/Child   Normally, when you share something, it gets smaller and smaller.

The children pass the loaf along, tearing off a piece as they go: get it down to five pieces.

But in the Gospel today we heard that Jesus took five pieces of bread like this...

Hold them up.   And fed 5,000 people.

(CD42.1)

(CD42.2)

(CD42.3)

(CD42.4)

Cartoons for this script

Script 43   Walking on Water

Proper 14
(The Sunday Closest to August 10)

Matthew 14:22-33

THEME

The Gospel today has many themes: Jesus' watchful care of us when we're in trouble; His ability to turn up, just when we thought He'd forgotten us; and His exhilarating call to "Come!" and share His adventures. We're going for the last one.

SET UP

- The liturgical color is Green.
- The "Holy Snakes and Ladders" game from the CD-ROM.
- Buy some inflatable (or bouncy) dice from a party/joke shop or make a couple by covering boxes with stiff white paper and drawing on the dots.
- Two Leaders should be wearing lace-up shoes (sneakers are fine).
- One Leader starts the session with their laces undone—choose a nice bouncy type, as they'll be asked to do a "prat fall" later on.

WELCOME *the children and lead them in* **The Sign of the Cross +** (p. xxxvi).

THE KYRIE   Lord Jesus, you came to earth to tell us how much God loves us,
Lord have mercy.
Lord have mercy.

Lord Jesus, you came to earth to help us,
Christ have mercy.
Christ have mercy.

Lord Jesus, you came to earth to forgive us,
Lord have mercy.
Lord have mercy.

Ask the children to repeat **The Prayer for Forgiveness** *after you* (p. xxxvi).

OPENING	Lord Jesus,
PRAYER	Thank you for bringing us together.
	Help us to hear you today:
	In the Gospel
	In our games
	And in our hearts. *Amen.*

BEFORE THE GOSPEL

Leader   Right, I thought I'd start this morning by showing *Name* there how to tie shoe laces. Look at that!

You wonder how she/he got to church at all this morning.

Set a couple of chairs and ask the other Leader to sit down.
Pull your laces undone and proceed to give a demonstration.

Okay, the way you tie your shoelaces is like this...

Ad lib your way through it, keeping your eyes on your own shoes.
The other Leader tries very hard, gets it totally wrong and ends up with both shoes tied together.
Both of you get up.

There, now you're safe to walk around.

And of course the other Leader crashes to the ground.
Pull the Leader up.

Well, at least you've learned something today—you've learned how *not* to tie your shoes.

Turn to the children.

And today, kids, we're going to learn how *not* to walk on water. This is one of the oddest stories in the Gospels, and we're going to hear it now.

THE GOSPEL PROCESSION

THE GOSPEL *Matthew 14:22-33*

Preface the Gospel reading with:

"After Jesus had fed the 5,000..."

AFTER THE GOSPEL

Go through the story with the children. Establish that the disciples were in the middle of the lake, that the water got rough and suddenly Jesus was there, coming towards them.

Leader	How did Jesus come? Was He swimming? (**No, He walked on the water.**)
	Then what happened? (**Peter tried.**)
	I love this story, especially the Peter bit.
	You see, people often tell it as though Peter failed.
	Well, he did in a way—but at least he jumped out of the boat. I notice the other eleven stayed very carefully inside.
	For a moment Peter really was walking on water—then he sank.
	Why did that happen? (**He got frightened/he felt the wind.**) *(Accept whatever the children say.)*
	Yup, he got distracted and took his eyes off Jesus.
	Peter shows us how *not* to walk on water.
	And he shows us something else:
	When Jesus says "Come!"
	Well, go—follow Him.
	But don't get distracted because you might sink.
	It's very easy to get distracted—TV can do it, or football, or anything we're frightened of.
	The secret is to keep looking at Jesus: there He is, standing on the water, doing amazing things—He'd love us to join Him but we have to keep our eyes on Him.

You might add that the kids are never ever to attempt to walk on water unless Jesus is right there, standing in front of them. And even then check to see His ID card.

ACTIVITY

"Holy Snakes and Ladders"

CD43.1 *Print up this game as large as you can. It works best by being played as a group game.*
Divide the children into two teams, a die each, and off you go.
The two little disciples, whose fortunes you follow round the board, go up the "ladders" when they keep their attention fixed on Jesus, and slither down the "snakes" when they don't.

FINAL	God our Father,
PRAYER	Thank you for Peter.
	Help us to be as brave as he was.
	Help us to reach out to Jesus, like him, when we're in trouble,
	And help us to love you as much as he did. *Amen.*

REHEARSAL

Practice your presentation for when you go back to church.

BACK IN CHURCH

*One Leader stands at the front of the church, the children line up at the back
Another Leader reads the script.*

Leader   This morning we learned how to walk on water.
              We found that the secret is to keep our eyes on Jesus.
              Name is going to stand in for Jesus—and it goes like this...

*The children come up the aisle, hands outstretched, as though they were walking a
tightrope: they make straight for "Jesus" and stand behind him.*

              There you are—it's easier than you think.

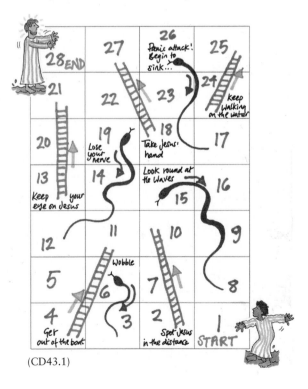

(CD43.1)

Script 44   Foreigners

Proper 15
(The Sunday Closest to August 17)

Matthew 15:21-28 plus 2 Kings 5:1-19

THEME

The Gospel today is about one of Jesus' most difficult encounters. A Canaanite woman follows Him and His disciples, demanding to be helped at the top of her voice. Jesus ignores the noise and it is not until He manages to get her to talk normally that He can reach out to help. Unfortunately their dialogue is one of those exchanges, so admired by our ancestors, of a sudden put-down and a smart reply, which nowadays comes across as simply rude. It's not easy to get children to appreciate the conversational nuances of earlier ages, but everyone can understand how Jesus helped a foreigner.

SET UP

- The liturgical color is green.
- Pictures from the CD-ROM. Doctor picture (**CD44.4**) with little plasticine or a reusable adhesive putty for "leprosy" spots (see below).

WELCOME *the children and lead them in* **The Sign of the Cross + (p. xxxvi).**

THE KYRIE   Jesus, friend of sinners, have mercy on us,
Lord have mercy.
Lord have mercy.

Jesus, healer of the sick, have mercy on us,
Christ have mercy.
Christ have mercy.

Jesus, help of Christians, have mercy on us.
Lord have mercy.
Lord have mercy.

Ask the children to repeat **The Prayer for Forgiveness** *after you* **(p. xxxvi).**

BEFORE THE OPENING PRAYER

Leader   Anyone here ever been to another country?

Go with the flow and ask if they had churches over there. Were you able to say your prayers?

Do you reckon God can hear you, even when you're not living in United States? (**yes**)

Yes, of course He can. But when Jesus was alive, people were very unsure whether God could be found in foreign countries—or even whether foreigners could pray to Him.

OPENING   God our Father,
PRAYER   Thank you for the world we live in.
Thank you for all the countries of the world,
And for all the people who live in them.
Help us to know that, wherever we go,
We will never be far from you. *Amen.*

BEFORE THE GOSPEL

Leader   Today we're going to hear a story in which Jesus went to a foreign country. He met a foreign woman there who was so desperate for help that she just yelled at Him. Jesus eventually got her to calm down and then He had a strange conversation with her. I'll stop when we get to that part so we can think about it.

THE GOSPEL PROCESSION

THE GOSPEL *Matthew 15:21-28*

Optional Paraphrase
Jesus left Palestine and went to the foreign lands along the coast. A Canaanite woman appeared from nowhere, shouting, "Sir! Son of David! Have pity on me, my daughter is being tormented by a devil."
But Jesus didn't say anything.
So His disciples pleaded with Him. "Give her what she wants," they said. "She's embarrassing us—she just goes on shouting!"
By this time the woman was kneeling at Jesus' feet.
"Listen," He said to her, "I'm supposed to be looking after the Children of Israel—you can't throw the children's food to the dogs."

Look up from the Gospel.

That's where I'm going to stop.
Because some people think that was very rude of Jesus.
But I don't think so.

Uncle Bert

You need an "Uncle Bert" story: somebody who insults you (or your team) to get you talking.
Something on the lines of:

> I remember when my Uncle Bert visited, my mother always used to ask him to stay for supper. He'd look delighted, rub his hands, and say: "Well, I'm not sure—have you learned to cook yet?"
> Mom always had a reply—and in the Gospel today the Canaanite woman had a reply too. Let's hear it.

Back to the Gospel:

> "Oh yeah?" she said. "You can't throw the children's food to the dogs, can you? Well, Lord, even the dogs can eat the children's crumbs."
> Jesus liked that answer, "Woman," He said, "you have great faith. What you wish will be done."
> And from that moment her daughter was healed.

AFTER THE GOSPEL

Leader   I think Jesus liked that woman—once she'd stoped yelling.
It's a pity we don't know her name, but we do know something about her—she wasn't a Jew. And she's in the Gospel because somebody remembered that Jesus had once helped a foreigner.
That was an important lesson to learn, because when Jesus went back to Heaven, His friends realized that they had to go to every foreign country they could think of to tell people that God loved them. Fortunately they got as far as here, which is why we're in church this morning.
There are lots of foreigners in the Bible. We're going to hear about one today. He was called Naaman.

Naaman the Leper

Read this story as freely as you can.

CD44.1   Naaman was a Syrian and the commander of the King's army—and one day he discovered he had leprosy.

Leprosy is a horrible disease that starts with sores all over your skin.

Ask a child to help you stick little bits of plasticine or a reuseable adhesive putty over Naaman's face.

CD44.2   Naaman had heard there was a famous holy man who lived in Israel, called Elijah.

Elijah was a prophet. He was very close to God and prayed to Him so often that he could sometimes guess the sort of things God was likely to do.

CD44.3   Naaman actually thought Israel was a trivial little country, but he journeyed all the way from Syria, just to see Elijah. As he was very grand he naturally came with all his chariots and horses, and his own personal servant.

Elijah felt sorry for Naaman and went away for a bit to pray. And Naaman hung around, hoping Elijah would do some magic spell—he didn't realize that God isn't really very keen on magic. He prefers you to talk to Him.

Anyway, Elijah prayed and came back and said to Naaman:

"God wants you to wash in the River Jordan seven times."

Naaman was furious. He hadn't come all this way to wash in a stupid Jewish river. He said: "We've got perfectly good rivers in Syria. Abana and Pharpar are better than all the rivers of Israel." And he went off in a huff.

But his servant said to him: "Sir, if the Holy Man had asked you to do something difficult, you would have done it; why *not* wash in the Jordan?"

CD44.4   So Naaman washed in the Jordan and, as he did so, his skin became as clear as a little child's—*(take off the spots)*.

The leprosy had disappeared. Naaman rushed back to Elijah to thank him.

"From now on," he said, "I'm going to pray to the God of the Jews."

"That's a VERY good idea," said Elijah.

ACTIVITY

There's been a lot of talking in today's session. I suggest you end with a game. Here are a couple of foreign games the kids may like.

Commander (from Taiwan)

One child is the Commander. He turns his back and counts one, two, three (as much as he likes) as everyone moves closer. The moment he finishes counting he turns and everyone freezes—one wobble and they're out. The aim is to get to the Commander and touch him.

Ice tag (from France)

One person is "it" and runs after the others. If they touch someone that person freezes. The frozen kid stands with its feet apart, and can't be unfrozen until another crawls through their legs. Play continues until everyone is frozen. The last person to be caught becomes "it" next time round.

FINAL PRAYER

See if you can manage a traditional prayer in a foreign language, for example:

+ The Sign of the Cross

Italian	+ Nel nome del Padre e del Figlio e dello Spirito Santo. *Amen.*
French	+ Au nom du Père, et du Fils, et du Saint-Esprit. *Amen.*
Latin	+ In nomine Patris et Filii et Spiritus Sancti. *Amen.*
German	+ Im Namen des Vaters und des Sohnes und des Heiligen Geistes. *Amen.*

BACK IN CHURCH

Leader	Today we heard how Jesus helped a foreign woman.
	We realized that God likes us to get along with each other.
	So we thought we'd pray to God in a foreign language.

*Then you, or some talented children say + **The Sign of the Cross** in whatever language you choose. The non linguists cross themselves.*

Script 45 Peter's Keys

Proper 16
(The Sunday Closest to August 24)

Matthew 16:13-17

THEME

Everybody likes keys, particularly when they're used for opening, rather than slamming something shut. When Jesus gave Peter the Power of the Keys He was drawing on a long Jewish tradition of priests and prophets locking and unlocking the Gates of Heaven. (But He was not impressed with the Pharisees for using this power to keep people out, see Matthew 23:13.)

So Peter, after his astonishing acclamation of Jesus as the Messiah, is given the Keys of the Gates of Heaven—with the strong implication that he (and the Church) will use them to open those gates and let people in.

SET UP

- The liturgical color is Green.
- Keys! Particularly old-fashioned ones. Can you get your hands on a very large key? Does your church door have one?
- Bring in anything you can open with a key—a padlock, a box, anything the kids could turn.
- Picture of Peter from the CD-ROM, or from an art book (he's normally got his keys somewhere to show who he is), or from the internet: searching on Peter Keys gives a good range of images.
- Picture of Heaven's gate and Peter from the CD-ROM—put the gate over Peter, so you can apparently open the gate and show him behind.
- Picture of a jailer or "turnkey" from the CD-ROM.
- Worksheet from the CD-ROM.

WELCOME *the children and lead them in* **The Sign of the Cross +** (p. xxxvi).

Leader	Today we're going to say a short Kyrie where all three prayers are said to Jesus—I'd like you to think about what we call Him in this prayer.

THE KYRIE   *Lord* have mercy.
Lord have mercy.

Christ have mercy.
Christ have mercy.

Lord have mercy.
Lord have mercy.

Ask the children to repeat **The Prayer for Forgiveness** *after you* (**p. xxxvi**).

BEFORE THE GOSPEL

Leader   What do we call Jesus? (**Lord, Christ**)
Those are big names.
When Jesus was alive on earth, a Roman Emperor was called "Lord"—not unimportant Jews like Jesus.
And "Christ" is even bigger—it's the Greek word for "Messiah."
The Messiah was the great hero that God was going to send to save the Jewish people. All the Jews were watching out for him.
Jesus' friends didn't call Him "Lord" or "Christ," they called Him "Teacher."
But one day everything changed.

THE GOSPEL PROCESSION

THE GOSPEL *Matthew 16:13-17*

Change the first verse to read.

Jesus went to the country round Caesarea Philippi and asked His disciples, "Who do people say I am?"

AFTER THE GOSPEL

Leader   Jesus asked His disciples, "Who do people say I am?"

Have the Bible on hand and be just as baffled as the children if they don't remember— look it up.

And the disciples said... ? (**John the Baptist back from the dead, Elijah, Jeremiah, a prophet**)
"Ah," said Jesus, "but who do *you* think I am?"
That's when He got a surprise, because Simon Peter said: "You are the Christ, the Messiah."

Jesus was so impressed with that answer that He gave Simon a new name—Peter—"Petrus" means rock in Latin—it was like calling him Rocky.

He said to Peter, "You are Peter the Rock, and on this rock I shall build my Church, and I shall give you the Keys of Heaven."

CD45.1   *Picture of Peter—point out the keys.*

Most paintings of Peter have his keys in somewhere.
Let's think about those keys.

Keys

Produce your keys.

I like keys—especially big ones.

Go through them.

Of course nowadays you can use swipe cards to open things, or you can click a car remote key—but nothing beats opening something with a key.

If you've got something the children could open, let them try now.

The trouble is, you can also close things with a key.
Think of a man in a dungeon as the door slams shut.

(Any key stories?)

I remember getting to a hotel, late at night, deep in the mountains, and hearing them getting ready to close—the door was shut, the bolts were rattling across, a great big key went clunk! in the lock. I hammered at the door and fortunately they let me in. Phew!

CD45.2   The old-fashioned name for a jailer was a "turnkey."

Now Jesus felt that some of the priests and religious people He knew were a bit like turnkeys: God had entrusted them with the Keys to Heaven, by teaching them the Jewish faith, but they used them to lock people out.

"You're not good enough for Heaven," they'd say—Slam! Clunk!

CD45.3   But Peter was given the Keys to let people in.

CD45.4   *Open up Heaven's Gate—there he is.*

ACTIVITY

CD45.5   *Hand out the worksheet in which the kids match keys to the things they open.*

FINAL PRAYER	We'll end by asking Peter for his prayers.

                      (*The response is:* **Pray for us**)

                      Holy Peter, Friend of Jesus,
                      Pray for us
                      Holy Peter, Key bearer,
                      Pray for us
                      Holy Peter, Rock of the Church,
                      Pray for us
                      Holy Peter, Head of the Church,
                      Pray for us
                      Lord Jesus,
                      Thank you for Peter.
                      Help us, like him, to hail you as the Messiah. *Amen.*

BACK IN CHURCH

Take in the Kingdom of Heaven picture.

Leader	Today we thought about keys.
	Some keys are used to shut doors...

Hold up the shut gate.

                      But Peter was given the Keys to Heaven...

Open the gate.

                      ...to open the Gate of Heaven—for everyone.

(CD45.2)

(CD45.3)

(CD45.4)

Sample cartoons for this script

Script 46   Take Up Your Cross

Proper 17
(The Sunday Closest to August 31)

Matthew 16:21-25

THEME

Being a Christian can be difficult and this Gospel suggests that Jesus found His vocation difficult too. Peter's well-meant suggestion that He should duck out of the suffering ahead is stopped in its tracks. "Don't go there!"
Without being too harrowing, this session suggests there are difficult moments ahead for all of us.

SET UP

- The liturgical color is Green.
- Flash cards which say:
  - Playing football
  - Doing homework
  - Watching TV
  - Going to church
  - Saying prayers
  - Chilling out
  - Being nice to your brother
  - Cleaning your bedroom
- Poster board or newsprint.
- Two cardboard boxes labelled "Easy" and "Difficult."
- Pictures from the CD-ROM.
- A crucifix or cross.

LEAVING CHURCH TO START THIS SESSION

Make sure that, whatever you do on other Sundays, the children process out of church behind the Gospel Book.

WELCOME *the children and lead them in* **The Sign of the Cross +** (p. xxxvi).

THE KYRIE   Lord, for the times we have forgotten to love you,
Lord have mercy.
Lord have mercy.

Jesus, for the times we have forgotten to love others,
Christ have mercy.
Christ have mercy.

Lord, we thank you for never forgetting to love us,
Lord have mercy.
Lord have mercy.

Ask the children to repeat **The Prayer for Forgiveness** *after you* (**p. xxxvi**).

BEFORE THE GOSPEL

Leader   Last week we heard how Peter realized who Jesus was—the Messiah.
The hero God was going to send to save Israel.
What Peter didn't realize was how tough it was to be the Messiah.
Jesus had to tell him—let's see how he reacted.

THE GOSPEL PROCESSION

THE GOSPEL *Matthew 16:21-25*

AFTER THE GOSPEL

Leader   So Jesus told His friends that being the Messiah meant He'd have to go to Jerusalem and suffer and be put to death.
What did Peter think of that? (**He didn't like it, he told Jesus not to do it**)
And what did Jesus say? (**"Get behind me, Satan!"**)
That's pretty fierce.
Why would Jesus say that?
Let's think about it. Look, here's some of the things we do—and here's a couple of boxes.

Produce flash cards and the two boxes.

    Right, which things are easy and which are difficult?

Ask the kids to put the cards in the relevant boxes (there might be some cross-overs).

Now let's think about Jesus, He had easy and difficult things to do as well.

*Show the pictures (**CD46.1–46.6**)—Jesus blessing children, healing people, being with His friends, being rejected, betrayed, carrying the Cross.*
Talk through the pictures with the kids:

It all ended with this...

Show the children a crucifix.

No wonder Peter was horrified.
And I don't suppose Jesus liked the idea much.
It's a tough thing to face suffering.
You need your friends.
And what you don't need is your friends telling you not to do it.
Jesus had to tell Peter to stop right there.

ACTIVITY

As this is quite a short session I've not colored in the pictures of Jesus. The children could do so, or better still make their own, and paste them horizontally along some newsprint. Get them in sequence: Jesus goes from the pleasant side of His Ministry to the difficult.

FINAL PRAYER

Form a prayer circle.
Place a large candle in the middle.
Pass the crucifix round as you say something on the lines of:

Jesus was the Messiah.
He realized that part of the Messiah's job was to die for His people.
So that's what He did.
And He warned us that, if He suffered, so would we.
BUT
Just like Him—
We'd get through our sufferings and come out the other side.

Light the candle.

Lord Jesus,
Light of the World,
Help us to take up our cross and follow you
Through this world and
All the way to Heaven. *Amen.*

SONG

Given the rather solemn theme it would be good to end with a song. "Take up thy Cross" (omitting verse 3) is an obvious one, but John Bunyan's great hymn "He who would valiant be" is more upbeat.

Exit

Give the "Back in Church" script on a slip of paper to each of your three readers (see below).
Line up behind the cross or crucifix and go back to church.

BACK IN CHURCH

The children process into church behind the cross or crucifix.

Child 1	At the start of the service we all processed out of church behind the Gospel.
Child 2	But we've come back behind the Cross.
Child 3	That's because, in the Gospel today, Jesus told us to "take up our cross and follow Him."

(CD46.1)

(CD46.2)

(CD46.3)

(CD46.4)

(CD46.5)

(CD46.6)

Cartoons for this script

Script 47   Time Out

Proper 18
(The Sunday Closest to September 7)

Matthew 18:15-17, 20

THEME

This Gospel gathers up some of the scattered sayings of Jesus: one about how to deal with an "erring brother" (i.e. a fellow Christian who's wronged you), and a famous one that assures us that even when there are only two or three Christians gathered together, Jesus is in the midst of them.

Children usually need no encouragement to rebuke their brothers or sisters so this session presents the saying from the sinner's point of view.

SET UP

- The liturgical color is Green.
- Pictures from the CD-ROM.
- Box with lid and slit in the top, labelled "Prayer Box."
- Slips of paper for prayers.

WELCOME *the children and lead them in* **The Sign of the Cross +** (**p. xxxvi**).

THE KYRIE   Lord, for the times we have forgotten to love you,
Lord have mercy.
Lord have mercy.

Jesus, for the times we have forgotten to love others,
Christ have mercy.
Christ have mercy.

Lord, we thank you for never forgetting to love us,
Lord have mercy.
Lord have mercy.

Ask the children to repeat **The Prayer for Forgiveness** *after you* (**p. xxxvi**).

OPENING	God our Father,
PRAYER	Thank you for bringing us here this morning.
	Thank you for the family of the Church.
	Help us to love one another
	And forgive one another
	Just as you love and forgive us. *Amen.*

BEFORE THE GOSPEL

Leader	In our prayer just now we thanked God for our family the Church.
	Let's just think about families.
	Anybody here got any little brothers and sisters?
	What are they like?

Take all answers.

What about big brothers and sisters? I imagine they're pretty super?

Take all answers—the question, as you'll have guessed, is designed to provoke an "Oh no they're not!" from some of the children.

I think brothers and sisters are difficult.
Obviously we're glad they're around—but they can be a bit irritating sometimes.
That's fine, Jesus' family sometimes found Him a bit odd.
He knew we'd have arguments, and He told us how to handle them.
Before we listen to the Gospel today I thought I'd introduce you to the all-time worst Little Brother.
His name was Charlie, but his family usually called him The Pest.

Pull out the pictures and go through Charlie's appalling career.

CD47.1	When Charlie was a baby he used his milk bottle as a water pistol.
CD47.2	When he was a toddler he shoved cookies into the DVD player.
CD47.3	When he was a little boy he zapped his brother's Gameboy, just as he'd got up to level a million in his Galaxy Blaster game.
CD47.4	When he went to school he poured syrup into the piano.
CD47.5	And when he grew up he became a professional soccer player—and in his very first match he got a yellow card and had to go and sit in the penalty box.
	Sitting in the penalty box was actually quite helpful, he had time to think about what a nuisance he was and how he could try and behave better.
	Jesus seems to have thought that having a moment of Time Out could be useful for irritating grown-up Christians as well. We'll hear that now.

THE GOSPEL PROCESSION

THE GOSPEL *Matthew 18:15-17*

Jesus said to His disciples: "If your brother does something wrong, go and have it out with him. But do it privately, just between your two selves. If he listens to you, you've won him back."
"But if he won't listen, talk it through with him and a couple of other people."
"If he still won't listen, tell the whole Church."
"And if he won't listen to the Church, treat him as if he weren't a member of the Church at all."

AFTER THE GOSPEL

Leader   "Treat him as if he weren't a member of the Church at all."
             That's a bit tough.
             But it would probably work.
             People sometimes need to have space, to sit alone in a pew for a moment and think about what's gone wrong.
             Especially as we all know that God, and the Church, will always welcome people back with open arms. Nobody stays in the penalty box for ever.
             Just after He said this Jesus went on to say, "Even if only two or three people gather together in my Name, I'll be right there with them."
             Well, there are more than two or three people here today. It's good to know Jesus is here among us and—with His help—I think we'll put together some prayers for people who are feeling angry or lonely or unhappy.

ACTIVITY

With the children's help write out some prayer slips for people like:

             The lonely.
             People who've stopped coming to church.
             People who don't know about Jesus.
             People everybody is angry with.
             People we don't like.
             The unhappy.

Post them in your Prayer Box.
Stop for a moment.

Do we know anybody like this ourselves?

Do *we* feel unhappy sometimes?

FINAL   I'm going to hand the box around and, as you get it, say the name of
PRAYER   somebody you want God to help.

It can be anyone: you, or a friend, or somebody you've heard of.

Say it to yourself—only God needs to hear.

Pass the Prayer Box around.
Hold up the Prayer Box.

Let us offer these prayers up to God in the words that Jesus taught us:

Our Father... (p. xxxvi)

BACK IN CHURCH

The children bring the Prayer Box back into church and one of them offers it to the priest.
If you're back in time for the Offertory it can be put in front of the altar and be part of the whole offering of prayer for the church. If you come back later in the service ask the priest to offer the Box of Prayers to God at some point during the week.
Take your cue from the priest.

(CD47.1)   (CD47.2)   (CD47.3)

(CD47.4)   (CD47.5)   *Cartoons for this script*

Script 48   The Ungrateful Servant

Proper 19
(The Sunday Closest to September 14)

Matthew 18:21-35

THEME

God forgives us over and over again and He wants us to forgive other people in return.

SET UP

- The liturgical color is Green.
- Two Leaders who have read the script beforehand.
- A child to help with the mini-drama.
- Mock up two large checks (poster board), one for $1,000 and the other for 50¢.

WELCOME *the children and lead them in* **The Sign of the Cross + (p. xxxvi).**

INTRODUCTION

Leader	Today we are going to think about what happens when we say sorry. When do we say sorry? (**When we do something wrong**)
	Supposing we were goofing around at dinner and spilled our soup all over the table—what would we say to Mom or Dad? (**Sorry**)
	Supposing we broke another kid's toy, what would we say to that kid? (**Sorry**)
	Supposing we mess around in church and don't say our prayers properly, what do we say to God? (**Sorry**)
	And what does Mom or Dad, or the other kid, or God say?

This is a rhetorical question—don't wait for an answer.

	They say, "Oh, that's all right."
	That means they have **forgiven** you—they're not mad, and everything is okay.

But supposing somebody does something awful to you? Perhaps a kid smashes *your* toy, or your baby brother scribbles on one of your books?

What happens then? (**They say, "Sorry."**)

And what do you do? (**You say, "That's okay."**)

You **forgive** them.

God is very keen on forgiveness. He will always forgive you when you do something wrong—and He expects you to forgive other people in return.

Let us ask God for His forgiveness now in the **Kyrie**.

THE KYRIE   God our Father,
We are sorry for all the things we have done wrong this week,
Lord have mercy.
Lord have mercy.

Lord Jesus,
We thank you for forgiving us every time we say we are sorry,
Christ have mercy.
Christ have mercy.

Holy Spirit,
Help us to forgive other people when they do wrong to us,
Lord have mercy.
Lord have mercy.

Ask the children to repeat **The Prayer for Forgiveness** *after you* (**p. xxxvi**).

OPENING PRAYER

Ask the children to join you in the **Our Father...** (**p. xxxvi**).
If you have a set of Our Father cards (see **p. xxiv**) *use these.*
Whether you have cards or not focus on:

"And forgive us our trespasses, as we forgive those who trespass against us."

What *are* trespasses? (**Things that we do wrong**)

Okay, so in this bit of the Our Father we ask God to forgive us the wrong things we do, just as we forgive other people when they wrong us.

We're going to think about that today.

BEFORE THE GOSPEL

Set up the following dialogue between two Leaders and a willing child. You can see the plot follows the parable—keep it light, lots of backchat.
Leader 1 approaches Leader 2 for a loan.

Leader 1	Listen, I need a loan of a thousand dollars.
Leader 2	What for?
Leader 1	Oh, a car—*(make it something extravagant).*
Leader 2	*(deliberates)*—Hmm, well, I'll need the money back in a month. Oh, all right.

Leader 2 puts Leader 1's name on the check for $1,000 and hands it over.
A kid then asks Leader 1 for 50¢ for a comic: Leader 1 makes a huge song and dance about it.

Leader 1	50¢! What a huge amount!
	What do you want with 50¢?
	A comic? Why don't you read a book?
	You'll have to take a check.

He writes the kid's name on the 50¢ check and hands it over—very reluctantly.

Leader 1	Well, I got my car and I had a super time driving around—then after a month, *Name* over there asked for her money back!

Leader 1 goes into cringe mode.

Leader 1	Listen, give me a week—I know I can pay it back then.
Leader 2	Okay, pay the money when you can.
Leader 1	Hmm, I need all the money I can get—
	where's that kid?!

He grabs the kid.

	Oi! Where's my 50¢?
Kid	I haven't got it.
Leader 1	Right! it's prison for you...

Stop the dialogue.

Leader 2	Do you think that's fair?

Take the answers but don't comment.

Jesus told a story like this once. Let's hear what *He* thought.

THE GOSPEL PROCESSION

THE GOSPEL *Matthew 18:21-35*

Use the same amounts of money that you used in your dialogue.

AFTER THE GOSPEL

Talk through the story:

Leader 2	What did the King eventually do to the man who owed him money? **(He threw him into jail)**
	Why? I thought the King was going to let him off? **(Because he wouldn't let off the man who owed him 50¢)**
	Let's look at the "Our Father" again,
	"Forgive us our trespasses as we forgive those who trespass against us."
	Jesus is telling us something about God.
	God will forgive us if we do something in return—what is it? **(If we forgive other people)**
	I think I'll let *Name* off paying me back that $1,000.
Leader 1	*(deep sigh)* So I suppose I'll have to let *Name* off that 50¢.
Leader 2	Did you hear the joke at the beginning of the Gospel?
	Peter asked Jesus how many times we should forgive somebody. Seven times?
	"*Seven* times!?" said Jesus, "70 times 7!"
	How many times is that? *(Some bright spark will work it out)* **(490)**
	Do you think God really counts up?
	No, He forgives us over and over again—and we must do the same. That is one of the reasons why Christians always shake hands in church before they go up to the altar. Shaking hands shows that we are trying to get along with each other.

Ask the children to stand.

FINAL PRAYER	**The Peace**
	Our Lord Jesus Christ asked us to love and forgive each other. Let us show we mean to do this by giving each other the Sign of Peace:
	Peace be with you. **And also with you.**

Everybody shakes hands with their neighbor as they say the Peace.

Lord God,
We thank you for always being ready to forgive us.
Help us to copy you this week and forgive others. *Amen.*

SONG

The hymn "God forgave my sin in Jesus' Name" *works very well here.*

BACK IN CHURCH

Leader 2   Today I gave *Name* a check for $1,000.

Leader 1 holds it up.

                    And *Name* gave *Name* another check for 50¢.

The child holds up their check.

                    Then it came to paying it back.
                    (Ad lib) That caused a bit of unpleasantness...
                    But, after we read the Gospel, I decided to forgive *Name* his debt.

Leader 2 tears up the $1,000 check.

Leader 1   *(Rather fed up)* So I realized that I'd better forgive *Name* his debt.

Leader 1 tears up the 50¢ check.
Leader 1 then turns to the kid.

                    Why did we do that?

Child   Because God likes us to forgive other people, just as He forgives us.

Script 49   The Laborers in the Vineyard

Proper 20
(The Sunday Closest to September 21)

Matthew 20:1-6

THEME

Children think this story is deeply unfair. It probably does them no harm to find the Gospel difficult once in a while, but obviously we have to help them get a grip on its meaning. In this session we concentrate on the generosity of God.

SET UP

- The liturgical color is Green.
- You'll need gold chocolate coins for everyone. Little medals cut out of gold paper are just as good—if you've got time to make them.
- You'll need a clear space for the children to run a race.
- If you meet in a confined space, bring along three nerf balls (see below).
- Set up some other adults, or big kids, to help you with the couple of dialogues below. Run through them before the session, they're very short.

WELCOME *the children and lead them in* **The Sign of the Cross + (p. xxxvi).**

Given the nature of the session, it might not be a bad idea to remind the kids that we don't always behave quite fairly or kindly and that this is a good moment to say sorry—in the confident knowledge that God will forgive us.

THE KYRIE   Lord Jesus, you came down from Heaven to tell us how much God loves us,
        Lord have mercy.
        Lord have mercy.

        Lord Jesus, you came down from Heaven and gave up your life for us,
        Christ have mercy.
        Christ have mercy.

Lord Jesus, You came down from Heaven to tell us that God will
    always forgive those who say they are sorry,
Lord have mercy.
Lord have mercy.

Ask the children to repeat **The Prayer for Forgiveness** *after you* (**p. xxxvi**).

BEFORE THE OPENING PRAYER

This is for use as long as the children are able-bodied, if there are disabled children in the group go on to the following section.

Leader   Has anybody had a birthday—did you get presents?
                  Can you remember what you got?

Continue this with a couple of kids and establish they got different presents.

On the day we were born, God gave us a load of presents. I'm going
to tell you what they were; point them out to me if you've got them.

Do this yourself as you go through the list.

Two eyes... two ears... a nose... a mouth... a heart... two hands and a
pair of legs.

If there are disabled children present then talk about some other gifts God has given us.

The sun... the earth... trees... water... and people to love us.
We all got the same presents.
God gives His children the same things whether they're big or small,
or good or bad. Everyone gets the same.
That's because God knows what we *need*.

OPENING   God our Father,
PRAYER   We thank you for making us
               and for giving us everything we need.
               Help us to be as loving and generous as you,
               Through Jesus Christ, our Lord. *Amen.*

BEFORE THE GOSPEL

The Olympic Games

Introduce the Olympics and attach the name of your town to them—the "Acton" Olympics for example.
Clear the floor.

Arrange the kids into three teams and appoint three leaders.
Set up a relay race and run it.
(In a confined space, put the teams in three lines and get them to pass a nerf ball rapidly between each other. If they drop it, they have to start again.)
Establish who came 1st, 2nd and 3rd.
Get the kids lined up in their teams and demand absolute quiet for the medal ceremony.
Start with the 3rds.

Leader   Right here's the leader of the 3rd team, you did really well, and here's one gold coin each!

Dish them out and encourage applause.
Exactly the same for the 2nds; then for the 1sts really build it up.

And the people who came first! A brilliant race. Step forward all of you, we have a prize for you as well. Yes! IT'S A GOLD COIN EACH!

Applause
Review the teams

So, we have this team who came third, hold up your prizes.
And this team who came second, hold up your prizes.
And lastly this fantastic team who came first, hold up your prizes.
Do you think that's fair? (**NO!**)
Well, once Jesus also told a story that some people thought was deeply unfair too.
Let's hear it.

THE GOSPEL PROCESSION

THE GOSPEL *Matthew 20:1-6*

This needs to be read very freely, change the "denarius" into "dollars," and the times into "9 o'clock," "lunch time" and so on.

AFTER THE GOSPEL

Go swiftly through the story.

Leader   So the man who owned the vineyard gave all the people who had been working for him their wages.
How much did he pay the people who had been working all day? (**A dollar**)

How much did he pay the people who started work in the afternoon? (**a dollar**)

How much did he pay the people who only worked in the evening? (**a dollar**)

Do you think that's fair? (**No!**)

And yet Jesus tells us that God is like that. It's something we need to think about.

Let's look at these two people.

Pull a couple of grown-ups or older children forward.

	This one has been working hard all day.
	What have you been doing?
1st person	*(Ad lib something:)* Well, I got up at 6 a.m., washed the car, fed the cat, cleaned the house, took the kids to school, went to work, made the supper, etc., etc.
Leader	Are you hungry?
1st person	I certainly am.
Leader	Well, here's $10.00 for a McDonald's...
	Now *this* shady character doesn't look as if she's been doing a thing. What *have* you been doing?
2nd person	*(Ad lib:)* Oh, well I slept late, had a cup of coffee, watched some daytime TV, played around on Facebook, then I went back to bed.
Leader	Disgraceful! Are *you* hungry too?
2nd person	Yup.
Leader	Okay, well, here's $10.00 for a McDonald's.

Sum up

Leader	You see, *Name* doesn't **deserve** any money, but she still **needs** her dinner.
	In the story we just heard, Jesus is telling us that God gives us what we *need*, even if we don't deserve it.
	It might not be **fair** to give people what they don't deserve, but it's very kind.
	God is **generous**.
	And that's a huge bit of luck for us!

FINAL	God our Father,
PRAYER	Thank you for your kindness to us
	And for your generosity.
	In the week ahead,
	Help us to share
	Help us to give
	Help us to be as generous as you,
	For Jesus Christ's sake. *Amen.*

BACK IN CHURCH

Line up the team leaders with their medals (or coins or whatever you've used).
Start with the 3rds.

Leader	So you led a team in the *Name* Olympics? (**yes**)
	Where did you come? (**3rd**)
	And what did you get? (**gold medal/coin**)

Make sure he/she shows it.
Same with the next two leaders.

To start with we weren't convinced this was completely fair, but we realized—after we'd read the Gospel—that God is not always bothered about giving people what they deserve, He gives them what they need.

We think that's a bit of luck for us...

Script 50 The Two Sons

Proper 21
(The Sunday Closest to September 28)

Matthew 21:28-32

THEME

This story was originally told by Jesus to warn the religious types of His day that they couldn't afford to be complacent: they might say they were serving God, but all sorts of sinful people were serving Him much better. However, this session skips the Pharisee versus Sinners debate and homes in on the basic moral: it's not what you say, but what you do, that counts.

SET UP

- The liturgical color is Green.
- Collection basket.
- A list of Qs (see below) written up on the board.
- Two grown-ups prepared to play in the mini-drama.

WELCOME *the children and lead them in* **The Sign of the Cross + (p. xxxvi).**

THE KYRIE   Lord Jesus, you came from Heaven to tell us how much God loves us,
Lord have mercy.
Lord have mercy.

Lord Jesus, you came from Heaven and gave up your life for us,
Christ have mercy.
Christ have mercy.

Lord Jesus, you came from Heaven to tell us that God will always forgive those who say they are sorry,
Lord have mercy.
Lord have mercy.

Ask the children to repeat **The Prayer for Forgiveness** *after you* (p. xxxvi).

OPENING	Jesus said,
PRAYER	"If anyone loves me they will keep my word,
	And my Father will love them."

Lord,
Help us this morning to hear your word
And keep it. *Amen.*

BEFORE THE GOSPEL

Leader	Today we're going to go for the land-speed record in children's worship.
	I guess we can get it down to 2 minutes flat.
	Let's try.
	We'll practice first.

*Point to each Q on the list, bring the kids in with a downward movement of the hand,
then do the "kill it" sign (a finger across the throat) to cut it dead.
The first Q is ROAR.
This is just any horrible noise made by the kids—the classic "blah, blah, blah" will
do, as long as they make it loud. Practice bringing them in on a Q, and killing it.
Then Q them to CROSS themselves quickly.
Say ALLELUIA at speed.
RUN on the spot.
SIT up straight with their arms folded.
Now do it faster.*

Leader 1	Okay, we're ready to begin.
	One day *Name—(your priest)—*asked for helpers for Children's Church.
	He told the congregation what a nice bunch of kids we had and asked people to come forward.
	One person—*(enter Leader 2)*—came forward at once. He said,
Leader 2	*(Ad lib something)* I should love to help—I *love* little children.
Leader 1	*Name* was deeply impressed and shook him warmly by the hand.
	But we still needed one more—so *Name* grabbed another person.

Grab another grown-up yourself.

	"Would you like to do children's liturgy?" he asked.
Leader 3	*(Ad lib something)* What me?! Certainly not—they are nothing but a bunch of raving little monsters!

Leader 1   The next Sunday the first person turned up for Children's Church, took one look at the kids...

Q ROAR and cut.

And hid behind the altar—*(he does so)*
But a few minutes later the second person came in. She looked at the kids...

Leader 3   Yuk, they give me a pain... but I suppose I'd better do it.
Leader 1   And she took Children's Church.

(All this is done at high speed.)

She took a collection—*(pour some money into a basket and put it on the altar)*
She prayed with the kids...

Q Sign of the + cut.

She sang with the kids...

Q ALLELUIA cut.

They did an activity together...

Q RUN cut.

And she read them the Gospel...

Q SIT cut.

At the end she was totally exhausted and looked round for the other helper. But he had gone and... *(his hand comes over the top of the altar)*...so had the collection.

The two stand forward.

Now which of these two had done what *Name* had asked?

Take answers, but don't comment.

Let's hear what Jesus has to say.

THE GOSPEL PROCESSION

THE GOSPEL *Matthew 21:28-31a*

(Down to Jesus' question...)

AFTER THE GOSPEL

Leader   So which of the boys did his father's will? (**The first one**)
Really? I thought he said "No!" (**Yes, but he went and worked all the same**)
Absolutely.

Jesus is telling us it isn't what you *say* that matters—it's what you *do.*

REHEARSAL

Split the group into Leaders (spare grown-ups and any older children who don't mind being villains) and all the rest of the children.
Practice the presentation below for when you go back to church.

FINAL	Let's try to do good things this week.
PRAYER	There's a lovely prayer by St. Teresa about using our hands and feet to do God's will. We'll say it now:

Christ has no body now on earth but ours,
No hands but ours,
No feet but ours,
Ours are the feet by which He is to go about doing good,
And ours are the hands by which He can bless the world. *Amen.*

End with a **Glory Be... (p. xxxvii).**

SONG

"Brother Let Be Be Your Servant" *is a useful song to finish with.*

BACK IN CHURCH

Line up in the two groups

Leader	Today I asked some people to help me with the presentation back in church. This group *(the villains)* said...
Villains	No problem!
Leader	Then they all disappeared.

The first group sit down abruptly.

	Then I asked the children to give me a hand, they said . . .
Kids	No way!
Leader	But they obviously changed their minds—because here they are.

The children stand round the Leader.

	Can one of you pass on what Jesus told us in the Gospel today?
A child from group 2	Jesus told us that it's not what you *say* but what you *do* that matters.

Script 51   The Farmer and his Tenants

Proper 22
(The Sunday Closest to October 5)

Matthew 21:33-43

THEME

It's a tough story today: listen up or God will move on. Jesus seems to have intended it as a warning to his fellow Jews—wake up, or you'll find the Messiah dead and disaster staring you in the face. Of course when He told the story it hadn't happened, but Christians can't help shuddering at what He foresaw.

Even so, be careful with the fierce language. The story is a wake-up call. It doesn't mean that God will actually reject a sinner, when it comes down to it. (Look at the difference between Jesus' solemn warning to Judas not to betray Him, and the way He calls him "friend" when he actually does it.)

SET UP

- The liturgical color is Green.
- Pictures from the CD-ROM.

WELCOME *the children and lead them in* **The Sign of the Cross + (p. xxxvi).**

Do a refresher course on the **Kyrie.**

Leader	This is one of the oldest prayers and comes from a time when most Christians spoke Greek.
	"Kurios" means "Lord" in Greek and saying "Jesus is Lord" was the very first creed. So the prayer that called Jesus "Kurios" really stuck.
	"Kyrie eleison" means "Lord have mercy."
	How good at Greek are you?
	What do you think "Christe eleison" means? (**Christ have mercy.**)
	Brilliant!
	All three prayers in the Kyrie can be seen as being addressed to Jesus.
	Two call Him "Lord', one calls Him "Christ."
	Let's do it in English, Greek and back to English.

THE KYRIE   Lord have mercy.
Lord have mercy.

Christ have mercy.
Christ have mercy.

Lord have mercy.
Lord have mercy.

Kyrie eleison.
Kyrie eleison.

Christe eleison.
Christe eleison.

Kyrie eleison.
Kyrie eleison.

Lord have mercy.
Lord have mercy.

Christ have mercy.
Christ have mercy.

Lord have mercy.
Lord have mercy.

Useful Knowledge

Leader   So the Kyrie was one of the first prayers a Christian learned.
Christians, and children, spend a lot of their lives learning things.
Raise your hands, those of you that go to school.
I thought so. I bet you guys know a fair amount already.
How many of you know the five times table?
Really? Okay, I'll test you—what's 2 x 5? **(10)**
Impressive—let's try something harder...

Do anything that seems feasible—telling the time, planets in the solar system, making the Sign of the Cross. No pop culture—keep to the sort of things kids learn from grown-ups.

But how do we *know* all this? Did we know it when we were babies?
(No—somebody taught it to us)
Quite so, we were taught: that's how we know most things.

OPENING	God our Father,
PRAYER	Thank you for the people who teach us:
	Our parents,
	Our teachers,
	The people who write our books.
	Most of all we thank you for sending us your Son
	Who came to tell us how much you love us. *Amen.*

BEFORE THE GOSPEL

Session with Old Testament pictures showing how God taught the Jews

Leader	Today we're going to think about learning about God.
	Most people have a vague idea about God, but to understand Him
	more, you have to be taught.
	So, right from the word go,
CD51.1	God taught His chosen people, the Jews. He did this by giving them
CD51.2	the Law...
	The Jews still think that that's the most precious thing He gave them.
	Then He sent them prophets.

Put up their pictures as you mention them.

CD51.3	Like Moses.
CD51.4	And Elijah.
CD51.5	And a mega prophet, John the Baptist.
	But some of the Jews wouldn't listen—they laughed at the prophets,
	or they put them in prison, they even killed a few of them.
CD51.6	So God decided to send His Son.
	And it's at that moment everybody behaved badly.
	The Romans, the Jewish priests, the people in the street, practically
	everyone rejected Jesus and killed Him.
	Jesus once told a story about that.

THE GOSPEL PROCESSION

THE GOSPEL *Matthew 21:33-43*

Leave out the "cornerstone" verse.
*Use the New Testament pictures (**CD51.7–CD51.11**) as you read the story:*
The Farmer.
The Vineyard.
The Tenants.
The Messengers.

The Farmer's Son.

AFTER THE GOSPEL

Leader   This sort of story is called an "allegory," that means that all the
                    people in the story stand for something.
                    The Farmer stands for God,
                    And the Vineyard stands for something very precious—the
                    knowledge that God gave His people.
                    Who do you think the tenants stand for? (**the Jews**)
                    And the messengers? (**the prophets**)
                    And the Farmer's Son? (**Jesus**)

Get the kids to pair the Old Testament pictures with the New Testament ones.

Sum up

Leader   So the story Jesus tells isn't about a farmer and a vineyard at all.
                    It's about God giving something very precious to His people:
                    the Law, and the Prophets and (eventually) His Son.
                    But, as they didn't listen, Jesus says that God will move on.
                    He'll turn to the Gentiles (that's us!).
                    And that's what God did.
                    Of course God still loves the Jews, but He's called us to be His chosen
                    people as well.
                    And He's sent us saints like Paul to tell us about Jesus,
                    And He's given us the Bible,
                    And the Church.
                    But we can't mess around.
                    We have to listen to God, learn about Him and pass it on to other
                    people.
                    Because if we don't, what do you think God will do?
                    He might try somebody else!

FINAL   *Ask the children to repeat after you:*
PRAYER   **Lord God,**
                    Help us to learn about you.
                    Help us to tell other people about you.
                    Through your Son, Jesus Christ. Amen

BACK IN CHURCH

Three children come to the front with a Bible, a picture of a prophet, and a picture of Jesus. They hold them up as they are mentioned.

Leader   Today we learned that God has sent us the prophets—

Hold up picture.

                And the Bible—

Hold up Bible.

                And His Son Jesus—

Hold up picture.

                So we can learn about Him—and pass it on.

(CD51.2)   (CD51.3)   (CD51.4)

(CD51.5)   (CD51.6)   (CD51.7)

Sample cartoons for this script

(CD51.8)

Script 52   The King's Party

Proper 23
(The Sunday Closest to October 12)

Matthew 22:1-6

THEME

This is another of Jesus' "Kingdom" parables. When Jesus told this story originally, He seems to have been warning the Jewish people to wake up: the invitations to the Heavenly Banquet had already been sent out and God would have no difficulty in finding guests. In this session we assure the children that everyone is invited to God's Party—as long as we remember to accept the invitation.

SET UP

- The liturgical color is Green.
- Put some little bowls of small food items—seedless grapes, candies, small cookies—on the table at the front.
- A couple of obvious party games, 'Hot Potato' or 'Pin the Tail on the Donkey' (CD52.1).
- Lots of balloons—out of reach (for the moment).
- A boom box with some disco music.
- Anything that will make the hall look festive.
- Write up some envelopes that appear to contain invitations to VIPs (see below).
- Make sure there are at least two Leaders at the front. Try and get a group of adults or teenagers to join you.

WELCOME *the children and lead them in* **The Sign of the Cross ✛ (p. xxxvi).**

THE KYRIE Lord Jesus, you came down from Heaven to tell us about God's
      love,
   Lord have mercy.
   Lord have mercy.

> Lord Jesus, you came down from Heaven and gave up your life for us,
> Christ have mercy.
> **Christ have mercy.**
>
> Lord Jesus, you came down from Heaven to tell us that God will always forgive those who are sorry,
> Lord have mercy.
> **Lord have mercy.**

Ask the children to repeat **The Prayer for Forgiveness** *after you* (**p. xxxvi**).

BEFORE THE GOSPEL

Meanwhile Leader 2 has been inspecting the stuff on the table.

Leader 2   What's all this for?

Leader 1   Ah well, today I'm going to have a party—we're going to have...

Hold up the games.

> games...

Hold up the sweets.

> and prizes...
> and some dancing.
> But first I need to send off the invitations.

Hold up the invitations—the names are very obvious.

> There's one to *Name...*
> and *Name...*
> and *Name...*

Read out the envelopes: put down whoever the current favorites are—include some very unlikely celebs like the President or the Bishop.

> Could you mail them for me?

Leader 2 pockets the invites and exits.

Leader 1   We've just got time to read the Gospel before the replies come back.

Look in the Gospel Book.

> Goodness, this seems to be about a party as well.

THE GOSPEL PROCESSION

THE GOSPEL *Matthew 22:1-10*

Substitute "party" for "wedding banquet" and leave out the poor man without a wedding garment at the end. He's strayed in from another parable.

AFTER THE GOSPEL

Leader 2 comes back with the replies—appear to read them out.

They all say   "No"—*(and give a poor excuse, for example):*
          "I'm staying in to watch TV."

You and the rest of the adults are disconsolate, all these nice games and nobody's coming. Talk among yourselves.

          What are we going to do?
          We've got all these balloons.
          What do you think Jesus would do?

Groan from somebody—Don't bring Jesus into this...

          But, He told that story in the Gospel... ?
Look it up.   The King had the same problem—and what did he do?
Read it out.   He called in all the riff-raff.

Look up at the kids, look at your helpers.

          I don't know...
          Where are we going to find riff-raff?

Leader 2 silently indicates the kids: pantomime horror from the other adults.

          You're kidding—not them!
          Shall we invite them?

Agonizing pause.

          Yeah, why not!

ACTIVITY

It's party time—games, conga, anything you like.
At the end, quieten the kids (good luck!)—a game of "Statues" might do it.

Sum up

Leader   Jesus told a story about a party in the Gospel today.
The King invited all sorts of people, did they come? (**no**)
What did he do then? (**He invited some other people.**)
Did they come? (**yes**)
Quite right. Anybody who wanted to come was welcomed in.
There are lots of meanings to this story, and *one* of them is that Jesus
was thinking about Heaven and the people God invites to join Him
there.
If some people are too lazy to turn up, then He invites other people.
Which is very lucky.
Because *we've* been invited—and it's up to us to turn up!

FINAL   God has invited us all to Heaven, let us remember some of the
PRAYER   people who are already there and ask them to pray for us.
After I say their name, you say:
Pray for us
(Add your patron saint to this list:)

Holy Michael
Pray for us
Holy Gabriel
Pray for us
Holy Raphael
Pray for us
All Holy Angels
Pray for us
Holy Mary
Pray for us
Holy Peter
Pray for us
Holy Teresa
Pray for us
All Holy Saints
Pray for us

Lord God, King of Heaven,
Hear the prayers of your saints in Heaven
And your children on Earth
And grant that one day we will all be together
With you in your Kingdom. *Amen.*

BACK IN CHURCH

There'll be no time to rehearse this one.
Everyone comes to the front.

Leader   Today the Leaders thought we'd give a party...

Pull out the invites.

We invited... *(name a few)*
But they were all too busy.
So we invited this group...

Indicate the kids—mock dismay, which turns into a grin.

We had a great time!

(CD52.1)

Script 53 Render unto Caesar

Proper 24, Ordinary Time 29
(The Sunday Closest to October 19)

Matthew 22:15-21

THEME

Christians are traditionally law-abiding but we have to know where the frontier is because, sometimes, the authorities can push us too far.

SET UP

- The liturgical color is Green.
- Some money: dollars and coins.
- A stamped envelope (make sure the stamp has a president on it).
- Picture of Tiberius Caesar (see CD-ROM).
- A picture of the President of the United States.
- A toy crown (a paper one will do).
- A cross.

WELCOME *the children and lead them in* **The Sign of the Cross + (p. xxxvi).**

THE KYRIE	Lord have mercy.
	Lord have mercy.
	Christ have mercy.
	Christ have mercy.
	Lord have mercy.
	Lord have mercy.

Ask the children to repeat **The Prayer for Forgiveness** *after you* (p. xxxvi).

INTRODUCTION

A Session on Presidents

Pull out a dollar bill and show it to the children.

Leader   Whose face is this? (**George Washington**)

Pull out some coins.

And whose faces are on these? (**Thomas Jefferson, Abraham Lincoln, etc.**)

Ditto with the envelope.

This is probably too small, but can you guess whose face is on the stamp? (**A President's!**)
Why do we have the presidents faces on our money and our stamps? (**Because they were famous leaders of our country**)

Put up a picture of the President.

Yes, the president is very important.
But there's somebody who is more important than he is.
Who's that?

They may well say other names, but lead toward Jesus, God.

What did we call Jesus just now in the Kyrie? (**Lord, Christ**)
Jesus is Lord.
Anybody know what a Lord is?

Work it out together, a Lord is somebody with power, who runs things.

When Jesus lived on Earth the Roman Emperor (or Caesar) was called "Lord" and people treated him very similarly to the way we treat our President.
They obeyed his laws and paid his taxes.
And these are very good things to do.
But all the time there was another Lord, the Lord God.
His laws are quite different from the laws made by Emperors, Caesars, Queens and our government leaders. They are about loving each other, and telling the truth, and going to church.
And we obey them not because God will put us into prison if we don't, but because we love Him.
Let's think about that as we pray.

OPENING   Lord Jesus,
PRAYER   Lord of Lords and King of Kings,
Help us to obey your laws,
And love and serve you. *Amen.*

BEFORE THE GOSPEL

Leader   The Jews were part of the Roman Empire and had to obey the
CD53.1   Emperor, Tiberius Caesar.
                  It was his face that was on the money and he was the one who
                  scooped up the taxes.
                  Tiberius Caesar was a pagan—he didn't believe in God—and the
                  Jews wondered if they should obey him.
                  Some of them asked Jesus.

THE GOSPEL PROCESSION

THE GOSPEL *Matthew 22:15-21*

AFTER THE GOSPEL

Leader   What did Jesus think about obeying Caesar?

Let the children tell you, and then sum up.

                  He said, you sorted out the things that were Caesar's, and did them—
                  and you sorted out the things that were God's—and did *them*.
                  And you didn't mix them up.
                  Of course, that's okay if your Caesar or King is good, but supposing
                  you had a bad one?
                  And suppose he told you to do things that God wouldn't like, what
                  did you do then?
                  Well, that happened once. We're going to tell that story together—
                  but first we have to get ready. I need some lions.

Get ready to run the story of Daniel in the lions' den.
Have the kids roar then, on a Q ("kill that') sign, stop roaring and freeze.
Then practice the Angel turning up and gently bopping them on the head to get them
to curl up and go to sleep.
Cast Daniel, Darius, the Angel, and some Persians (all the Q-ing is in the narration).

Daniel in the Lions' Den

Narrator   Once upon a time there was great King...

Kid with crown comes forward.

                  His name was Darius—and he was so rich and famous that one day
                  he made a new law.
                  He said that in future his people were not to worship God any more

but worship *him* instead.
So his people bowed down in front of Darius and prayed to him.

Persians bow down in front of Darius.

But there was a Jew living in his country—his name was Daniel.

Daniel comes forward.

And he refused to bow down to Darius, he shook his head and folded his arms...

Daniel does so.   And he said—"No, I will *serve* you, O King, but I will *not worship* you. I only worship God." And every day Daniel bowed down three times to God.

Daniel bows to the cross.

Well, the Persians went and told on him. They whispered in the King's ear...

The Persians go close to the King and whisper "psst, psst, psst" in his ear.

And the King had to punish Daniel. He was sorry to do so, because he liked him—but he wasn't going to be disobeyed.
He had a huge den of lions...

Indicate the rest of the children.

They were very fierce and they roared...

All the kids roar.

And he threw Daniel to the lions...

Daniel is chucked into the middle of the audience.

The King stood outside and called out:
"I hope your God saves you, Daniel!"
And then he closed up the den with a stone.

Somebody slams a door—Clonk!
Q Daniel and the lions to freeze mid-roar.

And that night the King couldn't sleep—he just walked up and down.

Darius does so.   And, as soon as it was light, he rushed to the den and shouted out.
"Daniel, are you okay?"
And Daniel called back,
"Certainly! God sent me an Angel...

Enter Angel, among the lions.

...and His Angel stopped the mouth of the lions...

The Angel gently bops the heads of the lions. The lions purr and curl up.

and I'm fine!"
So the King took away the stone and let Daniel out.

Pulls Daniel out.

He realized that he had made a silly law and he stopped pretending
to be God; he allowed his people to worship God properly, and he
just went on being King. And who was the person he trusted most in
his whole country?
Yup, Daniel.

Darius and Daniel shake hands.
Congratulate the children.

So the Bible tells us it is fine to be a good citizen and pay taxes and
obey the President—as long as they don't ask us to do something
that God would not like. God always has to come first.

FINAL   We'll end with a Jewish prayer that praises God our King.
PRAYER   *Ask the children to repeat after you*
        Blessed be God,
        King of the universe,
        Who reigns for ever and ever. *Amen.*

End with a **Glory Be... (p. xxxvii).**

BACK IN CHURCH

The Narrator and the child who played Daniel step forward.
The other children gather round.

Leader   Today we threw *Name* into a den of lions...

*Q the other children to roar and paw at him: allow for the fact that they may be
stricken with stage fright .*

But fortunately an Angel shut them up...

Do a "kill it" Q to the kids.

And saved Daniel.
And the King who had thrown Daniel to the lions realized he had
gone too far.

Daniel *(if he's up to it)*

God expects Kings to know their place.

Script 54 The Great Commandment

Proper 25
(The Sunday Closest to October 26)

Matthew 22:34-40

THEME

Christians aren't given lots of rules. In fact Jesus gave us just two: that we should love God and love everybody else.

SET UP

- The liturgical color is Green.
- Pictures from the CD-ROM (they include flash cards for the Ten Commandments).
- A Bible with a bookmark in Deuteronomy 5 (the Ten Commandments).
- Two flash cards for Jesus' two commandments.

WELCOME *the children and lead them in* **The Sign of the Cross + (p. xxxvi).**

Give the children a moment to think back over the week.

THE KYRIE   Lord, for the times we have forgotten to love you,
Lord have mercy.
Lord have mercy.

Jesus, for the times we have forgotten to love others,
Christ have mercy.
Christ have mercy.

Lord, we thank you for never forgetting to love us,
Lord have mercy.
Lord have mercy.

Ask the children to repeat **The Prayer for Forgiveness** *after you* **(p. xxxvi).**

OPENING
PRAYER

God our Father,
Thank you for bringing us together this morning.
Help us to do, with loving hearts,
All that you ask of us. *Amen.*

BEFORE THE GOSPEL

Leader

Today we're going to think about rules.
Let's think of some easy ones.
Raise your hands if you've ever been in a car.
Gosh, all of you...
Well, perhaps you'll know the answer to this.
If you're driving a car and come to a red traffic light, what must you do? Hands up... (**Stop!**)
What do you do when the light turns green? (**Go!**)
Who made these rules? (**the Government, the police, etc.**)
Okay, think about school.
There are school rules too, aren't there?
Can you tell me any?

For some reason children love this question. Hours pass as they tell you about the things they are not allowed to do.

Who made all these rules? (**teachers, the principal**)
God has given us some rules too.
Does anybody know where we find them?

Hold up the Bible as a clue.

The Bible.
There are a lot of them at the beginning of the Bible, the part written first of all for the Jewish people.
I've found some here—the Commandments.
How many Commandments are there?
It's easy, as many as the number of fingers you've got...

Write up a large **10 Commandments.**

How many do we know?

This might be a rhetorical question: stick up the Commandments, one by one.

CD54.1

Well, naturally the Jews didn't like so many rules, so they tried to get out of them. God found He had to give them some more laws—lots more laws—how many do you think?

Let them guess, then hone in on the number:

613

Write up   613 Laws

Laws Game

It was very difficult to remember all those Laws.
Let's see how good we'd be.

Stick the first series of pictures up on the board.

CD54.2   These are all the things a Jew is not supposed to eat.

Go through each picture.

They can't eat vulture, rabbit, bat, camel, crab, shrimp, tuna fish, snake or (and this is the tough one) pig. No bacon.
Look at the pictures for a minute and then we'll see how well you have remembered them.

Time them and remove the pictures.

So what things can't a Jew eat?
Hands up (absolutely no shouting out)

Stick the pictures back up as the kids remember them.
Help them if they get very stuck—a chance for your mime skills.

CD54.3   Okay, that was good. Here's another set of rules. These are the things a Jew shouldn't do on the Sabbath, that's Saturday. Saturday is the Jews" holy day.

Same business, go through the pictures again.

A Jew shouldn't touch money, or work, or go for a long walk, or cook.
Modern Jews aren't supposed to push an elevator button or switch on a light.

You might add that this makes the Sabbath rather a lovely day for the Jews, it's one they give to God.
See how many Sabbath rules the children remember.

You can see that's a lot of rules, we've only done...

Count them up. 15.

There are still 598 to go.
The Jews call their rules **The Law.**

Write it up.   How many rules do Christians have?

Take all answers, but don't comment.

Jesus talked about rules in the Gospel today, let's listen to Him.

THE GOSPEL PROCESSION

THE GOSPEL *Matthew 22:34-40*

Some Jews were pushing Jesus very hard with their questions and one said to Him:
"Master—which is the most important commandment in the whole Law?"
And Jesus said,
"It is: you must love the Lord your God with all your heart, with all your mind and with all your soul—this is the first and greatest commandment. And there is a second, very like it: you must love your neighbor as yourself. These two rules sum up the Law."

AFTER THE GOSPEL

Leader	So how many rules does Jesus give us? (**two**) What are they? (**You must love God and love your neighbor.**)

CD54.4   *Show them the flash cards of Jesus' commandments.*

Jesus said the second commandment was like the first one.
What do you think He meant?

See if they get it.

(**It's about love as well.**)
Yes, it's about love. And I think Jesus felt that it was like the first commandment—the one about loving God—because if you obey the second commandment and love your neighbor, you find it's a way to love God as well.
Just a minute. Who is your neighbor?

Accept all answers.

Well, it might be the person sitting next to you—but Jesus means everybody you meet. Especially people in need.
Actually that's quite tough.
It's something we need to practice. Let's do that now by giving each other the Peace.

Leader 2	Jesus said, "Peace be with you!" Let us offer one another the sign of peace.

Everybody, adults and children, offers each other the Peace.

SONG

"Shalom, my friends" *would fit in well here. Preface it by telling them that "Shalom" is the Jewish word for "Peace."*

Leader	It's good to connect with our Jewish friends when we pray.
FINAL PRAYER	Loving Lord, Help us to remember the two great commandments: Help us to love God with all our heart And love our neighbor as ourselves. *Amen.*

BACK IN CHURCH

The children come in with all the flash cards.

Leader	Today we discovered that the Jewish Law had 613 rules. We looked at ten of them...

Hold up the Ten Commandments.

	Then we read the Gospel and heard that Jesus said that all those laws could be summed up in two commandments:
Hold that up.	Love God...
Ditto.	And Love your neighbor...

These are some of the things a Jew wasn't allowed to eat.

(CD54.2)

Sample cartoon for this script

Script 55   Happy Endings
(David and Goliath)

Proper 26

(The Sunday Closest to November 2)

Matthew 23:1-12

THEME

Jesus' strictures on the Pharisees are best left for the grown-ups so, taking a cue from the last verse of the Gospel ("Those who make themselves great will fall, while those who humble themselves will be made great") this session tells the story of David and Goliath.

SET UP

- The liturgical color is Green.
- Plastic weapons for Goliath and three Jewish soldiers.
- A plastic breastplate would be useful and a toy caveman club would make Goliath even more effective.
- Toy crown.
- Five smooth stones.
- Small bouncy ball (sponge if possible).
- Scarf for a small sling.
- A watercolor tube full of red paint.

WELCOME *the children and lead them in* **The Sign of the Cross + (p. xxxvi).**

THE KYRIE   Lord Jesus, when you rose from the dead, you defeated evil,
Lord have mercy.
Lord have mercy.

Lord Jesus, when you rose from the dead, you washed away our sins,
Christ have mercy.
Christ have mercy.

Lord Jesus, when you rose from the dead, you set us free,
Lord have mercy.
Lord have mercy.

Ask the children to repeat **The Prayer for Forgiveness** *after you* **(p. xxxvi).**

OPENING PRAYER *from Psalm 130 or 13 (depending on the Bible translation)*

(*The response is:* **My trust is in the Lord**)

O Lord, my heart is not proud,
Nor haughty my eyes.
My trust is in the Lord.

As a child lies quietly in its mother's arms,
So my heart is quiet within me.
My trust is in the Lord.

O Israel, trust in the Lord,
Now and for ever.
My trust is in the Lord.

Leader   Today we have a very short Gospel reading.
Let's listen to it very carefully.

THE GOSPEL PROCESSION

THE GOSPEL *Matthew 23:12*

Jesus said:
"Those who make themselves great will fall, while those who humble themselves will
be made great."

AFTER THE GOSPEL

Leader   That was quick, wasn't it?
But very important.
Jesus was always telling people that the characters who make the
most noise, and push themselves forward, are heading for a fall.
He said God favored the small and the humble.
Sometimes that's quite difficult to believe—there seem to be such
a lot of big, noisy people in the world. But once the biggest and
noisiest of them all got a surprise.
His name was Goliath and we're going to tell his story today.

Casting

You need a good story-telling Narrator, who does all the dialogue except Goliath's roars, and Qs in the acting.
One of the grown-ups is Goliath, a dad preferably, or a large teenager. Get him secretly to squeeze some red paint into his left hand.
Then you need King Saul, who wears the crown, and three Jewish warriors—
Eliab, Abinadab and Shammah, all armed and terrified.
Cast a small child as David, he or she has the sling, stones and small sponge ball.
The other children line up behind either Saul or Goliath.

David and Goliath

Narrator	A very long time ago the Jews were having a lot of trouble with their enemies, the Philistines. The Philistines had an enormous soldier, nearly seven feet high. He carried a huge club in his hands, and he stood in front of his army and shouted at the Jews...
Goliath	*(Ad lib)* What are you doing here! Come on, one of you come forward and fight me You haven't got a chance!
Narrator	Saul, the Jewish King, and all his people, heard Goliath and were greatly afraid...

Bit of trembling here.

> Now one of the Jews was called Jesse, and he had sent some of his fine strong sons to fight for the King.
> They were Eliab, Abinadab and Shammah.

This trio is shoved to the front—Goliath moves towards them, swinging his club, they retreat hastily.

Narrator	Jesse kept his smallest son back. His name was David. David's job was to look after his father's sheep and run messages. One day his father told him to run to the army camp with some food for his brothers, and David crept up to the front line...

David sneaks up.

> And there he heard Goliath boasting away in front of the Philistine camp...

Off goes Goliath again.

Narrator	David was furious—but his brother Eliab saw him and said: "What are you doing here! Get back to your sheep!" But David asked King Saul for a chance to fight Goliath. David said, "Your majesty, I've been looking after sheep and fighting bears and lions all my life—I can handle Goliath." So the King gave David a chance, he gave him some splendid armor.—(And/or a sword, depending on your resources)

Take the armor off one of the others and put it on David.

Narrator	But David took it off—(he does)—and said: "I can't wear that, I'm not used to it." And he ran down to the brook and chose five smooth stones...

David shows them to the kids, then the Narrator pockets them, before David puts them in his sling.

	And he pulled out his shepherd's sling...

This is a scarf, knotted up as a sling.

Narrator	Then he went and stood in front of the Jewish army. Goliath roared when he saw David.

A few insults from Goliath here—he starts to approach.

Narrator	David said, "You come to me with a sword and a club, but my trust is in the Lord." Then Goliath charged at David, and David put his hand in his bag, and took out a stone (the small sponge ball), and slung it, and struck the Philistine on the forehead.

Impressive sling shot with the small bouncy ball.
Goliath claps his left hand to his forehead and leaves some red paint there.

Goliath	Ow!
Narrator	And he crashed to the ground.

He does a well-rehearsed fall.
(We'll omit the moment where David cuts off his head.)

Narrator	That was the end of Goliath, and the Philistines, and the Jews had a bit of peace for a while.

Congratulate the actors.

Health, Safety and Stones

As the ball will be bouncing all over the place you probably won't have to tell the children you used a ball instead of a stone—even so you might point out that slinging anything, particularly stones, is extremely dangerous. Don't do it.

Sum up

Leader That's one of the great stories, and it tells us something very important.

Big evil people are not as powerful as they look. They try to frighten us by making a lot of noise—but good people are strong in a way evil can't even guess at.

Good people know about God.

And God can fill their hearts with love and truth and courage, and help them stand up to evil. But only if they listen to Him.

That's why Jesus says quiet people are more blessed than big pushy people.

And that's why there are so many stories about little guys facing up to bad guys—it makes a good story, but it also happens to be true.

FINAL PRAYER

Gather the children into a prayer circle and light a candle.
Pass around the best of your swords.

Talk about it Swords are nice things to hold aren't they?

They swish...

But of course we use them for fighting.

Sometimes we feel we've got to fight—to protect the weak and combat evil.

But it's always better to find another way if we can.

Jesus said, "Blessed are the Peacemakers."

Sometimes soldiers are sent to dangerous areas to try and keep the peace.

Christians think it's okay to be a soldier.

But a sword does get in the way...

Try to shake hands with your neighbor.

Hmm, I think I'll put it down.

Look I've got an empty hand—

Now I can give my neighbor the Peace.

The Peace

Exchange the Peace all the way around the circle.

BACK IN CHURCH

Line up David, Saul and the three warriors at the front.
Goliath stays at the back of the church.

Leader   Today we had a lot of trouble with a giant.
                    His name was Goliath.
                    Fortunately we had a small kid who was handy with a sling...

Bring forward David.

                    His name was David.
                    And as a result it seems that Goliath...
Look for him.   Ah, there he is.
                    He wants to stay at the back of the church for the moment, where he
                    feels he'll be safe
                    It's helped us understand what Jesus told us in the Gospel—that
                    "Those who make themselves great will fall, while those who
                    humble themselves will be made great."

Script 56   Happy Endings
(The End of the World)
(Extra Lesson)
Matthew 24:3, 6-7, 13

THEME

Seeing that modern children have to cope with global warming (and "doom" movies) it seems a good idea to give them a Christian perspective on the End of Time.

SET UP

- The liturgical color is Green.
- A large nursery story book—*Sleeping Beauty* or *Cinderella*. (Make sure it's got a heroine.)
- Pictures from the CD-ROM.
- Two large tablecloths or sheets for the Presentation.

Giotto's "Last Judgement"

You may like to download the detail in Giotto's painting of an Angel rolling up the sky at the End of the World. It is in the Scrovegni Chapel in Padua, and can be found in the Web Gallery of Art www.wga.hu. Put Giotto Padua in the search engine and scroll down to the pictures of The Last Judgement. Left click on the thumbnails and they'll fill the whole screen. The images are very good and non-scary.

WELCOME *the children and lead them in* **The Sign of the Cross + (p. xxxvi).**

THE KYRIE   Lord, you always forgive those who say they are sorry,
Lord have mercy.
Lord have mercy.

Jesus, we are sorry for the times we have been unkind,
Christ have mercy.
Christ have mercy.

Lord, we thank you for always loving and forgiving us,
Lord have mercy.
Lord have mercy.

Ask the children to repeat **The Prayer for Forgiveness** *after you* (**p. xxxvi**).

OPENING PRAYER *from Psalm 144 or 145 (depending on the Bible translation)*

(*The response is:* **I will bless your Name for ever**)

I will give you glory, God my King,
I will bless your Name for ever,
I will bless your Name for ever

The Lord is kind and full of compassion,
Slow to anger and abounding in love,
I will bless your Name for ever

All your creatures will thank you, O Lord,
And your people will bless you,
I will bless your Name for ever.

BEFORE THE GOSPEL—Stories

Bring a chair forward, open a story book and settle down to a story.
Set up the opening.

Leader   How do fairy stories always begin? (**"Once upon a time'**)

Tell one of the stories—ad lib if you need to make it shorter.
Stop just before the end.

And how do you suppose it ended? (**"They lived happily ever after'**)
Exactly, when you hear that phrase, you know there's no more story
left.
It's the end.
But there's another sort of story...

Dr Who

Anyone here watch *Dr Who?—(Or any current adventure story)*

Get the children to tell you about it.

Does he live happily ever after?

Accept all answers.

He does in a sort of way. He wins—but then there's always another adventure.

A long time ago, there was a fabulous series you could see in the movies called *The Purple Monster*. There were 69 episodes and a typical one used to go like this...

The Purple Monster

Tell this story putting up the pictures as you go.

CD56.1   These stories always began where the last one left off, so our first picture is of Dick, the hero, hanging from a cliff, with a raging torrent below and some vultures circling above. And all the time he could hear the Purple Monster getting nearer and nearer.

It was a bad moment.

CD56.2   The Purple Monster looked over the cliff and grinned...

"Got you!" he said—and stamped on Dick's fingers.

CD56.3   "Ow!" said Dick, and promptly fell off the cliff, only to be caught by a tree, growing 10 feet below.

The Purple Monster was furious: he stamped his feet, and jumped up and down, and the cliff began to shake—and the tree began to wobble... *(wobble the picture)*

First one root, then another, gave way and Dick found himself sliding down the cliff face and crashing into a bundle of very prickly sticks.

"Ow!" said Dick. "No, wait a moment, this is rather good, I've landed in a bird's nest. Hmm, it's very big, I wonder what sort of bird... ?"

CD56.4   At which point he caught the eye of a very large, angry bird. The next minute he'd been booted off the cliff...

And this time he really did land in the raging torrent.

CD56.5   Fortunately he'd brought most of the nest with him and found that it made a perfectly nice boat. The only trouble was the chicks...

They were furious that their home had been made into a boat and started to peck him. Then the nest began to leak, and the current got faster, and Dick couldn't help noticing a strange purple glow in the water...

CD56.6   Suddenly!

"Oh NO!" said Dick.

CD56.7   But what happened then you'll have to discover next week.

THE END

Allow for a wail at this moment, not to say children coming up to you after the service to find out what happened next.

After the Story

Leader   Well, it's never much fun to see "THE END': but with a story like that you know there'll be another thrilling episode next week.

Now, the Universe God made is like a story.

It's got a beginning and an end.

And the end will be something like a fairy story, because we're definitely going to live happily ever after—but it'll be much more like a "Purple Monster" story, because once one episode has finished, another will begin.

Let's hear Jesus talk about the end of one of the chapters.

THE GOSPEL PROCESSION

THE GOSPEL *Matthew 24:3, 6-7, 13*

As Jesus sat on the Mount of Olives, His friends came up to Him privately and said, "Tell us what will happen at the End of the World."

Jesus answered, "You will hear the clash of battles close by, and a rumor of battles far off, but do not be afraid. Countries will fight countries, kingdoms will fight kingdoms, there will be famines and earthquakes and some people will lose their faith. But whoever holds out to the end will be saved."

AFTER THE GOSPEL

Leader   What do you think of that?

Is that scary?

Actually most kids view this Gospel with equanimity.

When do you suppose it's all going to happen?

Take all answers, but establish that the End of the World is not likely to happen for millions of years.

You see God didn't make this Universe to last for ever and one day this chapter will be over.

In one bit of the Bible it says God will one day fold away the Universe like an old cloak. I like that. It's like putting your toys away before you go to bed.

Optional Giotto

> Look here's a picture of the Universe being wrapped up...

Show them the Giotto picture of the Angel rolling up the sky.

> Can you see what's behind the Angel?—Gold!

Sum up

Leader God loves making new things. One day He'll wrap this Universe up
and give us a new one, even more beautiful and exciting than the one
we live in.
It'll be like starting a new chapter.
And of course some things will never change.
We'll be there, and so will Jesus.

REHEARSAL

Practice your presentation for when you go back to church (see below).

FINAL   Jesus said,
PRAYER "Stay faithful and I will give you the Crown of Life."
Lord Jesus,
Help us to know and believe that you are with us
To the end of time. *Amen.*

End with a **Glory Be...** *(p. xxxvii). (Emphasize: "As it was in the beginning, is now,
and ever shall be, world without end...")*

SONG

The spiritual "When the saints go marching in" *is a fine stirring way to finish, though
you may want to skip the verse about the moon turning to blood.*

BACK IN CHURCH

*The children enter with two tablecloths one rolled up and held by a couple of children,
the other held at each end by three or four kids.*

Leader Today we heard that one day, God would fold the world away like a
garment...

The children solemnly fold up the tablecloth, one of them drapes it over her arm.

> And then He'd make a new Heaven and Earth...

The kids with the folded tablecloth flap it free.

> Even more wonderful than the first.
> We're intending to be there!

Script 57   The Wise and Foolish Virgins

Proper 27

(The Sunday Closest to November 9)

Matthew 25:1-13

THEME

This story is one of the parables in which Jesus urged his fellow countrymen to get ready for God's Kingdom. However, modern Christians are often more interested (not to say shattered) by the wise virgins' decision not to share their oil. So, using a story about St. Francis, we're going to discover that being good is more complicated than it looks.

SET UP

- The liturgical color is Green.
- A pile of folded cloths: sheets, tablecloths, even altar cloths. (One should be red, or a striking color, and placed on the top.)
- You'll need three adults or some older children to read the script beforehand and be ready to play the parts of St. Francis, his Dad, and a passing Bishop. St. Francis should have a jacket on.
- Spare table.
- A full bottle of oil, and an empty bottle of oil.
- A Roman oil lamp, such as from the British Museum shop—or a DIY version.

DIY Lamp

You need a clear bowl, half filled with water, pour in a good amount of cooking oil, so that it eventually settles on the top in a layer about an inch thick.

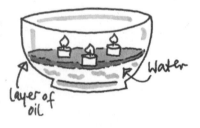

Chop a cork into slices, pierce each slice in the middle and insert a little twisted bit of string or wool for a wick. Float the corks on the oil and light them. Try this out before you bring it in!

WELCOME *the children and lead them in* **The Sign of the Cross + (p. xxxvi).**

THE KYRIE	Lord Jesus, we are sorry for the things we have done wrong,
	Lord have mercy.
	Lord have mercy.

Lord Jesus, we are sorry for forgetting to listen to you,
Christ have mercy.
Christ have mercy.

Lord Jesus, thank you for your promise to love and forgive us,
Lord have mercy.
Lord have mercy.

Ask the children to repeat **The Prayer for Forgiveness** *after you* (**p. xxxvi**).

| Leader | We've got a difficult Gospel reading today, so we're going to ask for God's help as we look at it together. |

OPENING PRAYER	God our Father,
	We thank you for giving us intelligence.
	Help us to think hard as we listen to your Word,
	So that we may hear and understand your Holy Gospel. **Amen**

BEFORE THE GOSPEL

| Leader | The Gospel today tells us that being good, and doing good, is sometimes quite complicated. To understand that we're going to think about something that happened to St. Francis. |

Cast: St. Francis, a beggar (one of the kids), St. Francis' dad, and a passing Bishop

The Story of St. Francis

| Narrator | When St. Francis was a young man he helped his father in the cloth trade. |

St. Francis and his dad set up a table.

His father was a very rich merchant and sold bolts of beautiful cloth.

St. Francis and his dad pile up cloths, the red one on the top.

One day Francis and his father were standing at the stall when a beggar approached them.

Enter beggar.   He had very little on and was freezing cold... *(Beggar acts cold.)*
But Francis' dad wouldn't give him anything and drove him away.

Exit beggar.

And then went off himself to see his friends... *(Dad exits.)*

St. Francis called the beggar over and, making the Sign of the Cross over the most expensive bolt there, gave it to the beggar.

Francis and the beggar act this and Francis gives the beggar the red cloth.

The beggar was delighted—and moved off quickly...

Exit beggar at speed.

At which point Dad came back...

Try to ad lib the next patch of dialogue—the story line is very simple. But it's okay if you read it.

Dad	Hey! I've got a buyer for that super red cloth I bought—Oi! Where is it???
Francis	Oh, I gave it to the beggar—
Dad	What do you mean, you gave it to the beggar?
	That was *my* bolt of cloth!
Francis	No, it wasn't, it was God's—I made the Sign of the Cross over it.
Dad	Oh did you!
	Well, you've got no right to give my cloth to God or anybody else.
Francis	Oh yeah? Well, you can have your bolts of cloth... *(Chuck them on the floor.)*
	And this stall... *(Shove it to one side.)*
	And everything you've paid for—this stupid jacket, you can have that... *(Take off jacket.)*
	And this sweatshirt/tie... *(Or remove whatever garment you feel you can remove.)*
	And these trousers...
Narrator	*(Hastily restrain Francis.)*
	Fortunately at this moment a Bishop passed by...

Enter Bishop.

Bishop	Stop!
	What are you doing!?
Narrator	And St. Francis explained...
	And his dad explained...

Make lots of wild gesticulations, pointing, fist shaking and so on.

And the Bishop told them to calm down...

Puts hands on their shoulders.

Take a walk—and listen to *him*...

Takes them off.

Narrator   *(Come forward to talk to the kids very directly:)*
What do you think the Bishop said?
Was Francis right to give away his father's stuff?

Take what comes, but establish that:

No, Francis wasn't right.
His father *should* have helped the beggar and it was *kind* of Francis to want to help the beggar. But it wasn't up to Francis to force his dad to be good, and he certainly shouldn't have used his father's stuff without permission. That wasn't fair or just.
And you must be just before you are generous.
Now we're ready for the Gospel.

THE GOSPEL PROCESSION

THE GOSPEL *Matthew 25:1-13*

AFTER THE GOSPEL

Leader   Right let's think about this:
First let's look at the lamps those bridesmaids had for the wedding.

Pull out the little Roman lamp.

It needs to be filled with oil, and have a wick put in...

Demonstrate or bring forward your bowl and show the kids the oil and the wicks.

How good are they?

Light them, pull down blinds, turn off light.

Not very...
Jewish wedding parties were held at night, so you can imagine how many of these lights they'd need.
The bridegroom in the story had arranged for the bridesmaids to turn up with their oil and lamps, and was expecting it to look marvellous.
But he and the guests took so long to come, and some of the girls were too stupid to save their oil, or get any more.
So they wanted the sensible girls to share.
We're always being told to share things, but this time the sensible girls said "No."
And Jesus agreed with them.
Can you see why?

Accept all answers.

Sum up

The girls were there for the bridegroom—it was his party, he expected them to be ready for him. It wouldn't be right to take his oil and give it to some girls just because they were stupid.

And anyway, it wouldn't work. That way, all the lamps would go out early, and everybody would be in the dark.

So, though it was tough to say "No," the sensible girls made the right decision.

Sometimes being good *is* tough, if you have to make the right decision and do something that's unpopular.

REHEARSAL

Practice the very short group shout for the presentation back in church (see below).

"Don't get locked out!"

FINAL	God our Father,
PRAYER	Help us to follow the example of Jesus this week,
	And do the right thing,
	Even if it's tough. *Amen.*

BACK IN CHURCH

Two children come in with the full and empty bottles of oil.

Leader	Today we heard how ten bridesmaids had to wait for a wedding party to turn up.
	Five ran out of oil...

Kid holds up empty oil bottle.

They got locked out.
But the other five were ready...

Kid holds up full bottle.

And they were able to greet the bridegroom.
In the same way Jesus expects Christians to be up and ready for Him.

Everybody	**"Don't get locked out!"**

Script 58   The Parable of the Talents

Proper 28

(The Sunday Closest to November 16)

Matthew 25:14-26

THEME

This parable is one of those difficult stories where people always feel sorry for the "villain': in this case the man who kept his talent to himself.

I think one of the points Jesus is making is that gifts are there to be shared, they don't work in isolation. (It's like hoarding your Easter Egg, eventually it goes bad—you don't enjoy it and nobody else can eat it either.)

SET UP

- The liturgical color is Green.
- Ask some of the children to be ready to give you a hand Before the Gospel.
- A soccer ball.
- Optional: any sort of musical instrument, preferably one some child can feasibly play—like a recorder or a keyboard.
- A CD player, or similar, with some dance music to play on it.
- A bag of gold chocolate coins for the Gospel.
- A picture of the Annunciation to the Virgin Mary (search on Google Images).

WELCOME *the children and lead them in* **The Sign of the Cross + (p. xxxvi).**

Ask everyone (children and Leaders) to think about the past week.

Leader	Did we do anything wrong? Did things get in a mess? Let's get rid of all that by saying we're sorry.

| THE KYRIE | Lord Jesus, you came to call sinners,
Lord have mercy.
Lord have mercy. |

Lord Jesus, you came to help the unhappy,
Christ have mercy.
Christ have mercy.

Lord Jesus, you came to tell us how much God loves us,
Lord have mercy.
Lord have mercy.

Ask the children to repeat **The Prayer for Forgiveness** *after you* (**p. xxxvi**).

INTRODUCTION

Talents

Ask the children what they are good at.

Can anyone here play soccer ball?
Who's good at drawing?
at texting?

Add other suitable skills—skateboarding, ballet, etc. Give everyone a chance to put their hand up.

What an amazing bunch of people!
Let's thank God for all the things we can do.

OPENING PRAYER

Ask the children to repeat after you:

God our Father,
We thank you for making us:
For giving us hands to work for you,
Hearts to love you,
And voices to praise you. *Amen.*

BEFORE THE GOSPEL

Bring forward one child plus soccer ball, and four others.

Leader   Right, I want to think about the talents we've got.
                Name here is good at games—
                Sometimes he plays with one kid...

They bounce the ball to one another.

Sometimes with two...

They play Piggy-in-the-Middle.

Sometimes with the whole group...

Throw the ball round the whole group—including the Leader.

So for this talent...

Tap first kid on shoulder.

You have the effect of loads of happy people

Indicate the others.
Do the same thing if you can rustle up somebody who can play a musical instrument.

The effect was that kid got so good she started a band.

Line some kids up behind.

And they got a recording contract...

Put on the CD.

And when other people heard the music they began to dance... *(They do.)*

Bring forward another child.

This kid had a talent as well...

The kid folds her arms.

But she never told anyone what the talent was...

The kid turns her back.

So nobody was made happy—not even the kid with the talent.
That's very sad.
Jesus told a story about it once.

THE GOSPEL PROCESSION

THE GOSPEL *Matthew 25:14-26*

Have the three servants at the front, they should either be big kids or grown-ups. The lazy servant should be another Leader.
Hand over the gold coins as you come to that bit of the story—make sure that the two good servants have spare coins in their pockets so that they can give you back the extra.
The lazy servant should look suspicious and sneak off to bury the money, only reappearing when emphatically gestured to present himself.
Calm the fierce biblical language down a bit.

At verse 24 use this rewrite
The servant who had received one talent came forward and said:
"Master, I knew you were difficult to please, so I didn't do anything. I just buried my talent in the ground. You can have it back again."
And the master said,
"You lazy ungrateful servant! Where did you get these ideas about me? Give your talent back. I'll give it to one of the others. You're fired. Get out of here—right now!"

AFTER THE GOSPEL

Leader　　　　So who were the good servants?
　　　　　　　And who was the lazy one?

They should get that right

　　　　　　　Why was the master so angry?

Take all answers, but establish

　　　　　　　It was because the lazy servant didn't even try.
　　　　　　　Do you think God gets that angry?
　　　　　　　We don't know—but I think we can guess He's very sad when people don't use their talents.
　　　　　　　Because if you don't *do* anything, that's it!
　　　　　　　All you've done is put a wrench in the works:
　　　　　　　Nothing happens.
　　　　　　　You see God won't *make* you do anything.
　　　　　　　He gives you talents, and chances, and loves you to try.

SONG

"God Forgave My Sin," *with its refrain,* "Freely, freely you have received, freely, freely give," *would fit in well here.*

FINAL　　　You never know how important your talent is.
PRAYER　　Let's think about somebody who used her talent really well...

Put up a picture of the Annunciation to the Virgin Mary

　　　　　　　God knew Mary was the right person to look after His Son, and He sent the Angel Gabriel to ask her if she would use her talent for Him. It was completely up to her and, thank goodness, she said "Yes." Let's ask her to pray for us.

End with a **Hail Mary...** *and a* **Glory Be... (p. xxxvii).**

BACK IN CHURCH

Rerun the soccer ball moment.
Bring forward the kid, the soccer ball and the others.

Leader   *Name* here is good at games.
                    Sometimes he/she played with one kid...

They bounce the ball to one another.

                    Sometimes with two...

They play Piggy-in-the-Middle.

                    Sometimes with the whole group...

Throw the ball around the whole group—including the Leader.

                    So for this talent, *tap first kid on shoulder...*
                    You have the effect of loads of happy people...

Indicate the others.

                    Just think how awful it would have been if *Name* had grabbed his
                    ball and kept it to himself! *(He does so.)*
                    Then nobody could have played at all...

All the kids sit down abruptly.

                    God likes us to use our talents.

Script 59   Christ the King

Proper 29 (The Last Sunday after Pentecost)
(The Sunday Closest to November 23)
Matthew 25:31-40

THEME

The Gospel today describes Christ as a hidden King. It also gives us a picture of Judgement and the famous division of saints and sinners into sheep and goats. It seems wrong to leave the goats out completely, but there's no need to dwell on their condemnation. Instead we concentrate on Jesus' presence in the poor and needy and introduce the children to the traditional list of good deeds in what is often called the Six Works of Mercy.

SET UP

- The liturgical color is White or Gold.
- A picture of President of the United States.
- Icon of Christ the King: you could download an image of Christ Pantocrator—search on Google Images—or use **CD59.1.**
- A dollar bill of any denomination and some coins.
- Pictures from the CD-ROM.
- A toy sheep and goat stuffed animal.
- Toy crown.
- A scruffy cardboard box to hide the crown in. (Before the session starts hide the crown in the not very conspicuous cardboard box. Label the box "Cardboard City," but turn its label to the wall and shove it in a corner.)

WELCOME *the children and lead them in* **The Sign of the Cross + (p. xxxvi).**

THE KYRIE   God, our Father, you always forgive those who say they are sorry, Lord have mercy.
Lord have mercy.

Lord Jesus, we are sorry for the times that we have been unloving and selfish,
Christ have mercy.

Christ have mercy.

God, the Holy Spirit, thank you for helping us to say sorry,
Lord have mercy.
Lord have mercy.

Ask the children to repeat **The Prayer for Forgiveness** *after you* (**p. xxxvi**).

OPENING	Lord Jesus,
PRAYER	You are the King of the Universe,
	And ruler of all.
	Help us to acclaim you as our King today. *Amen.*

BEFORE THE GOSPEL

Start with a quick session on the President—show his picture

Leader	Does anyone know who this is? (**The President**)
	Where does he live? (**The White House**—*or anything they come up with.*)
	Has anyone here ever seen him?

Go along with any President stories—or move on to seeing him on TV.

When do we see him on TV?
I bet some of us have got pictures of other presidents in our pockets.

Pull out a dollar bill, show them the picture.

They are even on our coins...

Pull out a couple.

If you live in the United States, you know exactly who the President is, and what he looks like.
But what about Jesus?
He's the King of the Universe.
Is He on our money? (**no**)
No, if we want to see what King Jesus looks like we have to look at pictures.
Like this one...

CD59.1 *Show the Christ Pantocrator picture from the CD-ROM—or one you have downloaded yourself.*

In these pictures, Jesus sits on a throne, and He looks straight at us
to bless us and—*(this is the important bit)*
He's got nothing but gold behind Him.
Gold, in this sort of picture, means Heaven.
That's where Jesus lives—and it's pretty difficult to get TV cameras
up there.
We believe that one day Jesus will come back to Earth and everyone
will know He's the King.
But for the moment, when He comes to Earth, He does it quietly.
Only people who love Him know He's here:
Jesus is in the Bread and Wine of the Eucharist;
He's in our hearts;
And He's somewhere else as well?
Let's find out where in the Gospel.

THE GOSPEL PROCESSION

THE GOSPEL *Matthew 25:31-40*

Optional Paraphrase

Jesus said: "At the end of time when the King shall come back, with
all His Angels, He will sit on His throne and everyone on Earth
will stand in front of Him. Then He will separate them, just as a
shepherd separates sheep from goats."

CD59.2   He will put the sheep on His right...

Stick the sheep picture to the far right of your display board.

CD59.3   And the goats on His left...

Stick the goats to the far left.
*Put up the pictures of the Works of Mercy as you mention them. They should stretch
from the sheep on the right hand side of the board to the goats on the left.*

And He will say to the sheep,
"Welcome! you that are blessed by my Father!
CD59.4   For I was hungry and you gave me food.
CD59.5   I was thirsty and you gave me drink.
CD59.6   I was a stranger and you made me welcome.
CD59.7   I was naked and you clothed me.
CD59.8   I was sick and you visited me.
CD59.9   I was in prison and you came to see me."
Then the sheep will say, "Lord, when did we ever see you hungry or
thirsty, a stranger or naked, sick or in prison?"

And the King will answer,
"I tell you solemnly, whenever you were kind to the least of my
brothers and sisters—you did it for me."

AFTER THE GOSPEL

Leader   Now the question is, what happens to the goats?

Pick up the sheep and goat toys, if you have them.

The bit of the Gospel we've read is only interested in the sheep.

Hold up the sheep.

So, I think the answer is to make sure you're a sheep.
God will sort the goats out...

Tuck the goat under your arm.

But us sheep have got to listen up...

Wiggle the sheep so it appears to look up suddenly.

Because Jesus is not just our Shepherd, He's our King.
He might live in Heaven, but He's still to be found on Earth. He's
right here, in our hearts and in the hearts of the poor and unhappy.
He's a hidden King and it's our job to find Him.

ACTIVITY

The children have to find Jesus, or rather His crown, in the room.
This is a controlled game, where you suggest a place they should look, and one of
them trots off to see. Adapt the script below as necessary. You could "plant" the room
by having a few more things in it than normal, for the children to peer into.

Hunt the Crown

Leader   Okay, Jesus is hidden somewhere in this room. We'll know we've
found Him when we find His crown.
Sit very still, and I'll think up places we could look.
Is He behind that door?
Name, could you look for me?
Nothing? Okay, we'll try again.
How about that cabinet?
He couldn't have got behind the piano, could He?
What about on the stage?

If you have a stage, you could send one kid to one wing, another kid to the other and so on.

>Is he behind those chairs?
>Or in our dressing-up box? *(and so on...)*
>Well, I think we've looked everywhere...

If the kids have spotted the box let them tell you about it.

>That beat-up old box—well, you can check it out...

Send several children over.

>(**We've found it!**)
>Good Heavens, bring the box and the crown over here.

Read the label on the box.

>"Cardboard City."
>Does anyone know what a Cardboard City is? (**It's a place where homeless people make shelters for themselves out of cardboard.**)
>Of course, that's just where Jesus would be.
>Right there with the homeless and the poor and the hungry. What a fantastic King He is.

REHEARSAL

Practice your presentation for when you go back to church (see below).

FINAL
PRAYER

(*The response is:* **We worship you.**)
Lord Jesus, King of the Church,
We worship you.
Lord Jesus, King of the Universe,
We worship you.
Lord Jesus, King of Saints,
We worship you.
Lord Jesus, King of Angels,
We worship you.
Lord Jesus, King of Kings,
We worship you.

SONG

The traditional hymns "At the name of Jesus" *and* "Ye servants of God" *have good tunes.*

BACK IN CHURCH

The children come in with the crown back in its box.

Leader   Today is the feast of Christ the King. But, as we read the Gospel today we realized that Jesus was a hidden King—so we thought we'd better find Him:
                  Where did we look, guys?

Let the children tell you.

                  (In the kitchen, behind the door, in the prop box...)
                  And where did we find Him?
Child 1   In this box.
Child 2   It's called "Cardboard City."
Child 3   It's where the homeless people live.
Child 4   That's where we found Jesus...

Child 5 pulls the crown out and holds it up.

(CD59.2)

(CD59.3)

(CD59.4)

(CD59.5)

(CD59.6)

(CD59.7)

(CD59.8)

(CD59.9)

Sample cartoons for this script

Script 60   Saint Spotting

Any Saint's Day

Revelation 7:9-12

THEME

This is an extra session, in case you find your church is celebrating a major saint and has, for once, ditched the Gospel of the Day.

As you'll see, the script accommodates any saint. If your one isn't mentioned just look him or her up and put them in. Wikipedia has a good section on saints under "saint symbolism." What you want to know is the *attribute* of the saint, the thing he/she holds in pictures. (St. Peter, for example, always holds keys.) This session is about recognizing saints by their attributes (their props), most of which you'll find you can replicate. (Though you'll have trouble with St. Agatha, her attribute is two breasts on a plate.)

However, we're not just into Spot a Saint we want the children to realize that there are millions of unknown saints and that they themselves are saints in training.

SET UP

- Pictures from the CD-ROM.
- There is a list of saints and their attributes at the end of the script, choose the ones you can do (adding to their number as you see fit).
- Stick the attributes in a large container, like a wastepaper basket.
- Create a "License plate," put it on some string so a child could wear it round their neck.

WELCOME *the children and lead them in* **The Sign of the Cross + (p. xxxvi).**

THE KYRIE   Lord Jesus, we are sorry for the things we have done wrong,
Lord have mercy.
Lord have mercy.

Lord Jesus, we are sorry for forgetting to listen to you,
Christ have mercy.
Christ have mercy.

Lord Jesus, thank you for your promise to love and forgive us,
Lord have mercy.
Lord have mercy.

Ask the children to repeat **The Prayer for Forgiveness** *after you* **(p. xxxvi).**

Leader	Today is St. *Name's* day, so we are going to think about all the saints in Heaven as we pray.
OPENING PRAYER	God our Father, Today we thank you for the holy men and women who are your saints. May they pray for us as we try to follow their example. We ask this through Jesus our Lord. **Amen**
	When the saints lived on earth they were just like us. They behaved badly, just like us, and they asked God to forgive them. Let's follow their example.

SAINTS AND THEIR PROPS

Prop Show

Pull out the prop basket, it should be bristling with interesting things like large rulers and plastic axes
Talk through how many saints there are, and how difficult it is to remember their names

Leader	It is even more difficult if you want to make pictures of them. How do you know if a painting is of St. Peter? You could put his name underneath of course, but the painting would look like a cartoon. So painters have come up with a cunning wheeze—they give the saint a "prop." Something to do with the sort of person they were. So when you see the prop you know the saint. Can anybody remember what St. Peter's prop is? **(Keys)**

If the children can't remember, just put up the picture

CD60.1	What's St. Peter holding? **(Keys!)** Yes, Jesus gave him the Keys of Heaven.
CD60.2	OK, let's think of another saint. St. Agnes. "Agnes" means lamb—what do you think her prop is? **(Lamb)**

Put up the picture.

> Quite right.
>
> Now, we've got a basket of props here, all belonging to various saints.
>
> Let's get the saint attached to his or her prop...

Start pulling out props, get kids at the front to hold them.

> Ah, this scythe is for St. Isidore—*(swish it)*—he is the patron saint of farm workers...

Put Isidore's name up on the board.

> This chalice is for St. John.
>
> Have we got a John or a Joanna here?
>
> Great, hold that—ugh, what's inside? *(A plastic snake)*
>
> John always holds a chalice with a snake in it because somebody once tried to poison him.

Write John's name up.

And this Ruler—*(or triangle ruler)*—is for St. Thomas.
He holds that because he's supposed to have been an architect.

And so on—see list of saints and props at the end of this script.
At the end you should have an impressive line-up of saints.

Game

Put all the props back and invite the kids up to take a prop—but they can only have
it if they can remember the saint to whom it belongs. (Give some outrageous hints.)

Finish

Leader   How many saints do you think there are?
              Nobody knows, not even the Bible. There are **millions** of saints—
              and there'll be even more when we get to Heaven.
              Let's hear about them in the Bible.

BIBLE READING *Revelation 7:9-12*

AFTER THE READING

Leader   There are lots of odd things in that part of the Bible, but you get the
              picture there are loads of saints, around the throne of God.
              But if we were there we'd know who they were immediately.
              If we saw a saint with eyeballs, for example, we'd know it was?
              (**St. Lucy**—*they always remember her*)
              Now here's a saint you probably haven't heard of.

Call a victim to the front.

              This is Saint *Name.*
              Do you think this kid's a saint? (**No!**)
              Well, what does saint mean? (**Holy**)
              And what are Christians called?

This is a rhetorical question.

              "The Holy People of God."
              Well, if Christians are holy, young *Name* here must be holy, and so
              has got to be a saint. What attribute do you think St. *Name* should
              have?
              I know what I think... *(give them the license plate)*
              A learner saint
              And so are we.

FINAL PRAYER   Learners need lots of help, so let's ask the saints to pray for us...

Get a line of kids at the front, holding the saint props, and construct the litany round their names.

Litany   Holy Peter
         Pray for us
         Holy Helena
         Pray for us

And so on. Finish with:

God our Father,
We thank you for the saints.
May their prayers help us,
And may we join them one day,
to live with you for ever in
Heaven. **Amen**

SONG

There are many modern and traditional hymns for this day. "For all the saints" *is the classic, but* "Be thou my vision" *and* "He who would valiant be" *are stirring calls to service. If you have focused on the children's capacity for sainthood,* "I the Lord of sea and sky" *fits in well.*

BACK IN CHURCH

Line up the kids and props—as you point to them, each child calls out the name of his or her saint and attribute:

"I'm St. Isidore, and I've got a scythe.'

Even so you might have to go along the line and gently extract the information. End with the learner saint.

SAINTS AND THEIR ATTRIBUTES

Peter	Keys (of Heaven and Purgatory).
St. John	Chalice (borrow a spare) with rubber snake: John was offered a poisoned chalice once, and survived.
St. Isidore	Plastic scythe (he is the patron saint of farm workers).
St. Joseph	Toy hammer or saw.
St. Olaf	Toy axe (Olaf used an axe as a unique method of converting the heathen).
St. Paul	Toy sword.
St. Gabriel	A lily (actually the lily belongs to Mary; he must have plucked it in one crucial picture and has been stuck with it ever since).
St. Lawrence	Gridiron, grill, grill tray from oven (he was grilled).
St. Roche	Toy dog (who used to beg for him—St. Roche had plague and couldn't approach people, so his dog got bread for him instead).
St. James	A cockle shell: the badge of the pilgrims who go to St. James's shrine in Spain.
St. Andrew	A (chocolate) fish: he was a fisherman.
Sts. Cosmas & Damian	Toy stethoscope: they were brothers and doctors.
St. Stephen	Stones (get some from the Lent desert): he was stoned to death.
St. Thomas	Long ruler or triangle ruler: he was an architect.
St. Leonard	Chains: he is the patron of prisoners.
St. George	Toy dragon or an England flag: he's the patron saint of England.
St. Patrick	Shamrock or clover leaf (a large cardboard version) or a plastic snake (he ejected all the snakes from Ireland).
St. David	A dove.
St. Lucy	Eyeballs, you can actually find these among the children's section in various tourist shops, or joke shops. Making a couple out of a pair of ping pong balls is just as good. St. Lucy was blinded.
Mary	Baby Jesus: borrow the Infant Jesus from the Nativity set.

Ping Pong ball

draw in pupil and cornea

(Totally awful but children love it!)

St. Mary Magdalene	A jar of oil (see-through so the kids can see the oil; it's the oil she brought to the Tomb).
St. Clare	A lamp—another pun, she shines as clear (Clara) as light.
St. Helena	Either a wooden cross, or some nails: she found the True Cross.
St. Mary of Egypt	Plastic skull: she meditated on skulls and things as a hermit in the desert.
St. Catherine	A wheel—they tried to kill her on a wheel, but it didn't work. The wheel went out of control and killed 50 heathen philosophers.
St. Agnes	A woolly lamb (a pun on her name).

You don't have to do all these saints, pace the session and do as many as keeps it zingy. Balance out the male and female saints.

Stories for Children in Distress

In the 17 years we have been running Children's Church groups we have had to cope with several deaths. Children have also shared a variety of other griefs with us, ranging from family troubles and illness to anxieties about exams and moving on to secondary school.

You may find the following Gospel stories helpful if it becomes apparent that a child is in distress. Try to tell these stories in the context of a prayer circle, so that the narrative can immediately spill over into prayer. (And always talk to the child's parents afterwards.)

Emmaus—Luke 24:13-35

Tell the story very simply, stressing the unhappiness of the two disciples who were walking to Emmaus and the way Jesus walked along beside them. He was there all the time, listening to them and loving them, but their unhappiness was so great they simply couldn't see Him.

Even so, He got through: their hearts lightened up as He talked to them and, at the climax of the story, they suddenly realized who He was as He broke the bread at supper time.

Walking on water—Matthew 14:22-32

It's useful to have a little toy ship for this, to show how greatly it was tossed about, and how Jesus brought it to rest.

Describe the set up. The disciples are separated from Jesus and go off, across the lake, in a boat by themselves.

For a while everything is fine and the disciples get to the middle of the lake. Then a storm blows up. They are terrified, "Where's Jesus?' And all the time, He's been watching them, from the side of the lake, and patiently walks across the raging water towards them. By the time He arrives the disciples are so panicked they can barely recognize Him (they think He's a ghost) but they hear His call, "Do not be afraid!' And the storm dies down.

Index of Biblical References

Gospel	Reference	Story	
Acts	1:7-12	Detecting the Ascension	153
Acts	2:1-21	Pentecost	158
John	1:1-18	The Word	27
John	1:29-42	Behold the Lamb of God	38
John	2:1-11	Wedding at Cana	48
John	3:1-5	Nicodemus (and Noah)	92
John	4:5-42	The Samaritan Woman	99
John	9:1a, 6, 11-12	Jesus Heals a Blind Man	104
John	10:1, 7-15	"I am the Gate'	135
John	6:8	The Feeding of the 5,000	215
John	11:17, 20-27, 33-44	Lazarus	109
John	14:1-14	Mansions	139
John	14:15-21	Jesus Packs Up	144
John	17:1, 6, 11	Staying Together	149
John	20:1-9	Easter Sunday	120
John	20:19-23	Pentecost	158
John	20:19-29	Doubting Thomas	125
Luke	24:13-35	The Walk to Emmaus	130
Luke	24:50-51	Detecting the Ascension	153
Matthew	1:18-21	St. Joseph	18
Matthew	2:13-23	The Flight into Egypt	22
Matthew	3:1-6	'Repent!'	7
Matthew	3:1, 6, 13-17	The Baptism of Jesus	33
Matthew	4:1-11	Jesus in the Desert	85
Matthew	4:18-24	Fishers of Men	43
Matthew	5:1-12	The Beatitudes	52
Matthew	5:14-16	Lights and Bushels	60
Matthew	5:29-30	Staying Good	64
Matthew	5:38-48	Turning the Other Cheek	69
Matthew	6:24-34	Trusting in God	74
Matthew	7:24-27	The Two Builders	169
Matthew	9:9-12	The Call of Matthew	174
Matthew	10:1-4	Jesus' Twelve Friends	178
Matthew	10:26-31	Shouting from the Housetops	183
Matthew	10:40-42	A Cup of Cold Water	187
Matthew	11:2-6	'Rejoice!'	12
Matthew	11:28-30	My Yoke is Easy	193
Matthew	13:1-9	The Sower	198

Matthew	13:24-30	Wheat and Tares	203
Matthew	13:31-33, 44-46	Mustard Seeds	208
Matthew	14:13-21	The Feeding of the 5,000	215
Matthew	14:22-33	Walking on Water	220
Matthew	15:21-28	Foreigners	224
Matthew	16:13-17	Peter's Keys	229
Matthew	16:21-25	Take Up Your Cross	233
Matthew	17:1-8	The Transfiguration	80
Matthew	18:15-17, 20	Time Out	237
Matthew	18:21-35	The Ungrateful Servant	241
Matthew	20:1-6	The Labourers in the Vineyard	246
Matthew	21:1-3, 6-11	Palm Sunday	114
Matthew	21:28-32	The Two Sons	251
Matthew	21:33-43	The Farmer and his Tenants	255
Matthew	22:1-16	The King's Party	260
Matthew	22:15-21	Render unto Caesar	265
Matthew	22:34-40	The Great Commandment	270
Matthew	23:1-12	David and Goliath	275
Matthew	24:1-14	The End of the World	281
Matthew	24:42-44	Advent 1 "Watch Out!'	1
Matthew	25:1-13	The Wise and Foolish Virgins	286
Matthew	25:14-26	The Parable of the Talents	291
Matthew	25:31-40	Christ the King	296
Matthew	28:1-10	Easter Sunday	120
Matthew	28:16-20	Trinity Sunday	163
Revelation	7:9-12	Saint Spotting	302